Implementing VxRail HCI Solutions

A complete guide to VxRail Appliance administration and configuration

Victor Wu

BIRMINGHAM—MUMBAI

Implementing VxRail HCI Solutions

Group Product Manager: Wilson Dsouza

Publishing Product Manager: Meeta Rajani

Senior Editor: Rahul Dsouza

Content Development Editor: Sayali Pingale

Technical Editor: Nithik Cheruvakodan

Copy Editor: Safis Editing

Project Coordinator: Neil Dmello

Proofreader: Safis Editing

Indexer: Manju Arasan

Production Designer: Joshua Misquitta

First published: May 2021

Production reference: 2220621

Published by Packt Publishing Ltd.

Livery Place

35 Livery Street

Birmingham

B3 2PB, UK.

ISBN 978-1-80107-048-5

www.packt.com

Contributors

About the author

Victor Wu has over 14 years of system infrastructure experience. Currently, he works as a senior solutions expert at BoardWare Information System Limited in Macau.

He is the only qualified person in Macau with a certificate in VMware VCIX-DCV, and he has been awarded the vExpert certification from 2014 to 2021, Cisco Champion from 2017 to 2020, Veeam Vanguard from 2019 to 2021, and Nutanix Technology Champion in 2021.

His professional qualifications include VCIX-DCV, VMware Certified Master Specialist – HCI 2020, Implementation Engineer – VxRail Appliance, Systems Administrator – VxRail Appliance, Nutanix Certified Professional 5, NetApp HCI Implementation Engineer, and Knowledge Sharing Author from 2018 to 2020.

He is the author of *Mastering VMware vSphere Storage* and *Cisco UCS Cookbook*, published by Packt Publishing in July 2015 and March 2016, respectively.

About the reviewer

Venkata Krishna Mallemarapu is a senior systems integration advisor with over 12 years of experience in information technology, currently working as a systems advisor at one of the largest healthcare systems in the United States. He holds certifications in the fields of hyper-converged, virtualization, storage, networking, and hardware. He completed his education in the fields of computer science, information technology, electronics, and biomedical engineering.

He loves exploring new places, playing ping-pong, tennis, and volleyball, and gardening. He is people-friendly and loves social gatherings.

To my wife, Sruthi: Thank you for your love, support, and encouragement. I am so thrilled I get to spend the rest of my life with you.

To my family: Thank you for the unconditional love, for always being supportive, and for always being there for me.

To my friends: Thank you for the birthdays, inside jokes, food, laughs, and all the board and card game nights we've shared.

Table of Contents

Preface

Section 1: Getting Started with VxRail HCI System

1

Overview of VxRail HCI

What is a VxRail Appliance?	4	VxRail system architecture	14
What's in a VxRail Appliance?	9	VxRail system features	18
VMware SDDC	9	VxRail system management	23
VxRail HCI System Software	10	VxRail resources	24
Data protection options	10	Summary	27
VxRail licensing	11	Questions	28

2

VxRail Installation

Technical requirements	32	Mounting the VxRail appliances	44
Environment	32	Cabling VxRail appliances	44
Site preparation for VxRail Appliance	35	VxRail Appliance initialization	46
Top-of-Rack switch requirement	36	Configuring a laptop for VxRail Manager connectivity	47
DNS requirements	42	Building a VxRail cluster	48
Power and rack space requirements	43	VxRail validation	62
VxRail Appliance hardware installation	43	Summary	63
		Questions	63

Section 2: Administration of VxRail

3

VxRail Administration Overview

Technical requirements	70	VxRail system virtual machines	85
VxRail management interfaces	70	vDS and port groups	86
VMware vSAN	74	VxRail disk groups	87
Overview	75	vSAN services	89
vSAN objects	77	VxRail storage policy	90
vSAN storage policy	78	**Summary**	**91**
VxRail cluster configuration	85	**Questions**	**91**

4

VxRail Management Overview

Technical requirements	96	VxRail events in vCenter	110
VxRail Manager overview	96	**VxRail roles and permission management**	**112**
The VxRail Manager plugin at the cluster level	97	Creating a user account with an HCIA Management role	114
The VxRail Manager plugin at the host level	104	**Summary**	**117**
VxRail monitoring	106	**Questions**	**117**
The VxRail Manager plugin for vCenter	107		

5

Managing VMware vSAN

Technical requirements	122	Advanced options	128
VMware vSAN service configuration	122	**Defining vSAN storage policies**	**130**
vSAN Deduplication and Compression	123	Overview of VM storage policies	130
vSAN Encryption	124	Creating VM storage policies	133
vSAN Performance Service	126	Applying VM storage policies	139
The vSAN iSCSI target service	127	**Monitoring a vSAN cluster**	**140**

vSAN health   140
vSAN virtual objects   142
vSAN resyncing objects   143
vSAN capacity   144
vSAN cluster level   144
vSAN host level   145
vSAN VM level   146

vSAN availability   **147**
Overview of vSAN fault domains   147
Creating vSAN fault domains   150
vSAN maintenance mode   152

Building VMs   **158**
Summary   **163**
Questions   **164**

6

VxRail Upgrade

Technical requirements   **167**
VxRail disk group upgrade   **168**
Drive expansion procedures   169
Drive upgrade in the disk group   171

VxRail software upgrade   **175**
Accessing the VxRail upgrade procedure 176

Downloading the VxRail software   180
Upgrading the VxRail software from
version 4.7 to version 7.0   183

Summary   **193**
Questions   **193**

7

VxRail Scale-Out Operations

VxRail scale-out rules   **198**
Environment   198

VxRail cluster expansion   **199**
Preparation   200

Scale-out operation   203

Summary   **214**
Questions   **215**

Section 3: Advanced Solutions for VxRail

8

Active-Passive Solution for VxRail

Technical requirements   **222**
**Deploying an active-passive
solution for VxRail**   **222**
Solution with VR and SRM   223

SRM appliance deployment   **225**
VR deployment   **240**
Configuring SRM inventory

mappings   255
Protecting virtual machines   264
Creating SRM recovery plans   269

Summary   271
Questions   272

9

Active-Active Solution for VxRail

Technical requirements   276

Overview of the active-active
solution
for VxRail   277
VxRail cluster configuration   279
vCenter Server requirements   280
Network requirements   281

Deploying the active-active
solution for VxRail   283

Deploying a vSAN stretched cluster
witness   283
Configuring the VxRail vSAN stretched
cluster   294

Overview of the active-active-
passive
solution for VxRail   304
Summary   306
Questions   306

10

Migrating Virtual Machines into VxRail

Technical requirements   312

Understanding migration
methodologies for VxRail   312

Migrating a virtual machine into
VxRail with vSphere Replication 313
Environment   314
Migration flow   314
Creating a virtual machine replication
session   315

Failing over a virtual machine   320

Migrating a virtual machine into
VxRail with Storage vMotion   322
Environment   323
Migration flow   324
Using Storage vMotion   324

Summary   328
Questions   329

Assessments

Chapter 1 – Overview of VxRail
HCI   333
Chapter 2 – VxRail Installation   333
Chapter 3 – VxRail
Administration Overview   334

Chapter 4 – VxRail Management
Overview   334
Chapter 5 – Managing VMware
vSAN   335
Chapter 6 – VxRail Upgrade   335

Chapter 7 – VxRail Scale-Out
Operations   336

Chapter 8 – Active-Passive
Solution for VxRail   336

Chapter 9 – Active-Active

Solution for VxRail   337

Chapter 10 – Migrating Virtual
Machines into VxRail   337

Why subscribe?   339

Other Books You May Enjoy

Index

Preface

Hyper-converged infrastructure (**HCI**) can help you simplify the provisioning and daily operations of computing and storage. With this book, you'll understand how HCI can offload the day-0 deployment and day-to-day operations of a system administrator. You'll explore the VxRail Appliance, which is an HCI solution that provides life cycle management, automation, and operational simplicity.

Who this book is for

If you are a system architect, system administrator, or consultant involved in planning and deploying VxRail HCI or want to learn how to use VxRail HCI and its active-active solution, then this book is for you. Equivalent knowledge and administration experience with ESXi and vCenter Server will be helpful.

What this book covers

Chapter 1, *Overview of VxRail HCI*, discusses the VxRail system; you will get an overview of the VxRail HCI platform.

Chapter 2, *VxRail Installation*, describes the installation of the VxRail Appliance. You will learn how to plan and design the VxRail Appliance pre-deployment and post-deployment activities. This includes preparation of the pre-installation site checklist, hardware and software installation, network environment validation, and VxRail initialization and configuration.

Chapter 3, *VxRail Administration Overview*, describes an overview of VxRail administration. We will learn about the management panel that is used in VxRail appliances. Since the VxRail platform runs on VMware **virtual SAN** (**vSAN**), we will explain the vSAN architecture and its concepts.

Chapter 4, *VxRail Management Overview*, describes an overview of VxRail management. We will learn about the functions of the VxRail Manager Plugin for vCenter. We will become familiar with how to monitor the status of VxRail appliances with the VxRail Manager Plugin for vCenter.

Chapter 5, Managing VMware vSAN, describes an overview of VMware vSAN configuration and operation in a VxRail cluster. This includes different vSAN services, the management of vSAN storage policies, the monitoring of vSAN objects in a VxRail cluster, and vSAN availability.

Chapter 6, VxRail Upgrade, provides an overview of VxRail drive expansion and software upgrade procedures. We can easily upgrade the vSAN capacity in our VxRail cluster based on the disk group configuration rules.

Chapter 7, VxRail Scale-Out Operations, covers the process of adding a node to your VxRail cluster. The cluster expansion is performed with the VxRail Manager Plugin in VMware vCenter Server.

Chapter 8, Active-Passive Solution for VxRail, covers what the disaster recovery solutions for VxRail are. This includes a solution with VMware **Site Recovery Manager** (**SRM**) and **vSphere Replication** (**VR**).

Chapter 9, Active-Active Solution for VxRail, covers what a vSAN stretched cluster on VxRail is. This includes the active-active-passive solution with VMware SRM. We will learn how to plan and design this solution in this chapter.

Chapter 10, Migrating Virtual Machines into VxRail, covers how to migrate virtual machines into VxRail appliances from the vSphere environment, including different migration methodologies based on various scenarios.

To get the most out of this book

Make sure your workstation (laptop) is running on the Windows platform and a web browser is installed onto your laptop. The latest versions of Firefox, Google Chrome, and Microsoft Internet Explorer 10 or above are all supported. You need to run the VxRail software at version 4.7.300 or above.

Software/hardware covered in the book	OS requirements
Microsoft Windows platform	Windows 7, 8, or 10
VxRail software	VxRail 4.7.300 or above
VMware SRM	Version 8.2 or above
VMware VR	Version 8.2 or above

Download the color images

We also provide a PDF file that has color images of the screenshots/diagrams used in this book. You can download it here: `http://www.packtpub.com/sites/default/files/downloads/9781801070485_ColorImages.pdf`.

Conventions used

There are a number of text conventions used throughout this book.

`Code in text`: Indicates code words in text, database table names, folder names, filenames, file extensions, pathnames, dummy URLs, user input, and Twitter handles. Here is an example: "The default internal VLAN is `3939`."

Bold: Indicates a new term, an important word, or words that you see onscreen. For example, words in menus or dialog boxes appear in the text like this. Here is an example: "Click **Flash** from Etcher to write the image."

> **Tips or important notes**
> Appear like this.

Get in touch

Feedback from our readers is always welcome.

General feedback: If you have questions about any aspect of this book, mention the book title in the subject of your message and email us at `customercare@packtpub.com`.

Errata: Although we have taken every care to ensure the accuracy of our content, mistakes do happen. If you have found a mistake in this book, we would be grateful if you would report this to us. Please visit `www.packtpub.com/support/errata`, selecting your book, clicking on the Errata Submission Form link, and entering the details.

Piracy: If you come across any illegal copies of our works in any form on the Internet, we would be grateful if you would provide us with the location address or website name. Please contact us at `copyright@packt.com` with a link to the material.

If you are interested in becoming an author: If there is a topic that you have expertise in and you are interested in either writing or contributing to a book, please visit `authors.packtpub.com`.

Reviews

Please leave a review. Once you have read and used this book, why not leave a review on the site that you purchased it from? Potential readers can then see and use your unbiased opinion to make purchase decisions, we at Packt can understand what you think about our products, and our authors can see your feedback on their book. Thank you!

For more information about Packt, please visit packt.com.

Section 1: Getting Started with VxRail HCI System

In this section, we will have an overview of VxRail HCI System and VxRail installation, which will include the VxRail architecture and software, and the management and preparation of VxRail deployments.

This section of the book comprises the following chapters:

- *Chapter 1, Overview of VxRail HCI*
- *Chapter 2, VxRail Installation*

1
Overview of VxRail HCI

In the digital economy, most applications provide a 24 x 7 **Service-Level Agreement** (**SLA**) for every customer. So, SLAs are very important for all customers. The service provider often faces the expectation that the application service will be available anytime, anywhere, and on any device, and will provide real-time updates, automatically scale up/out, and so on. Actually, most of the traditional infrastructure architecture has some hardware, software, and day-to-day operational limitations, and so on. These limitations mean that the service providers or end users do not have the expertise for planning, upgrading, and reconfiguring the system properly, for example, hardware scaling, software package upgrade, resource planning, central management, **Life Cycle Management** (**LCM**), and so on.

The **Hyper-Converged Infrastructure** (**HCI**) platform is well integrated with hardware and software. It facilitates simplified solutions created from these limitations. The HCI platform can deliver simplified infrastructure deployment and management. One benefit that HCI gives users that traditional architecture cannot is that the end user can easily manage and perform administrative tasks from a central management control place, which is fully integrated with VMware vCenter. In the current market, the Dell EMC VxRail appliance is one such HCI platform engineered and developed by Dell EMC with VMware collaboration. In this chapter, we will discuss the VxRail system; you will get an overview of the VxRail HCI platform.

In this chapter, we're going to cover the following main topics:

- What is a VxRail Appliance?
- What's in a VxRail Appliance?
- VxRail licensing
- VxRail system architecture
- VxRail system features
- VxRail system management
- VxRail resources

What is a VxRail Appliance?

The **VxRail Appliance** (as seen in *Figure 1.1*) is developed and powered by **Dell EMC** and **VMware**. It is an HCI appliance that is exclusively integrated and pre-configured with **VMware vSphere** and **Software-Defined Storage** (**SDS**). VxRail HCI systems are fully integrated with the VMware **vCenter Server Appliance** (**VCSA**) with the **VxRail Manager plugin**. The VxRail Appliance can deliver resiliency and centralized management to a system administrator and can easily perform all operations and configurations via the VxRail Manager plugin in **VMware vCenter Server**:

Figure 1.1 – Front view of the VxRail system on the Dell 14th-generation PowerEdge server

The VxRail HCI system is pre-configured in Intel-based **Dell EMC PowerEdge servers** with VMware vSphere and **Virtual SAN (vSAN)**. The VxRail Appliance provides different options for hardware configuration, for example, Intel and AMD processors with options for the number of cores, MEM RAM, 10 Gbps or 25 Gbps network connectivity, a **Graphics Processing Unit (GPU)**, storage drives, and so on. VxRail models are available in different form factors, that is, four nodes in a two-unit chassis, one unit per node, and two units per node. These allow customers to buy what they need now. This is one benefit of HCI, that the customer is able to buy and build the system configuration from day one. Since VxRail appliances are fully integrated with VMware products, they are also supported by other VMware solution products, including VMware vRealize, NSX, and SRM, and work as a foundation for **SDDC (Software Defined Data Center)** and private clouds like **VCF (VMware Cloud Foundation)**. You can go to the VMware website (https://vmware.com) if you want to learn about these VMware products in more detail.

The VxRail Appliance architecture is designed so that customers buy and grow their appliances based on forecasts for their hardware requirements (Dell EMC engineers use the Live Optics sizing tool for VxRail design). **Live Optics** is online software we can use to collect data about our IT environment and workloads. Live Optics provides data analysis to help us understand our workload performance. The customer can choose different hardware configurations for their different scenarios. The Dell EMC VxRail family includes six types of platforms, that is, E (entry-level) Series, P (performance-optimized) Series, V (VDI-optimized) series, D (durable-platform) Series, S (storage-dense) series, and G (general-purpose) Series.

In VxRail 4.7.100, a two-node VxRail cluster is available. This configuration is only supported on VxRail E Series appliances, which is directly attached across two nodes.

Now we will introduce each model of the Dell EMC VxRail appliance:

Figure 1.2 – Front view of VxRail E (entry-level) Series on the Dell 14th-generation PowerEdge server

The VxRail E Series appliance has three options: NVMe, hybrid, or all-flash. If you want high performance, you can choose the NVMe or all-flash option, whereas if you want a general-purpose one, you can choose the hybrid option. Each node is a **One-Unit (1U)** form factor system that is used for every scenario. It is based on Dell EMC PowerEdge R640 server technology, and it supports 1 GbE, 10 GbE, and 25 GbE network interfaces:

Figure 1.3 – Front view of VxRail P Series on the Dell 14th-generation PowerEdge server

The VxRail P Series appliance has three options: NVMe, hybrid, or all-flash. Each node is a **Two-Unit (2U)** form factor system that is used for high-performance and data-intensive application scenarios. It is based on Dell EMC PowerEdge R740xd server technology, and it supports 1 GbE, 10 GbE, and 25 GbE network interfaces:

Figure 1.4 – Front view of VxRail V Series on the Dell 14th-generation PowerEdge server

The VxRail V Series appliance only has two options: hybrid or all-flash. Each node is a 2U form factor system that is used for **Virtual Desktop Infrastructure (VDI)** optimized for specialized scenarios. It is based on Dell EMC PowerEdge R740xd server technology, and it supports 1 GbE, 10 GbE, and 25 GbE network interfaces. Only V Series can support GPU cards.

Figure 1.5 shows the VxRail D Series appliance:

Figure 1.5 – Front view of VxRail D Series on the Dell 14th-generation PowerEdge server

The VxRail D Series appliance only has two options: hybrid or all-flash. Each node is a 1U form factor system that is designed to withstand extreme conditions, such as intense heat, cold, humidity, and so on. It is based on Dell EMC PowerEdge XR2 platform technology, and it supports both a 10 Gb and 25 Gb network interface. VxRail D Series is a MIL-STD 810G certified configuration:

Figure 1.6 – Front view of VxRail S Series on the Dell 14th-generation PowerEdge server

The VxRail S Series appliance only has the hybrid option. Each node is a 2U form factor system that is used for the higher storage capacity at the server level, for example, big data, analytics, archive data, and so on. It is based on Dell EMC PowerEdge R740xd server technology, and it supports 1 GbE, 10 GbE, and 25 GbE network interfaces:

Figure 1.7 – Front view of VxRail G Series on the Dell 14th-generation PowerEdge server

The VxRail G Series appliance has two options: hybrid or all-flash. Each node is a Two-Unit (2U) form factor system that is used for general purposes and computes dense scenarios. It is based on Dell EMC PowerEdge C6420 server technology, and it supports 1 GbE, 10 GbE, and 25 GbE network interfaces. Each VxRail G Series chassis can install four nodes.

> **Important note**
>
> In a standard VxRail cluster, the first three VxRail nodes in a cluster must
> be identical models. In a two-node VxRail cluster, system expansion is not
> supported. The G Series VxRail nodes in a chassis must be identical models.
> Hybrid and all-flash nodes cannot mix in a VxRail cluster. There can also be no
> mixing of all-flash and NVMe nodes in the same cluster.

This table shows a summary of the hardware configurations on each VxRail series:

VxRail Series	E Series	P Series	V Series	D Series	S Series	G Series
Roles	Entry level	High performance	VDI scenario	Durable and rugged	Dense storage	Dense compute
Options	Hybrid, all-flash, NVMe	Hybrid, all-flash, NVMe	Hybrid, all-flash	Hybrid, all-flash	Hybrid	Hybrid, all-flash
CPU Cores	4 to 56	4 to 112	8 to 56	4 to 48	4 to 56	4 to 56
Memory	64 GB to 3,072 GB	64 GB to 6,144 GB	192 GB to 3,072 GB	64 GB to 1,024 GB	64 GB to 3,072 GB	64 GB to 2,048 GB
Disk Slots	10	24	24	8	12	6
Disk Groups	2	4	4	2	2	1
Base Network	10 Gb SFP+, RJ45, 25 Gb SFP28	10 Gb SFP+, RJ45, 25 Gb SFP28	10 Gb SFP+, RJ45, 25 Gb SFP28	10 Gb RJ45, 25 Gb SFP28	10 Gb SFP+, RJ45, 25 Gb SFP28	10 Gb SFP+, 25 Gb SFP28
Additional Network	Supported	Supported	Supported	Supported	Supported	Supported
Fibre Channel	Supported	Supported	Supported	N/A	Supported	N/A
GPU	Supported	N/A	Supported	Supported	N/A	N/A
Unit	1 unit	2 unit	2 unit	1 unit	2 unit	1 unit

Now you know the different types of VxRail appliances and which option is suitable for
different scenarios.

What's in a VxRail Appliance?

A VxRail Appliance is a turnkey solution for managing and deploying VMware infrastructure. VMware vSphere is pre-installed and pre-configured on each VxRail appliance. vSphere is a powerful hypervisor that can provide the embedded and cost-effective SDS feature, that is, **vSAN**. Customers can purchase VxRail with different types of vSAN licenses, such as Enterprise Plus, Enterprise, Advanced, or Standard. vSphere can provide different, powerful features, for example, VMware **High Availability** (**HA**), **vSphere Storage vMotion**, data protection of virtual machines, and **Storage Policy-Based Management** (**SPBM**). There are three groups of software components in a VxRail cluster: VMware SDCC, VxRail HCI System Software, and data protection options. This table shows a summary of each type of software on a VxRail appliance:

VMware SDDC	VxRail HCI System Software	Data Protection Options
vCenter Server	VxRail Manager	Dell EMC RecoverPoint for Virtual Machines (RP4VM)
vRealize Log Insight	Secure Remote Support (SRS)	VMware vSphere Replication (VR)
vSphere Ready	VxRail Analytical Consulting Engine (ACE)	N/A
vSAN Ready	N/A	N/A
VMware Cloud Foundation (optional)	N/A	N/A

With the preceding table, we know what component is included in each piece of software. Now we will discuss each piece of software.

VMware SDDC

VMware vSphere is a hypervisor that can provide different virtualization-based services, such as VMware vSphere, ESXi (hypervisor), software-defined storage and networking, and so on.

> **Important note**
> vSphere licenses are not included in the VxRail Appliance; we can reuse existing vSphere licenses or order new licenses for each VxRail node.

The VxRail Appliance is bundled with a VMware vCenter Server instance that's used for all virtual machine management. VMware VCSA is a virtual appliance that provides a centralized management dashboard for day-to-day activities and the configuration of all virtual machines. With the embedded VxRail Manager plugin, we can administer VxRail appliances hosted from within the vCenter.

VMware vSAN is SDS that is bundled with the kernel of the vSphere hypervisor. VMware vSAN features are enabled on each VxRail appliance.

VMware vRealize Log Insight is a virtual appliance that is used to monitor the system events and provide the system log management of a VxRail cluster.

VMware Cloud Foundation on VxRail is used to build up the SSDC. This platform runs on VMware vSphere and enables the VMware vSAN, NSX, and vRealize features.

Important note

VMware Cloud Foundation is an optional software feature on VxRail; this software is not included in VxRail appliances.

VxRail HCI System Software

VxRail Manager is a virtual appliance that delivers the central management dashboards in HTML and it is fully integrated with VMware VCSA, and it can provide LCM, system scale-out, and automatic deployments. All VxRail operations can be performed on vCenter Server via the VxRail Manager plugin.

VxRail **ACE** (**Analytical Consulting Engine**) is a cloud-based platform that can provide proactive system monitoring of VxRail HCI systems. VxRail ACE does not require optional costs for the customer if they are using VxRail HCI System Software. It collects all system events and logs from VxRail HCI systems and performs the system analysis.

ESRS (**Secure Remote Services**) is a 24 x 7 remote support service provided by the Dell EMC support team. They can deliver an immediate, secure response to VxRail system event reports, such as error alerts, which can greatly increase the availability of your VxRail system.

Data protection options

Dell EMC **RP4VM** is a **Continuous Data Protection** (CDP) solution and can deliver the data protection of virtual machines with its point-in-time synchronization or asynchronization in a local VxRail cluster or across VxRail clusters between two separate locations. RP4VM is directly managed by vCenter Server.

> **Important note**
>
> The RP4VM license includes five virtual machine licenses per node (E, P, V, D, and S Series) and 15 virtual machine licenses per chassis for the G Series.

VMware VR is a hypervisor-based disaster recovery solution; it can provide the data protection of virtual machines asynchronously in a local VxRail cluster or across VxRail clusters between two separate locations. VR is directly managed by vCenter Server. VR can also work with VMware **Site Recovery Manager** (**SRM**) to provide automated failover and failback to minimize downtime.

> **Important note**
>
> VMware SRM requires optional licenses for enabling disaster recovery. You need a license for at least 25 virtual machines per site.

Now we understand which software components are bundled with the VxRail Appliance.

VxRail licensing

When we purchase a VxRail cluster (a minimum of three nodes), the suite of software licenses bundle includes VxRail HCI System Software. The following VMware software is included:

- VMware vCenter Server Standard edition
- VMware vSphere ESXi
- VMware vSAN (SDS)
- VMware vRealize Log Insight
- VMware VR

Dell EMC software includes the following:

- Five virtual machine CDP licenses per node (E, P, V, D, and S Series) and 15 virtual machine CDP licenses per chassis for the G Series

VxRail also follows a **Bring-Your-Own (BYO)** license model. We can purchase a new vSphere license with the VxRail appliance or reuse any existing qualified vSphere licenses. The VxRail system supports several VMware vSphere license editions, such as Enterprise Plus, Standard, **Remote Office Branch Office (ROBO)** editions, and so on. This table provides an edition summary of all the supported vSphere licenses:

VMware vSphere Package	vSphere Functional Level	Input Unit
vSphere Enterprise Plus	Enterprise Plus	Per CPU
vSphere Enterprise	Enterprise Plus	Per CPU
vSphere Standard	Standard	Per CPU
vSphere ROBO Advanced	Standard (no DRS feature)	Per VM (Qty: 25)
vSphere ROBO Standard	Standard	Per VM (Qty: 25)
vSphere Desktop	Enterprise Plus	Per-User (Qty: 100)
vSphere with Operations Management Enterprise Plus	Enterprise Plus	Per CPU
Horizon Enterprise	Enterprise Plus, virtual desktop only	Per-User (Qty: 10 or 100)
Horizon Enterprise	Enterprise Plus, virtual desktop only	Per-User (Qty: 10 or 100)
Horizon Enterprise	Enterprise Plus, virtual desktop only	Per-User (Qty: 10 or 100)
vCloud Suite	Enterprise Plus	Per CPU

VxRail supports a flexible vSAN licensing option; the customer can order the vSAN license included with VxRail or applied via a vSAN **Enterprise License Agreement (ELA)** from VMware. The VxRail system supports several VMware vSAN license editions, including Standard, Advanced, Enterprise, and Enterprise Plus. *Figure 1.8* shows an edition comparison:

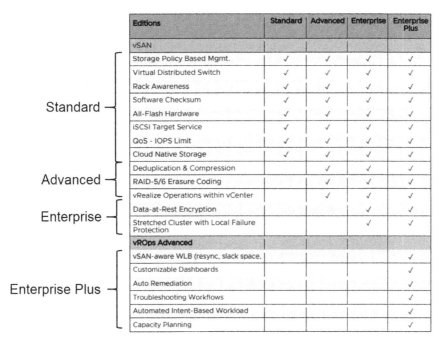

Figure 1.8 – Flexible vSAN licenses with VxRail; this information is copyright of VMware

A VMware vCenter Server license is included with a VxRail cluster. During VxRail initialization, VxRail Manager applies this license to the embedded vCenter Server.

> **Important note**
>
> Please note that transferring a bundle vCenter license to any vCenter Server is not supported. We prepare a new VMware vCenter license for an external vCenter Server if we choose the external vCenter Server during VxRail initialization.

With *Figure 1.8*, we can choose the different types of VMware vSphere and vSAN licenses on our VxRail appliance based on the required functions.

VxRail system architecture

The VxRail system has been integrated, tested, and validated as a turnkey solution by Dell EMC. Each node is built on a Dell PowerEdge server; it includes the following hardware components:

- Intel Xeon Scalable Gen 1 and Gen 2 processors with single, dual, or quad cores (up to 28 cores per processor) or a single 2nd-generation AMD EPYC processor with up to 64 cores.

- An up-to-24-DDR4 dual in-line memory module (memory capacity ranges from 64 GB to 6 TB).

- A mirrored pair of Boss SATA M.2 cards (stores the ESXi operating system) installed on the node.

- A 10/25 Gb **Network Daughter Card** (**NDC**) used to connect to VxRail's foundation network (ESXi management, vMotion, vSAN, and virtual machine network).

- If VxRail is hybrid configured, it contains a single SSD flash disk for caching (the cache tier) and multiple HDD disks for capacity (the capacity tier).

- If VxRail is all-flash configured, it contains all SAS SSD or NVMe drives for both cache and SAS or SATA SSD for capacity.

Important note

Each VxRail series has a different maximum hardware configuration, such as the number of disk groups, the number of additional network ports, the amount of memory, the number of CPU cores, and so on.

Now we will discuss the software architecture of VxRail:

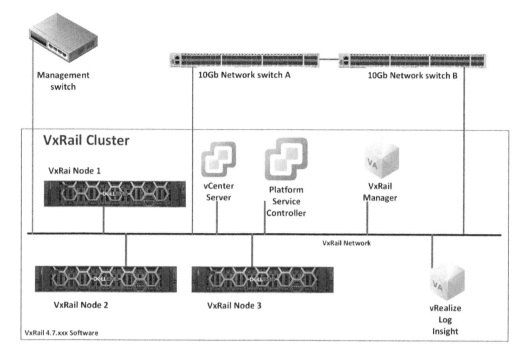

Figure 1.9 – The high-level architecture for the VxRail 4.7 software platform

In this VxRail cluster environment, there are the following hardware and software components:

- The first three VxRail appliances must be the same module in any series in a VxRail cluster, and the VMware vSphere hypervisor re-configured vSAN feature is enabled on the VxRail cluster.

- Two 10 Gb network switches for VxRail connectivity (minimum network requirement).

- One 1 Gb network switch for **Integrated Dell Remote Access Controller** (**iDRAC**) management on each VxRail node.

- One VxRail Manager virtual machine.

- One VMware VCSA.

- One VMware vCenter **Platform Service Controller** (**PSC**).

- One vRealize Log Insight virtual appliance (optional).

If you order the VxRail 7.0 platform, its architecture is slightly different from the VxRail 4.7 platform. The vCenter PSC virtual machine is not available in a VxRail cluster after initialization. The PSC is embedded with the VCSA. *Figure 1.10* shows the high-level architecture for the VxRail 7.0.x software platform:

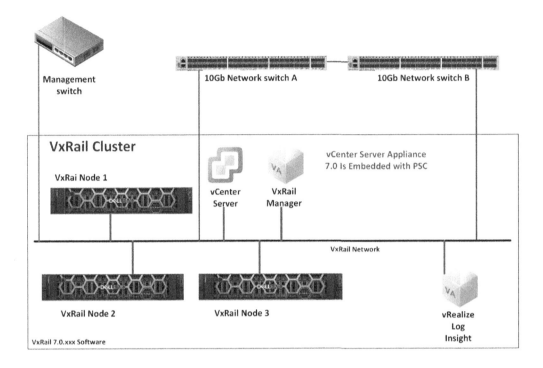

Figure 1.10 – The high-level architecture of the VxRail 7.0 software platform

> **Important note**
>
> The VxRail nodes are connected to **Top of Rack** (**ToR**) network switches. Customers can use their existing switches or purchase them directly from Dell EMC.

In a VxRail cluster environment, there are two sets of network switches for a VxRail network connection. One is used for the VxRail cluster (ESXi management network, vSAN network, vMotion network, and virtual machine network), and the other is used for the iDRAC on each VxRail node. You can go to *Chapter 2, VxRail Installation*, of this book for more details.

The architecture of VxRail 4.7 is different from VxRail 7.0. When you initialize the VxRail Appliance, we can see that both welcome pages are different. You can check *Chapter 2, VxRail Installation,* for more details:

Figure 1.11 – Welcome page of VxRail 4.7

In *Figure 1.12,* you can see the welcome GUI of VxRail 7.0 is different from VxRail 4.7:

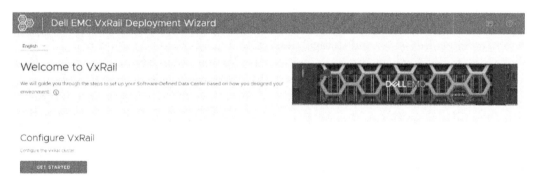

Figure 1.12 – Welcome page of VxRail 7.0

During VxRail initialization, there must be three nodes with the same mode connecting to the VxRail network so that it can automatically build the VxRail cluster. When the VxRail cluster is built, the vSphere and vSAN features are enabled on the VxRail cluster. By default, there are four virtual machines running in the VxRail cluster; they are VxRail Manager, VMware VCSA, VMware vCenter PSC, and vRealize Log Insight. All virtual machines must be running in the VxRail cluster except vRealize Log Insight. Otherwise, the service of the VxRail system cannot be working in normal status.

> **Important note**
>
> VxRail 4.7.x is shipped with VMware VCSA 6.7. VxRail 7.0.x is shipped with VMware VCSA 7.0.

Now you understand the architecture of the VxRail system and the core components.

VxRail system features

The Dell EMC VxRail system can provide different features, such as a single management dashboard, deployment automation, LCM, flexible scale-out, SPBM, CDP, single vendor end-to-end support, and so on. The system administrator can easily handle daily operations with these features.

When the system engineer deploys the VxRail system for the first time, they do not spend much time on the operating system deployment and storage configuration. In a traditional system architecture (server and storage), the system engineer requires many manual procedures for deployment and configuration. In a VxRail system architecture, when the top of the switch and network connections to the VxRail system are ready, the system engineer can easily deploy the operating system and enable the SDS on the VxRail system with the VxRail deployment wizard shown in *Figure 1.13*. Using VxRail can minimize the deployment time:

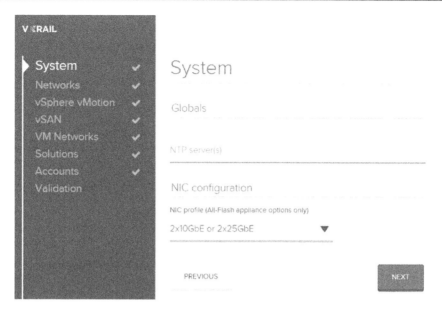

Figure 1.13 – VxRail deployment wizard

All of VxRail's operations can be executed with the VxRail Manager plugin in vCenter Server. You can see all the operation functions in VxRail's **Configure** menu in *Figure 1.14*, such as **System**, **Updates**, **Add VxRail Hosts**, **Support**, and so on:

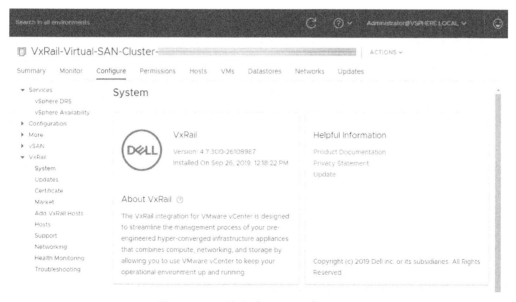

Figure 1.14 – VxRail system information

LCM is one of the core features of the VxRail system. When a system has been alive a few times, software package and operating system upgrades are required; however, the system administrator may spend much of their time on the preparation and dependency verification before the software upgrade. VxRail's one-click upgrade feature can easily and flexibly handle LCM; they can bypass all dependency and software version compatibility. Because VxRail's software package is a single image that is pre-validated with Dell EMC and VMware, the system administrator can perform a one-click upgrade in vCenter Server with the VxRail Manager plugin shown in *Figure 1.15*. The upgrade components including VMware vCenter Server Appliance, VMware vSphere ESXi, VxRail Manager, and VxRail Manager VIB, and so on. You can check *Chapter 6*, *VxRail Upgrade*, for more details:

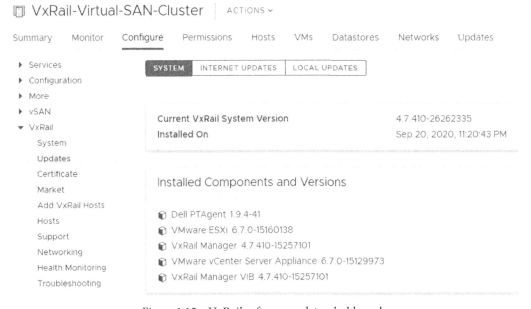

Figure 1.15 – VxRail software updates dashboard

VxRail's architecture can deliver cost-effective and flexible scale-out. The customer can scale out the computer and storage capacity when adding a new node to the existing VxRail cluster (*Figure 1.16*). You can go to *Chapter 7, VxRail Scale-Out Operations*, for more details:

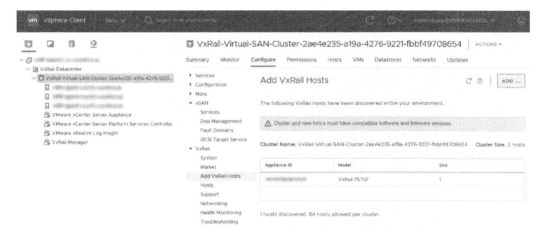

Figure 1.16 – The Add VxRail Hosts dashboard

SPBM is an embedded feature in a VxRail cluster. In *Figure 1.17*, we specify the name of the VM storage policy in SPBM. It has four steps to create a VM storage policy, for example, we can choose policy structure, **RAID-1 (Mirroring)**, **RAID-5/6 (Erasure Coding)**, and so on. You can go to *Chapter 5, Managing VMware vSAN*, for more details:

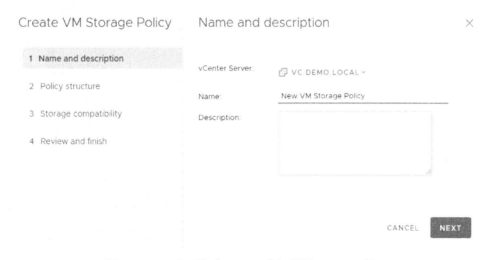

Figure 1.17 – Specify the name of the VM storage policy

Dell EMC RP4VM can deliver the data protection of virtual machines with its point-in-time synchronization or asynchronization in a local VxRail cluster or across VxRail clusters between two separate locations. In *Figure 1.18*, the management panel of RP4VM is fully integrated with vCenter Server:

Figure 1.18 – Dell EMC RP4VM dashboard

VxRail's support service can deliver single vendor support from Dell EMC for both hardware and software. This support service is working with ESRS, which provides a 24 x 7 remote support service provided by the Dell EMC support team. The Dell EMC technical support team has the deep VMware knowledge to resolve the VMware issue in each service request. The customer does not involve any VMware support team to resolve technical problems. VxRail's support service includes three types of service support-level agreement: Basic, ProSupport, and ProSupport Plus. You can refer to *Figure 1.19* for more details:

Feature	Basic	ProSupport	ProSupport Plus
Remote technical support	9x5	24x7	24x7
Covered products	Hardware	Hardware Software	Hardware Software
Onsite hardware support	Next business day	Next business day or 4hr mission critical	Next business day or 4hr mission critical
Automated issue detection and case creation		●	●
Self-service case initiation and management		●	●
Access to software updates		●	●
Priority access to specialized support experts			●
3rd party software support			●
Assigned Technology Service Manager			●
Personalized assessments and recommendations			●
Semiannual systems maintenance			●

Figure 1.19 – Dell support comparison; this information is copyright of Dell Technologies

With *Figure 1.19*, you can choose the different support services to support the VxRail system based on the Dell support service agreement.

VxRail system management

VxRail Manager is a single virtual machine that runs on the VxRail Appliance. After the initial deployment of the VxRail cluster, VxRail Manager is fully integrated through the VxRail Manager plugin for vCenter. In *Figure 1.20*, we can see that the VxRail Manager plugin for vCenter can deliver VxRail cluster management from the vSphere HTML5 client, and it can mainly provide four functions: deployment, update, monitoring, and maintenance. VxRail's deployment function can deliver over 200 automated tasks, such as node discovery, node configuration, VxRail cluster building, and so on:

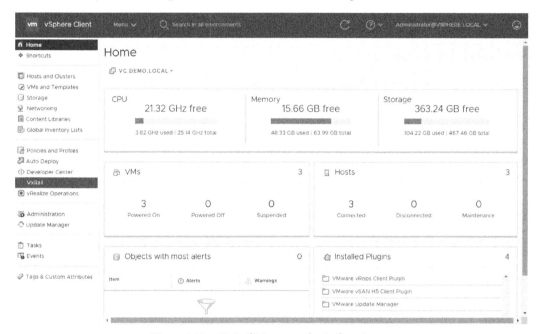

Figure 1.20 – VxRail Manager plugin for vCenter

The VxRail update function can deliver online and offline bundle updates for hardware and software components; this includes VxRail Manager updates, hypervisor updates, VCSA updates, firmware updates, BIOS updates, other hardware component updates, and so on. All update components are delivered as a single software package that has already been tested and validated by Dell EMC.

The VxRail Manager for vCenter plugin can monitor system health with deep hardware intelligence and a user-friendly GUI. It also supports integration with the management packs for VMware vRealize Operations Manager. A VxRail management pack is a free software management pack with VMware vRealize Operations Manager that delivers system monitoring and troubleshooting for the VxRail cluster.

> **Important note**
>
> The VxRail management pack does not bundle software on the VxRail system; it is an optional feature on the VxRail system.

When the system administrator performs maintenance operations on the VxRail system, such as hardware replacement, hardware upgrade, system scale-out, software package upgrade, and so on, they can execute these operation tasks via the VxRail Manager plugin for vCenter and can deliver it in VMware vCenter Server; this can minimize the VxRail cluster's service interruption during maintenance windows.

VxRail resources

In this section, we will discuss VxRail documentation and resources. This includes the Dell EMC support site, Dell EMC SolVe, and VMware documentation.

As we can see in *Figure 1.21*, the Dell EMC support site provides access to technical documentation, a knowledge base, and downloads for Dell EMC products. The VxRail documentation can be accessed from `https://www.dell.com/support/home/en-us/product-support/product/vxrail-gen2-hardware`:

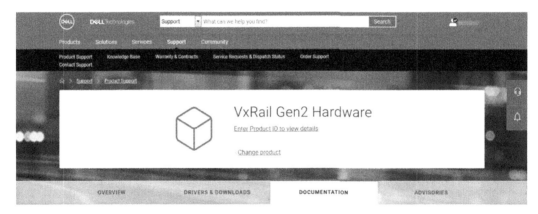

Figure 1.21 – Dell Technologies support portal

Dell EMC SolVe is interactive software used by Dell EMC employees, partners, and customers. It has two versions: SolVe Online (*Figure 1.22*) and SolVe Desktop (*Figure 1.23*). Dell EMC SolVe is used to generate the detailed step-by-step procedures for installing and configuring Dell EMC products, such as VxRail appliances, Unity XT storage, RP4VM, and so on:

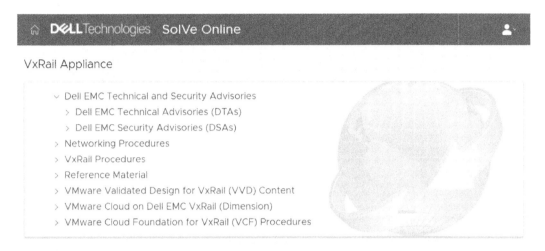

Figure 1.22 – Dell Technologies SolVe Online

SolVe Online is a web-based application. You can access SolVe Online with this link: `https://solveonline.emc.com/solve/products`.

SolVe Desktop is Windows-based software. To access SolVe Desktop, you can download and install the SolVe Desktop utility from the Dell EMC support site at `https://support.emc.com`:

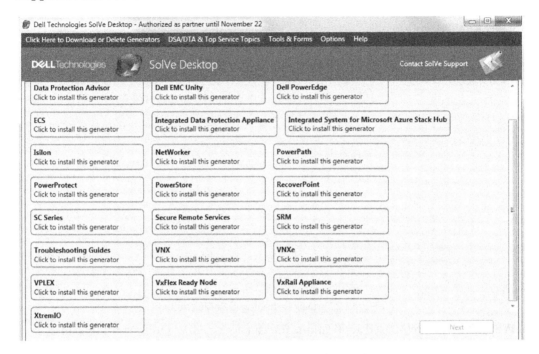

Figure 1.23 – Dell Technologies SolVe Desktop

> **Important note**
>
> You need a Dell EMC employee, partner, or customer account to access both SolVe Online and Desktop.

Since VMware vSphere with vSAN is running on VxRail, the VMware documentation is also valid for the VxRail environment. As shown in *Figure 1.24*, you can find the VMware vSphere and vSAN documentation at `https://docs.vmware.com/`:

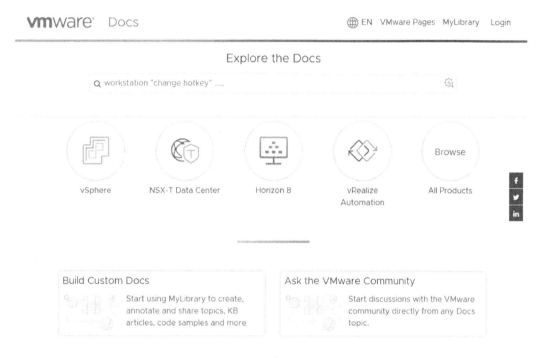

Figure 1.24 – VMware documentation website

If you have any technical or support questions about your VxRail Appliance, you can use the preceding tools to find relevant information.

Summary

In this chapter, we learned about hardware, the different series of VxRail, configuration minimums and maximums, licensing, and architecture for VxRail, which will help us make decisions based on Live Optics gatherings when building a new system.

In the next chapter, we will learn about VxRail installation, including the preparation and installation procedures of a VxRail Appliance.

Questions

1. Which series does not exist for the VxRail Appliance?

    a. M Series

    b. E Series

    c. D Series

    d. P Series

    e. S Series

2. Which licenses are bundled with the VxRail Appliance?

    a. VMware vRealize Log Insight

    b. VMware vCenter Server Appliance

    c. VMware vSAN

    d. VMware vSphere

    e. Dell EMC RecoverPoint for Virtual Machines

3. Which series does not have the all-flash option in the VxRail Appliance?

    a. M Series

    b. E Series

    c. D Series

    d. P Series

    e. S Series

4. If the customer is planning to deploy VDI into a VxRail system, as a VxRail consultant, which VxRail option should you propose to the customer?

    a. VxRail E Series hybrid

    b. VxRail P Series hybrid

    c. VxRail P Series all-flash

    d. VxRail V Series all-flash

    e. VxRail S Series hybrid

5. With which license can the customer reuse their existing license after the VxRail cluster initialization?

    a. VMware vSphere license

    a. VMware vCenter Server Appliance

    c. VMware vSAN license

    d. VMware vRealize Operations Manager

    e. Any VMware product license

6. Which of these is an unsupported configuration in the VxRail system?

    a. VxRail V Series all-flash

    b. VxRail S Series all-flash

    c. VxRail V Series NVMe

    d. VxRail P Series NVMe

    e. VxRail E Series hybrid

    f. All the above

7. What are the main software components that exist in the VxRail system?

    a. VxRail Manager

    b. VMware vSphere Replication

    c. VMware Site Recovery Manager

    d. VMware vSAN

    e. VMware vSphere

8. Which VxRail Service-level agreements can provide access to software updates?

    a. ProSupport

    b. Enterprise Plus

    c. ProSupport Plus

    d. Basic

    e. Enterprise

    f. None of the above

9. Which resources do we use to access the step-by-step installation procedures for the VxRail system?

    a. VMware documentation

    b. Dell EMC support site

    c. Dell EMC SolVe Online

    d. MyVMware support site

    e. Dell EMC SolVe Desktop

10. Which unit is used to manage the VxRail cluster?

    a. VxRail Manager

    b. vCenter Server Appliance

    c. VxRail Manager for vCenter plugin

    d. vSphere Client

    e. vRealize Operations Manager

11. Which software component does not exist on the VxRail 7.0. platform?

    a. VxRail Manager

    b. vCenter Server Appliance

    c. vCenter Service Platform Controller

    d. VxRail Manager for vCenter plugin

    e. vRealize Log Insight

12. Which VxRail series includes 15 virtual machine licenses of RP4VM per chassis?

    a. VxRail P Series

    b. VxRail S Series

    c. VxRail E Series

    d. VxRail G Series

    e. VxRail D Series

2

VxRail Installation

The previous chapter provided you with an overview of VxRail Hyperconverged Infrastructure. You learned what Dell EMC VxRail Hyperconverged Infrastructure is and its key functions. VxRail Appliance can deliver a lot of features that can offload the system administrator's daily operation and configuration. The initial setup of VxRail requires three identical nodes running in a VxRail cluster. According to different business requirements, the system administrator can purchase a suitable model for deploying a VxRail cluster.

This chapter will describe the installation of VxRail Appliance. You will learn how to plan and design VxRail Appliance pre-deployment and post-deployment activities. This includes preparation of the pre-installation site checklist, hardware and software installation, network environment validation, and VxRail initialization and configuration. By the end of this chapter, you will have learned the step-by-step installation procedure for VxRail Appliance and network environment validation. Now we will begin to discuss each of these topics.

In this chapter, we're going to cover the following main topics:

- Site preparation for VxRail Appliance
- VxRail Appliance hardware installation
- VxRail Appliance initialization
- VxRail validation

Technical requirements

In this chapter, we need to prepare a laptop for VxRail initialization. For VxRail initialization, we will use a four-port configuration on the **Network Daughter Card (NDC)** – an onboard network adapter. Make sure Microsoft Windows 7 or above is running on this laptop, and that the web browser is installed on your laptop. The latest versions of Firefox, Google Chrome, and Microsoft Internet Explorer 10 or above are all supported.

Environment

In this chapter, we will discuss VxRail installation based on the architecture in *Figure 2.1*. There are three VxRail nodes (P570 model), two 10 Gb network switches, and one 1 Gb network switch. The following table is the summary of each hardware component. The two pairs of 10 Gb switches are used to network VxRail Appliance, and the 1 Gb switch is used for the **Integrated Dell Remote Access Controller** (**iDRAC**) network:

Components	Network Port	Network Role
VxRail Node A	Port 1	ESXi Management
	Port 2	Virtual Machine
	Port 3	vSAN Network
	Port 4	vMotion Network
	iDRAC Port	iDRAC Network
VxRail Node B	Port 1	ESXi Management
	Port 2	Virtual Machine
	Port 3	vSAN Network
	Port 4	vMotion Network
	iDRAC port	iDRAC Network
VxRail Node C	Port 1	ESXi Management
	Port 2	Virtual Machine
	Port 3	vSAN Network
	Port 4	vMotion Network
	iDRAC port	iDRAC Network
10 Gb Top-of-Rack (TOR) switch A	Six 10 Gb ports enabled	ESXi Management
		Virtual Machine
		vSAN Network
		vMotion Network
10 Gb Top-of-Rack (TOR) switch B	Six 10 Gb ports enabled	ESXi Management
		Virtual Machine
		vSAN Network
		vMotion Network
1 Gb Out-of-Band (OOB) switch	Three 1 Gb ports enabled	iDRAC Network

According to the preceding table, we know the network configuration of each piece of equipment:

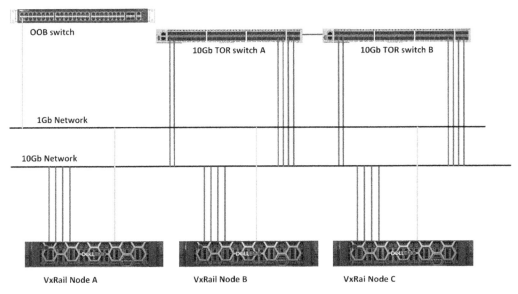

Figure 2.1 – The network connections of each hardware component

In *Figure 2.1*, you can see that there are three network groups. These are the **iDRAC network**, the **Management and Virtual Machine network**, and the **vSAN and vMotion network**.

Site preparation for VxRail Appliance

Prior to VxRail initialization, we must complete the validation of network settings and the **Domain Name System** (**DNS**) settings for VxRail Appliance. Each VxRail series appliance includes a 10/25 Gb NDC and one iDRAC port. Each NDC is bundled with either four 10 Gb SFP+ ports or two 10/25 Gb SPF+ ports. Each VxRail model series offers different choices in terms of network connectivity. Now it shows some of the physical network port options for each VxRail series. In *Figure 2.2*, you can see four 10/25 Gb NDC ports and one iDRAC port on the VxRail E Series:

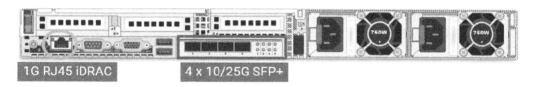

Figure 2.2 – Back view of the VxRail E Series on Dell's 14th-generation PowerEdge server

In *Figure 2.3*, you can see four 10/25 Gb NDC ports and one iDRAC port on the VxRail V, P, and S Series:

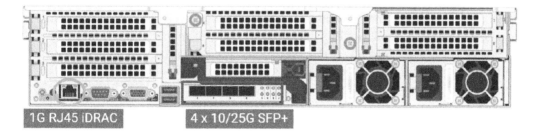

Figure 2.3 – Back view of the VxRail V/P/S Series on Dell's 14th-generation PowerEdge server

In *Figure 2.4*, you can see two 10/25 Gb NDC ports and one iDRAC port on the VxRail G Series:

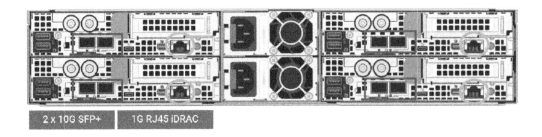

Figure 2.4 – Back view of the VxRail G Series on Dell's 14th-generation PowerEdge server

Based on the network connectivity of *Figures 2.2*, *2.3*, and *2.4*, you know the number of network cables required to connect to each Ethernet switch, in other words, 10/25 SPF+ and 1 Gb network uplinks.

Top-of-Rack switch requirement

When the network connections of VxRail Appliance are ready, we should verify the network settings on each Ethernet switch. We can download the **Network Validation Tool** (**NVT**) for VxRail from the Dell support website (`https://dell.com/support`) before VxRail deployment. The NVT is used for validating switch port definitions with a Dell EMC partner or Dell EMC engineer. The validations include the switch configuration, edge port configuration, VLAN configuration, and so on. First, we must download the VxRail Appliance **Pre-Engagement Questionnaire** (**PEQ**) from `https://psapps.emc.com/central/solution/PEQ`. The PEQ is used to prepare all the requirements regarding VxRail installation, such as IP addresses for the components on the VxRail external management network (embedded vCenter, ESXi hosts, VxRail Manager, and so on), DNS, and VxRail accounts.

> **Important note**
> Dell EMC employees and their partners can access the VxRail Appliance PEQ.

Now we will describe all the network requirements for VxRail internal and external network settings (the third column) in the following table based on the PEQ:

Network Component	Category	Description
System	VxRail internal Management VLAN ID	This is the VxRail internal management network. The default VLAN ID is 3939.
	Global settings	Time zone
		NTP server
		DNS server

Now we will describe each of these components in turn.

System: These are the global settings on the VxRail cluster, and we need to provide a native VLAN ID for the VxRail management network, and the IP addresses of the **Network Time Protocol** (**NTP**) server and the **Domain Name Server** (**DNS**). There is also a default VLAN of 3939 configured on each VxRail node that comes from the Dell factory. This VLAN ID must be configured on the TOR switches:

Network Component	Category	Description
Networks	ESXi hostnames and IP addresses	Domain name
		ESXi hostname prefix
		Starting IP address for the IP pool
		Ending IP address for the IP pool
	vCenter Server	vCenter Server hostname
		vCenter Server IP address
	Platform Services Controller	Platform Services Controller hostname
		Platform Services Controller IP address
	VxRail Manager	VxRail Manager hostname
		VxRail Manager IP address
		VLAN ID for external management; this is untagged/native
		Subnet mask for VxRail Management Network
		Gateway for VxRail Management Network

Networks: This setting includes three parts, in other words, the IP address and hostname of each VxRail node, the site name of the vCenter **Platform Services Controller** (**PSC**), and the network information of VxRail Manager. There are three network settings for each VxRail system virtual machine:

1. Define an IP address pool for each VxRail node, its hostname, and its domain name. This IP pool range is at least three IP addresses. You may reserve more IP addresses for future cluster expansion.

2. During VxRail initialization, it can deploy a vCenter Server virtual appliance or it can be pointed to an external vCenter and a vCenter PSC virtual machine on the VxRail cluster. We need to define the hostname and IP address for both the vCenter Server and the PSC.

3. We now need to define the IP address, network gateway, and VLAN ID for VxRail Manager's virtual machine:

Network Component	Category	Description
vMotion	vMotion Network	Starting address for vMotion's IP pool
		Ending address for vMotion's IP pool
		The subnet mask of vMotion Network
		The VLAN ID of vMotion Network

vMotion Network: We need to define a vMotion IP address pool and VLAN ID for each VxRail node. This IP pool range is at least three IP addresses. You may reserve more IP addresses for future cluster expansion:

Network Component	Category	Description
vSAN	vSAN Network	Starting address for vSAN's IP pool
		Ending address for vSAN's IP pool
		The subnet mask of vSAN Network
		The VLAN ID of vSAN Network

vSAN Network: We need to define a vSAN IP address pool and VLAN ID for each VxRail node. This IP pool range is at least three IP addresses. You may reserve more IP addresses for future cluster expansion:

Network Component	Category	Description
VM Networks	Virtual Machine Networks	VM Network Port Group Name
		The VLAN ID of VM Networks

VM Networks: This setting is used for the virtual machine's network connection: we need to configure at least one VM port group in this setting:

Network Component	Category	Description
Solutions	vRealize Log Insight	vRealize Log Insight's hostname
		vRealize Log Insight's IP address

Solutions: This is the log server configuration. There are three options in this configuration: deploy vRealize Log Insight, connect to the existing Syslog server, and do not install any Syslog servers:

Network Component	Category	Description
Accounts	vCenter Server management account	vCenter Server management username
	The credentials for all virtual appliance accounts	The root account for all virtual appliances in the VxRail cluster
	VxRail Manager Service account (Username: "mystic")	VxRail Manager service account's password
	ESXi root account	ESXi root account's password
	ESXi management account	ESXi management account's username
		ESXi management account's password

Accounts: In this configuration, we need to define three pieces of account information.

We need to create an Active Directory account (with **Administrator role** or **VMware HCIA Management role**) for vCenter Server's management account.

- vCenter Server's management account is used to manage services in vCenter Server.
- The root account for all virtual appliances runs in the VxRail cluster. It includes vCenter Server's root, administrator, and management accounts, the PSC root account, VxRail Manager's root account, and vRealize Log's root and administrator accounts.
- The VxRail Manager service account is used to manage services in VxRail Manager's virtual appliance. By default, the username of this account is *mystic*.

- ESXi root and management accounts are used to manage services in each VxRail node:

Network Component	Category	Description
iDRAC	iDRAC network for each VxRail node	Starting address for iDRAC's IP pool
		Ending address for iDRAC's IP pool
		The subnet mask of iDRAC Network
		Gateway of iDRAC Network

iDRAC is the management and control panel embedded in the motherboard of Dell PowerEdge 14th-generation servers. The network connection is connected to the **Out-of-Band (OOB)** management Ethernet switch.

We must create the required VLAN IDs (3939, vMotion VLAN, vSAN VLAN, and VxRail Manager management VLAN), and IPv6 multicast needs to be enabled for VxRail loudmouth on private management network on the TOR switches or existing Ethernet switches. When the preceding network requirements are ready on TOR and OOB Ethernet switches, we can go and prepare the DNS requirements.

> **Important note**
>
> Please ensure that all VxRail external management networks (Internal vCenter, ESXi hosts, VxRail Manager, and so on), as well as vMotion and vSAN networks, are non-routable and all on the same subnet.

DNS requirements

When we prepare all the IP addresses and hostnames of each VxRail component, we go to the DNS to add the related DNS entries for VxRail in the DNS according to the preceding Ethernet switch requirements. The following table provides example DNS entries:

VxRail Component	Host Name	FQDN (Fully Qualified Domain Name)
VxRail Node A	esxi01	esxi01.<your domain name>
VxRail Node B	esxi02	esxi02.<your domain name>
VxRail Node C	esxi03	esxi03.<your domain name>
vCenter Server Appliance	vc	vc.<your domain name>
vCenter Platform Services Controller	psc	psc.<your domain name>
VxRail Manager	vxm	vxm.<your domain name>
vRealize Log Insight	vrealize	vrealize.<your domain name>

We must confirm that both the forward and reverse entries for the VxRail management components were created in DNS Manager:

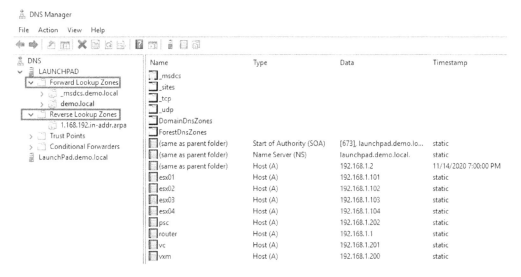

Figure 2.5 – DNS Manager

When you add both forward and reverse entries for all VxRail management components to the DNS, please use the nslookup FQDN and the nslookup IP address for each VxRail management component.

Power and rack space requirements

Prior to VxRail hardware installation, we should check the power and rack space requirements for the VxRail nodes and Ethernet switches. The following table is a summary of the power and rack space requirements based on the architecture in *Figure 2.1*:

Components	Rack space	Number of power cords required
VxRail Node A	Two units of rack space	Two c19 power cords
VxRail Node B	Two units of rack space	Two c19 power cords
VxRail Node C	Two units of rack space	Two c19 power cords
Top-of-Rack switch A	One unit of rack space	Two c19 power cord
Top-of-Rack switch B	One unit of rack space	Two c19 power cord
Out-of-Band switch	One unit of rack space	One c19 power cord

> **Important note**
>
> Each VxRail series model requires different rack space and power consumption. Refer to the Dell EMC VxRail Appliance Specification Sheet for more details at `https://www.delltechnologies.com/resources/en-hk/asset/data-sheets/products/converged-infrastructure/h16763-vxrail-spec-sheet.pdf`.

Before powering on all the previously mentioned hardware, please ensure that the data center can provide enough power to all VxRail appliances and TOR switches.

VxRail Appliance hardware installation

Once the site preparation for VxRail Appliance is complete, we can start the VxRail hardware installation, which includes the following steps:

1. Mounting VxRail appliances needs to be done in a specific order, starting with the lowest serial number at the bottom of the rack and stacking them up as the numbers ascend in the customer-provided rack.

2. Mount the TOR switches into the customer-provided rack if the latter does not provide TOR switches.

3. Cable TOR switches to VxRail Appliance nodes.

Mounting the VxRail appliances

In the best practices of VxRail Appliance deployment, we should install the VxRail appliances in a specific order, starting with the lowest serial number at the bottom of the rack and stacking them up as they ascend, and install the TOR switches at the top of the rack:

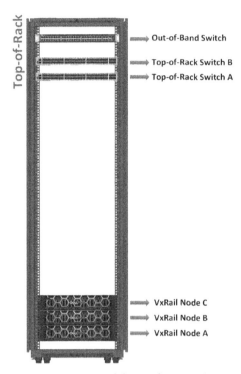

Figure 2.6 – Rack layout for VxRail

Figure 2.6 shows mounting appliances from bottom to top by serial number.

Cabling VxRail appliances

When the hardware mounting is complete, we can implement network connections between the VxRail nodes and Ethernet switches. Use two **Top-of-Rack** (**TOR**) switches for **high-availability** (**HA**) applications, and effect network connections between two TOR switches. In each VxRail series model, a DNC is built into each VxRail node, which has two options – four 10 Gb ports and two 25 Gb ports. If the configuration is four ports with 10 Gb, two ports are shared with both management and the VM network, others are shared with both vSphere vMotion and the vSAN network. If the configuration is two ports with 10 Gb or 25 Gb, two ports are shared with management, vSphere vMotion, vSAN, and VM network. Both two ports are four ports are active/passive configurations.

In this configuration, the DNC is built with four 10 Gb ports. There are four 10 Gb SFP+ cables connected to TOR switches – two cables (ports 1 and 3) connected to TOR switch A, and the others (ports 2 and 4) connected to TOR switch B, and one 1 Gb RJ45 cable connected to an OOB switch. For other VxRail nodes, you can repeat the same procedures for the network connections:

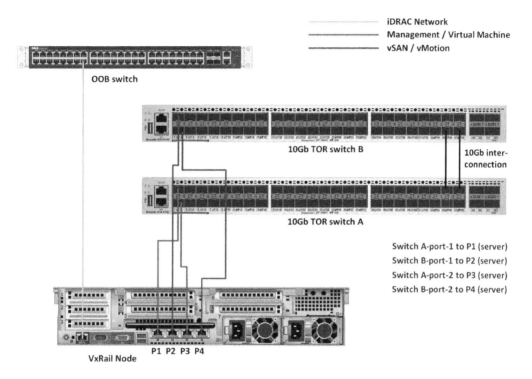

Figure 2.7 – The cable connection diagram for each VxRail node

> **Important note**
>
> The VxRail system traffic is connected to the DNC. VxRail system traffic includes the ESXi management, vSAN, vCenter Server, and vMotion networks. It does not support the migration of system traffic to optional PCIe ports. Ensure that multicast traffic for IPv4 and IPv6 are forwarded between the two TOR switches.

Once all the cable connections between VxRail appliances and TOR switches are complete, then we can validate the network settings on each TOR switch with the **NVT**. We generate the JSON file from the **PEQ**, then upload this JSON file into the NVT for network validation. If the validation is no problem, then we can proceed to the next section.

VxRail Appliance initialization

Once the VxRail hardware installation is complete, we can begin VxRail Appliance initialization. First, we must prepare a laptop for VxRail initialization and configuration. The operating system is the Windows platform. Connect the laptop to a port on the TOR switch, or to a VLAN that can access the VxRail appliance:

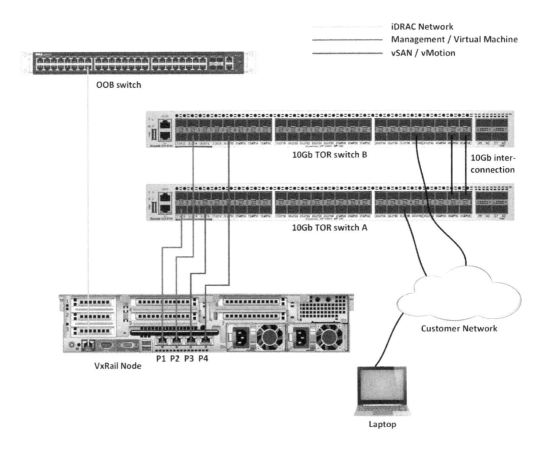

Figure 2.8 – The cable connection diagram for the management laptop

Now we can move on to the next section, where we will configure the connectivity of VxRail Manager.

Configuring a laptop for VxRail Manager connectivity

To configure a laptop for VxRail Manager connectivity, perform the following steps:

1. Set up an IP address on the same subnet as the permanent address to be assigned to VxRail Manager (the default IP address for VxRail Manager is 192.168.10.200).

2. We configure an IP address (192.168.10.101/24) on the laptop to connect on the same subnet as VxRail Manager:

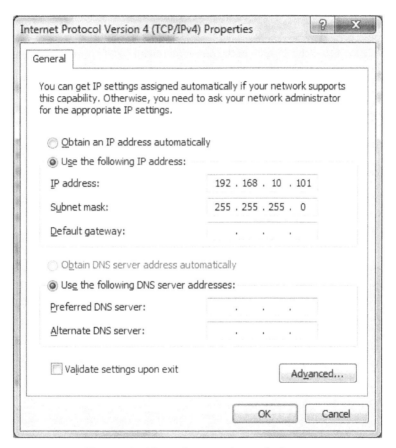

Figure 2.9 – Network properties on the laptop

3. Now we can power on the VxRail node. The power button is located in the upper-right corner:

Figure 2.10 – The location of the power button on Dell PowerEdge nodes

When the VxRail node is powering on, the **light emitting diode** (**LED**) shows a blue light.

Building a VxRail cluster

In our scenario, there are three VxRail nodes:

1. First, we must power on the first VxRail node (**VxRail Node A** in *Figure 2.1*). Each VxRail node requires about 5 to 6 minutes in order to power up successfully, and then we can see the vSphere ESXi management page. After this, we can access the VxRail Manager virtual machine once the first VxRail node bootup is successful. Now we can start to build up the VxRail cluster:

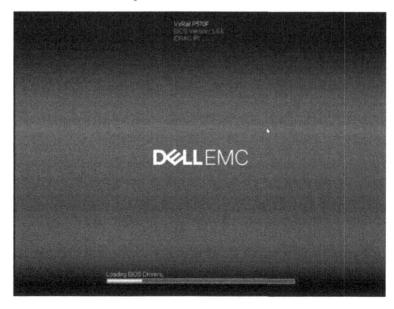

Figure 2.11 – VxRail node bootup

2. Launch a browser on your laptop and input this IP address – `192.168.10.200`, which is the default IP address of VxRail Manager. Since VxRail Manager is a VM running within the hypervisor of a node, we need to make sure the VM network is configured properly. This could be the `192.169.10.x` network. We can change the VM network tag on ESXi from the DCUI by entering `esxcli network vswitch standard portgroup set -p "VM Network"`. Or, we can make requirements on the switch/laptop, such as L2 connectivity to talk to VxRail Manager. Then, when you can see the VxRail welcome page, click **GET STARTED** to build up the VxRail cluster. Now we can power on the remaining VxRail nodes (VxRail nodes B and C). Once VxRail nodes B and C have booted up fully, we can proceed to the next step:

Figure 2.12 – VxRail Welcome page

3. Click **ACCEPT** to accept the end-user license agreement:

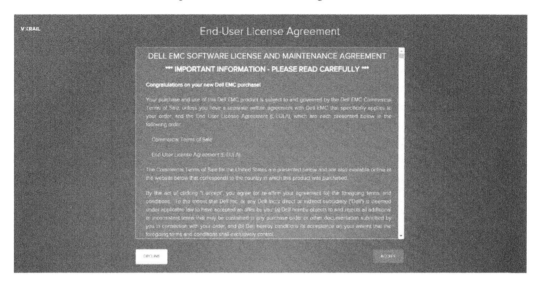

Figure 2.13 – End-User License Agreement of VxRail

4. On this page, three VxRail appliances are revealed. You can see a blue home icon at the top of the VxRail appliance, which is the first VxRail node. Select the **I confirm I want to configure the listed VxRail nodes** checkbox and then click **NEXT**:

Figure 2.14 – Scanning for VxRail nodes

5. There are two options to configure VxRail; these are **Step-by-step** and **Configuration file**. If you select **Step-by-step**, you enter the required VxRail configuration settings step by step. If you select **Configuration file**, you will be prompted to select the JSON file created by the PEQ. In this chapter, we will use **Step-by-step** to configure VxRail. Then, click **NEXT**:

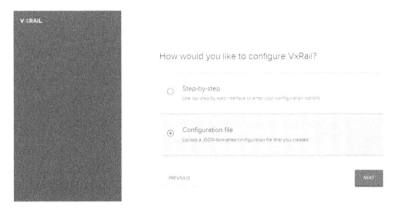

Figure 2.15 – How would you like to configure VxRail?

6. According to the information provided in the preceding *Site preparation for VxRail Appliance* section, input the IP address for **NTP server**, select **4x10GbE** under **NIC configuration**, and then click **NEXT**. In our scenario, each VxRail node has four 10 Gb ports:

Figure 2.16 – Selecting the NIC configuration on VxRail

7. Under **Top Level Domain**, you need to input the domain server. In **ESXi Hosts**, you need to complete the **Host names, Starting IP address**, and **Ending IP address** fields for ESXi management's IP pool:

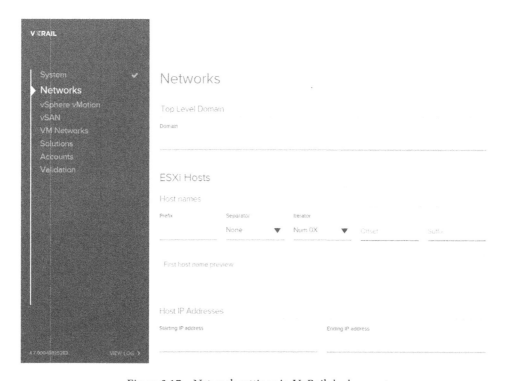

Figure 2.17 – Network settings in VxRail deployment

8. Under **vCenter Server**, if we select **Join existing vCenter Server**, the VxRail cluster would be part of the existing vCenter and no new vCenter would be created. If we don't select **Join existing vCenter Server**, then it will create an internal vCenter for this VxRail cluster/appliance. In our scenario, we will deploy an internal vCenter. We need to complete the **hostname** and **IP address** fields for **vCenter Server** and **Platform Services Controller**:

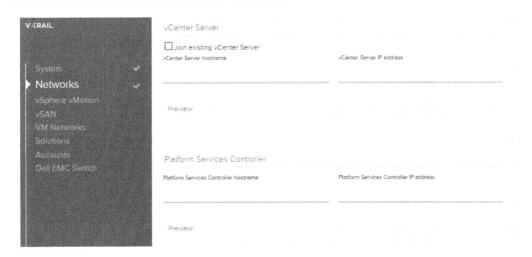

Figure 2.18 – Network settings in VxRail deployment

9. Under **VxRail Manager**, complete the **VxRail Manager hostname** and **IP address** fields. Under **Networking**, complete the **Management Subnet mask**, **Management Gateway**, **Management Network VLAN ID**, and **DNS server(s)** fields for each VxRail node. Then, click **NEXT**:

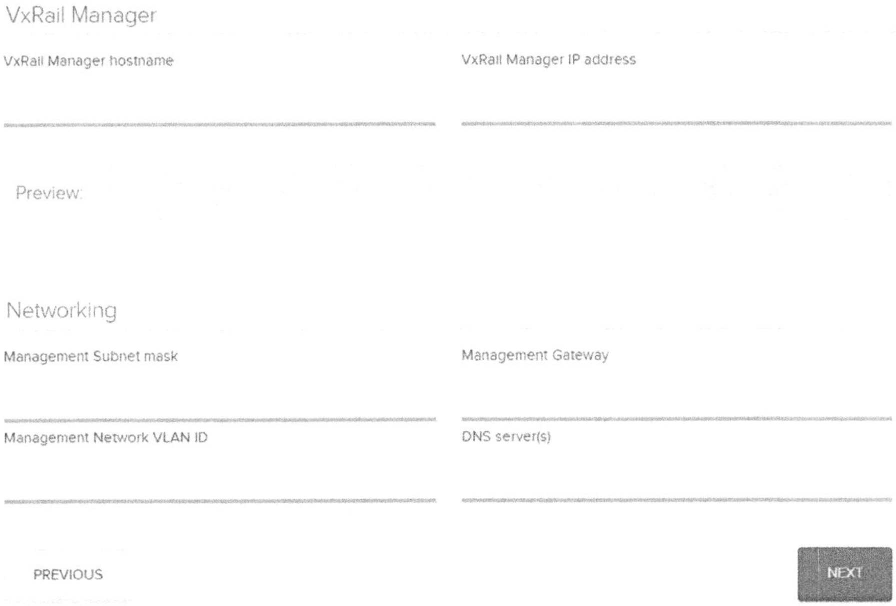

VxRail Manager

VxRail Manager hostname   VxRail Manager IP address

Preview:

Networking

Management Subnet mask   Management Gateway

Management Network VLAN ID   DNS server(s)

PREVIOUS   NEXT

Figure 2.19 – Network settings in VxRail deployment

10. Under **vSphere vMotion**, complete the **Starting address**, **Ending address**, **Subnet mask**, and **VLAN ID** fields for the vSphere vMotion network. Then, click **NEXT**:

Figure 2.20 – vSphere vMotion settings in VxRail deployment

11. Under **vSAN**, complete the **Starting address**, **Ending address**, **Subnet mask**, and **VLAN ID** fields for the vSphere vSAN network. Then, click **NEXT**:

Figure 2.21 – vSAN settings in VxRail deployment

12. Under **VM Networks**, complete the **VM network name** and **VLAN ID** fields for the virtual machine network port group. Then, click **NEXT**:

Figure 2.22 – VM Networks settings in VxRail deployment

13. Under **Solutions**, select **vRealize Log Insight** under **Select logging** and complete the **vRealize Log Insight hostname** and **vRealize Log Insight IP address** fields. Then, click **NEXT**:

Figure 2.23 – Solutions settings in VxRail deployment

14. Under **Accounts**, select **Use the same credentials for all virtual appliance accounts**. If you select this option, you use the same password for all accounts (vCenter root, administrator, and management accounts, the PSC root account, VxRail Manager's root account, and vRealize Log Insight's root and administrator accounts). Then, define the username in the **vCenter Server management account username** field.

Under **Shared password for all non-ESXi accounts**, we define the password for all accounts (vCenter root, administrator, and management accounts, the PSC root account, VxRail Manager's root account, and vRealize Log Insight's root and administrator accounts).

Under **VxRail Manager Service account**, we define the password for this account:

Figure 2.24 – Account settings in VxRail deployment

15. Under **ESXi accounts**, you define **Root password**, **Management username**, and **Management password**. Then, click **NEXT**:

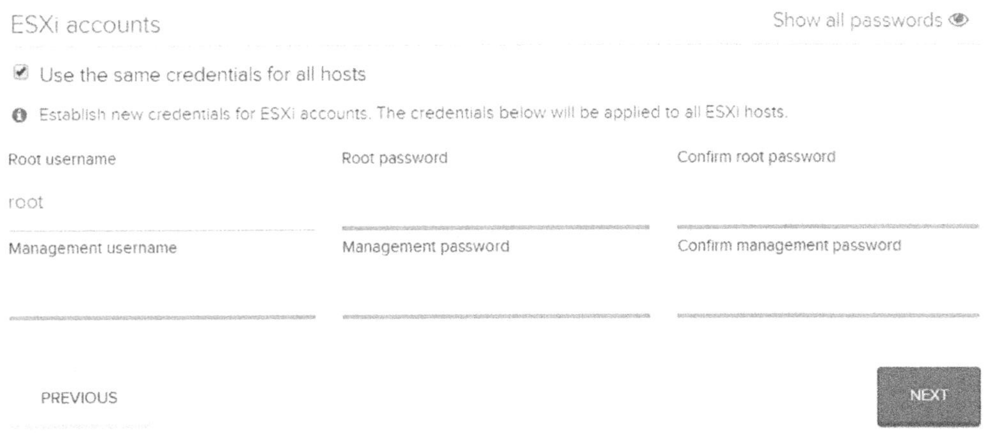

ESXi accounts   Show all passwords 👁

☑ Use the same credentials for all hosts

ℹ Establish new credentials for ESXi accounts. The credentials below will be applied to all ESXi hosts.

Root username   Root password   Confirm root password

root

Management username   Management password   Confirm management password

PREVIOUS   NEXT

Figure 2.25 – Account settings in VxRail deployment

16. Under **Validation**, click **VALIDATE** to start the validation process of VxRail deployment:

Figure 2.26 – Review and validate in VxRail deployment

17. When validation is successfully completed without any errors, you can see that it displays a **BUILD VXRAIL** button. Before we click **BUILD VXRAIL**, we need to click **DOWNLOAD JSON**. This is an important document for site handover and future reference. Then, click **BUILD VXRAIL** to build a VxRail cluster:

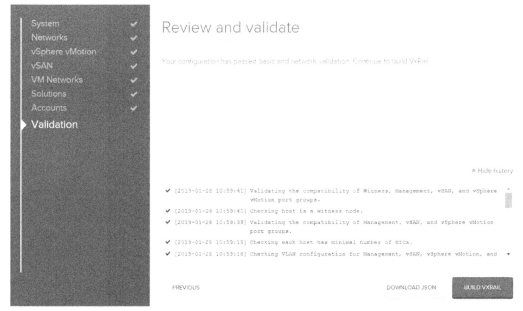

Figure 2.27 – Review and validation in VxRail deployment

This process starts to build up the VxRail cluster. It requires about 30 to 40 minutes to complete the whole process:

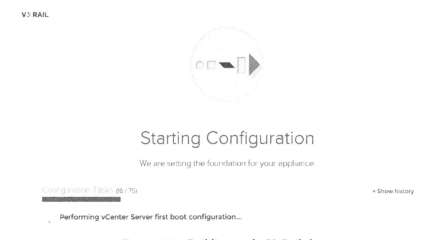

Figure 2.28 – Building up the VxRail cluster

18. The **Hooray!** screen is displayed when the VxRail cluster building process completes successfully. Click **MANAGE VXRAIL** to access the VxRail cluster:

VX RAIL

Please apply your vSAN license as soon as possible. The evaluation license will only last for 60 days.

VxRail is set up and ready to use.   MANAGE VXRAIL >

4.7.000-10825283

Figure 2.29 – VxRail cluster building process completes successfully

> **Important note**
> We need to manually add the vSAN license to each VxRail node once VxRail initialization is completed successfully.

19. This will take you to vCenter Server automatically, and we then use VxRail's administrator account (`administrator@vsphere.local`) to log in to vCenter Server:

Figure 2.30 – vCenter Server web client

20. Finally, you need to add the VMware vSAN licenses to the VxRail node. Go to the **Administration** menu and select **Licensing**, and then **Licenses**. Then, click **Add New Licenses** to add the license:

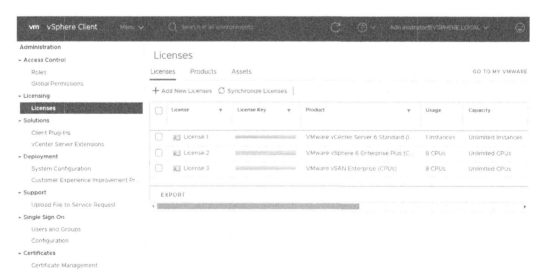

Figure 2.31 – License management in vCenter Server

Once the license is added to each VxRail node, VxRail cluster deployment is completed successfully:

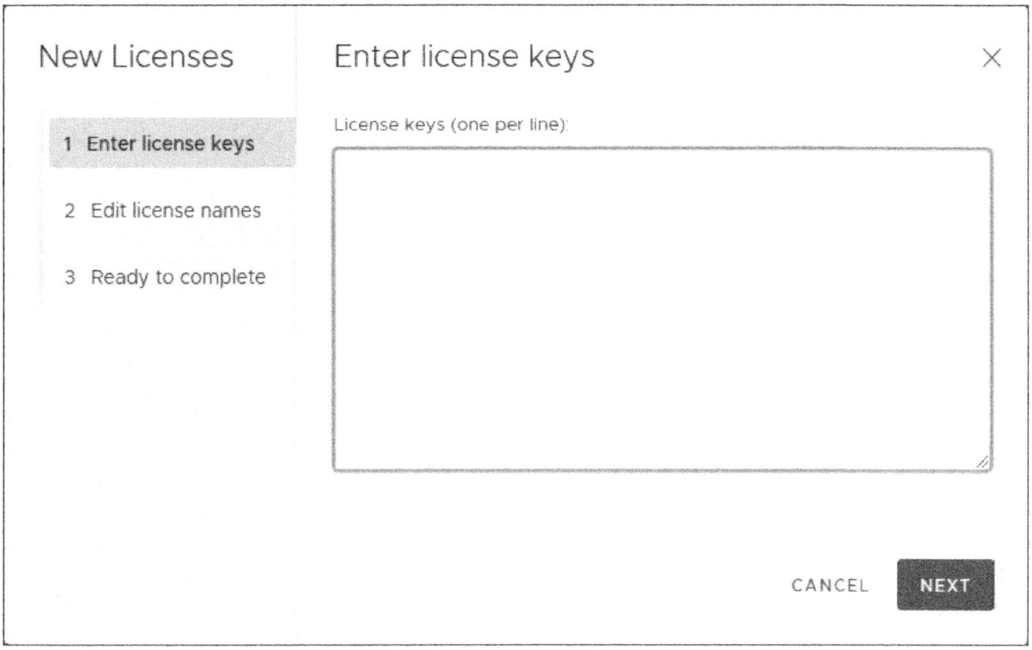

Figure 2.32 – Adding new license keys to the VxRail cluster wizard

Now we can move on to the final section – validating the VxRail cluster.

VxRail validation

Once VxRail initialization is complete, we need to verify the status of the core components in the VxRail cluster:

1. We go to the **Monitor** tab and select **Health** under **vSAN**, making sure that all vSAN services are running with a green icon, including **vSAN Build Recommendation**, **Network**, **Physical disk**, **Data**, **Cluster**, **Capacity utilization**, **Hardware compatibility**, and **Performance service**:

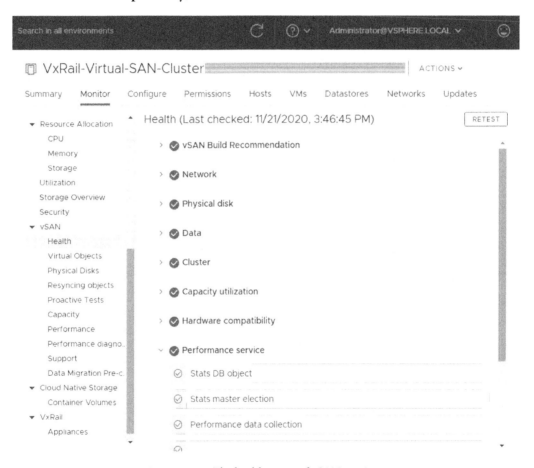

Figure 2.33 – The health status of vSAN services

2. Finally, we go to **VxRail Dashboard** on the home menu and verify that **System Health** shows as **Healthy**. At this point, VxRail cluster deployment has completed successfully:

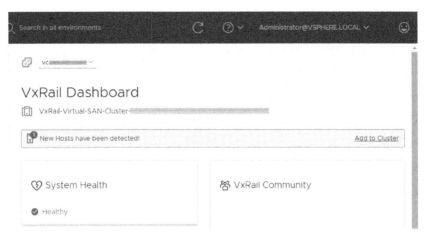

Figure 2.34 – VxRail Dashboard

Now that this VxRail cluster is healthy, you can start to deploy the virtual machines based on your requirements regarding this VxRail cluster.

Summary

In this chapter, we described the VxRail Appliance installation procedures and how to prepare all the requirements. Compared with traditional server deployment, VxRail HCI installation is more intelligent and automatic. We don't spend a lot of time deploying the server and storage because VxRail Appliance includes compute and storage nodes.

In the next chapter, you will get a VxRail administration overview. This includes the VxRail management dashboard and vSAN configuration.

Questions

1. How many network ports are there on the DNC in the VxRail P Series model?

   a. Two

   b. Three

   c. Four

   d. Five

   e. Six

2. Which network setting is required to define the IP address pool during VxRail initialization?

   a. vSAN and vMotion Network

   b. ESXi Management and VMs Network

   c. vCenter Server Network

   d. vRealize Login Insight Network

   e. Platform Services Controller Network

3. What are the configuration requirements in DNS Manager prior to VxRail initialization?

   a. Forward Lookup Zone

   b. Revise Lookup Zone

   c. Both Forward and Revise Lookup Zones

   d. Either Forward or Revise Lookup Zones

   e. None of the above

4. How many TOR switches support the high-availability network connection on VxRail Appliance?

   a. 1

   b. 2

   c. 3

   d. 4

   e. 5

5. What is the default IP address of VxRail Manager?

   a. `192.168.10.10`

   b. `192.168.10.100`

   c. `192.168.10.20`

   d. `192.168.10.200`

   e. None of the above

6. Who can access the VxRail Appliance PEQ?

    a. Any customers

    b. Dell EMC partners

    c. Dell employees

    d. VMware partners

    e. Dell employees and Dell EMC partners

7. Which network's VLAN is an untagged native during VxRail initialization?

    a. vCenter Server Management Network

    b. vSAN Network

    c. vMotion Network

    d. VxRail Manager External Management Network

    e. VMs Network

8. How many configuration methods are supported for VxRail initialization?

    a. 1

    b. 2

    c. 3

    d. 4

    e. 5

9. What license do you need to manually add to each VxRail node once VxRail initialization is complete?

    a. VMware vSphere license

    b. VMware vCenter Server license

    c. VMware vSAN license

    d. VMware vRealize Log Insight license

    e. VxRail Manager license

10. Which screen(s) will be displayed once VxRail initialization is completed successfully?

    a. VxRail Manager screen

    b. vCenter Server Login screen

c. The "Hooray" screen

d. VMware vRealize Log Insight administration screen

e. All the above

11. What are the VLAN IDs for VxRail's internal management network?

a. 3900

b. 3929

c. 3939

d. 3949

e. All the above

12. How many VxRail Manager virtual machines will deploy to the VxRail cluster once VxRail initialization is completed?

a. 0

b. 1

c. 2

d. 3

e. 4

Section 2: Administration of VxRail

In this section, we will learn the administration of VxRail, e.g. VxRail management, vSAN storage policy, VxRail software upgrade and VxRail cluster scale-out, etc.

This section of the book comprises the following chapters:

- *Chapter 3, VxRail Administration Overview*
- *Chapter 4, VxRail Management Overview*
- *Chapter 5, Managing VMware vSAN*
- *Chapter 6, VxRail Upgrade*
- *Chapter 7, VxRail Scale-Out Operations*

3
VxRail Administration Overview

In *Chapter 2, VxRail Installation*, we discussed an overview of VxRail installation. You learned how to prepare the hardware and software requirements for a VxRail installation. You can see from the whole deployment that it is more flexible and automated than the deployment of traditional servers and storage. These features help us minimize the deployment and configuration time, which is why we choose VxRail appliances for new system deployment.

In this chapter, we will describe an overview of VxRail administration. We will learn about the management panel that is used in VxRail appliances. Since the VxRail platform runs on VMware **Virtual SAN** (**vSAN**), we will explain the vSAN architecture and its concepts. You will see a review of the core components of a VxRail appliance by the end of this chapter, such as the VxRail Manager plugin for vCenter, **vSphere Distributed Switch** (**vDS**), vSAN configuration, and so on. Now, we will begin to discuss each topic in this chapter.

In this chapter, we're going to cover the following main topics:

- VxRail management interfaces
- VMware vSAN
- VxRail cluster configuration

Technical requirements

In this chapter, we will make sure that our workstation is a Windows platform, and a web browser is installed. The latest versions of Firefox, Google Chrome, and Microsoft Internet Explorer 10 or above are all supported. The VxRail software should be version 4.7.300 or above.

VxRail management interfaces

In this section, we will introduce the VxRail management interfaces, such as vSphere Client, vSphere Web Client, VxRail Manager, the VxRail Manager plugin for vCenter, and the **Integrated Dell Remote Access Controller (iDRAC)**. Prior to VxRail 4.7.100, VxRail Manager and vCenter Server were two separate management interfaces in a VxRail appliance. For virtual machine operation tasks, we needed to perform them with vCenter Server. For VxRail operation tasks, such as hardware replacement, node scale-out, software upgrades, and so on, we had to perform them with the VxRail management interface. There was no full integration and management with both vCenter Server and VxRail Manager. Starting with VxRail 4.7.100, the VxRail Manager Plugin for vCenter is available, which can provide central management of the VxRail cluster, and can be accessed with vSphere Client. Let's learn about these interfaces in more detail. *Figure 3.1* shows the VxRail management interface:

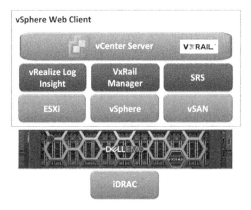

Figure 3.1 – VxRail management interface

Now we will discuss each management interface:

- **VMware vSphere Client** and **vSphere Web Client** are web browser-based user interfaces, and we can directly connect to ESXi and vCenter Server with these two clients. vSphere Client is a Flash-based interface, and vSphere Web Client is an HTML5-based interface. Only vSphere Web Client can support the VxRail Manager plugin for vCenter.

  In VxRail 4.5.xxx, the VxRail Manager plugin for vCenter is not available. We cannot manage VxRail Manager directly with vSphere Client and Web Client. Starting from VxRail 4.7.100, we can manage VxRail Manager directly with vSphere Web Client. For efficient performance, vSphere Web Client is recommended to use as a management interface.

- The **VxRail Manager plugin for vCenter** can provide administration tasks in the VxRail cluster, such as storage provisioning, virtual machine configuration, node scale-out, life cycle management, system monitoring, and so on.

In *Figure 3.2*, we can see the VxRail Manager plugin for vCenter on the **Home** menu after logging in to vCenter Server:

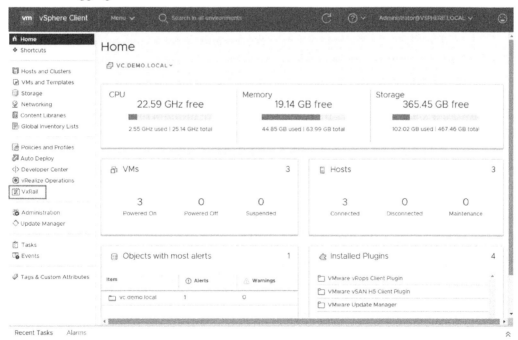

Figure 3.2 – VxRail Manager plugin for vCenter

Most of VxRail's configuration tasks can be executed through the VxRail Manager plugin for vCenter in vCenter Server.

- **VMware vCenter Server** is a central management dashboard for managing the virtual machines in a VxRail cluster; it includes the virtual machine operations, virtual network configuration, virtual storage configuration, ESXi management, and so on.

We can access VMware vCenter Server with vSphere Client for VxRail administration tasks. VMware vCenter Server can provide central management in the HTML5 interface for managing the virtual machine in a vSphere environment. We can see the core management components in a VxRail appliance in *Figure 3.1*, that is, **VxRail Manager**, **vCenter Server**, **iDRAC**, and so on.

- **VxRail Manager** is a virtual machine that can deliver deployment, configuration, and ongoing administration tasks in the VxRail cluster. Starting with VxRail 4.7.100, the VxRail Manager plugin for vCenter provides the central management HTML5 dashboard of the VxRail appliance from VMware vSphere Web Client. When we log in to the management IP address of vCenter Server, we can see the VxRail Manager plugin for vCenter displayed on the home page of vCenter Server.

We can use the VxRail Manager plugin to monitor the system's health. It can also be used to check the VxRail software versions and updates, and access the online **VxRail Community** and **Knowledge Base** (refer to *Figure 3.4*). VxRail appliances support the proactive monitoring of system health. Dell **Secure Remote Services** (**SRS**) is a secure remote connection between Dell EMC products and Dell EMC customer support services that can deliver remote monitoring, diagnoses, and repairs. If we enable SRS on a VxRail cluster, the Dell EMC support team can remotely monitor the VxRail appliance with 24x7 service and notify us if there are any hardware or software problems in the VxRail appliance. SRS is included with Dell premium support agreements of VxRail appliances. In *Figure 3.4*, we can find information on the system health, support, **VxRail Community**, and **Knowledge Base**:

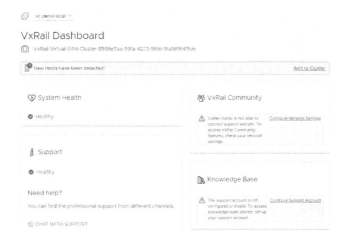

Figure 3.3 – VxRail Dashboard

The VxRail Manager plugin can be used to perform maintenance operations such as hardware replacement, adding drives, adding nodes, software upgrades, and so on. In VxRail Market, we can access qualified software products for a VxRail cluster, such as Dell EMC RecoverPoint for virtual machines, VxRail Management Pack for vRealize Operations, and so on. In *Figure 3.5*, we can find the installed version of the VxRail software, in this case, **4.7.300-26108987**:

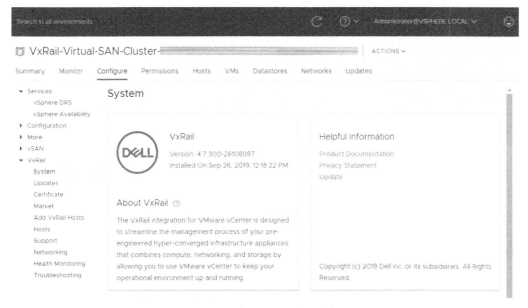

Figure 3.4 – VxRail Manager plugin for vCenter

- **VMware vRealize Log Insight** is an optional virtual appliance running in a VxRail cluster. We choose whether or not to deploy this virtual appliance during VxRail initialization. It can deliver real-time monitoring and log management on a VxRail cluster; it can also provide notifications to us when there are any problems, such as on the software, hardware, or virtual machines.

In each series VxRail node, there is an iDRAC port on the Dell PowerEdge server. We can remotely monitor the hardware status of a VxRail node through this port:

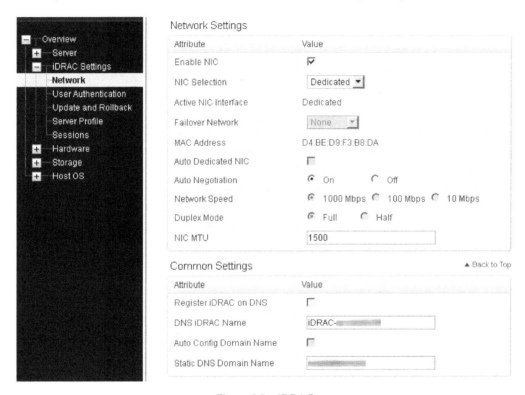

Figure 3.5 – iDRAC

We have now covered an overview of the core management interfaces in a VxRail appliance. In the next section, we will have an overview of VMware vSAN.

VMware vSAN

In this section, we will discuss the vSAN architecture, components, and fault tolerance concepts. VxRail appliances are powered by VMware **vSAN**. VMware vSAN is the software-defined storage across the vSphere cluster.

Overview

A vSAN cluster supports up to 64 nodes; four nodes are the recommended configuration. Each vSAN node must contain at least one **disk group**, which includes one Flash device as the cache tier and one magnetic drive as the capacity tier. The network requirement of each vSAN node is a 10 Gb or 25 Gb network interface. They can support 1 GbE as well on single-processor models. *Figure 3.7* shows a sample configuration of the vSAN architecture. You can see that there are four physical servers, which are validated and certified hardware from VMware for VMware vSAN deployment. Each vSAN node (VxRail appliance) includes one Flash device and three magnetic drives and could be All-Flash as well. In this vSAN cluster, there are four ESXi hosts and it has one disk group on each node. A disk group must consist of two components: the cache tier and the capacity tier. VMware vSAN has two configuration options: **hybrid** and **All-Flash** configuration. In a **hybrid configuration**, the cache device is utilized as a 70% read cache and a 30% write buffer. In an **All-Flash configuration**, the cache device is utilized as a 100% write buffer. A vSAN node can have at most five disk groups, each containing one Flash device as a cache drive and up to seven capacity devices could be Flash or magnetic drives. All vSAN nodes deliver a software-defined storage pool across a vSAN cluster:

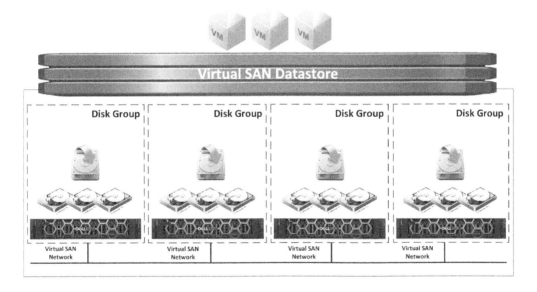

Figure 3.6 – The architecture of VMware vSAN

There are different services in a vSAN cluster, such as **Storage Policy-Based Management** (**SPBM**), deduplication and compression, RAID-5/-6 erasure coding, data-at-rest encryption, stretched clusters, and so on.

SPBM is a virtual machine storage policy tool that provides the data services and storage object protection of virtual machines with vCenter Server. In the virtual machine storage policy, we need to define the availability and the different advanced policy rules.

In the **Availability** settings, we can define the following:

- **Site disaster tolerance**: Define whether the vSAN cluster is a standard cluster or a stretched cluster across two sites.

- **Failures to tolerate**: Define the protection option of virtual machines, such as **RAID-1 (Mirroring)**, **RAID-5 (Erasure Coding)**, **RAID-6 (Erasure Coding)**, and so on. You can refer to the *vSAN storage policy* section of this chapter for more details:

Figure 3.7 – Availability settings under a virtual machine storage policy

In the **Advanced Policy Rules** settings, we can define the following:

- **Number of disk stripes per object**: Define the number of drives across which each replica of a storage object is striped.

- **IOPS limit for object**: Define the **Input/Output Operations Per Second (IOPS)** for the disk.

- **Object space reservation**: Define whether the space type of the storage object is thick provisioning or thin provisioning.

- **Flash read cache reservation**: Define the Flash read cache for each storage object:

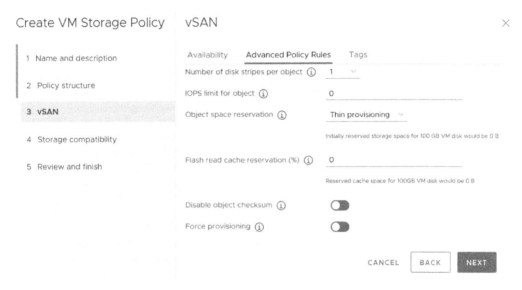

Figure 3.8 – Advanced Policy Rules under the virtual machine storage policy

Before you define the virtual machine storage policy, you need to know what a vSAN object is first. In the next section, we will discuss what a vSAN object is.

vSAN objects

A **vSAN object** is a logical volume that consists of data and metadata distributed across a vSAN cluster. These objects include **Virtual Machine Disks** (**VMDKs**), VM home, VM swap, memory, and VM snapshots. In *Figure 3.9*, we can see there are four vSAN objects in a **VxRail Manager** virtual machine; there are two VMDKs, one VM home, one VM swap object, and VM snapshots.

We can assign the different virtual machine storage policies to each vSAN object; you can see two storage policies, **vSAN Default Storage Policy** and **VXRAIL-SYSTEM-STORAGE-PROFILE**, in the **VxRail Manager** virtual machine. You can assign a storage policy or different storage policies to each vSAN object of the same virtual machine:

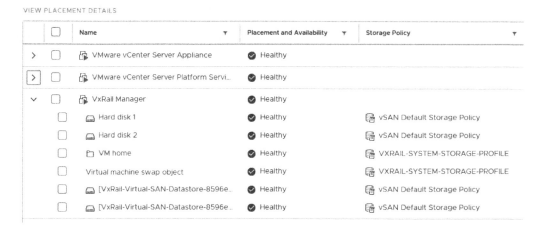

Figure 3.9 – VMware vSAN objects of the virtual machine

We can define different virtual machine storage policies to protect the vSAN object in a virtual machine.

vSAN storage policy

Before we create the virtual machine storage policy, we must know what the definitions of **Failure To Tolerate** (**FTT**) and **Failure Tolerance Method** (**FTM**) are. We must define these two parameters in the virtual machine storage policy.

FTT is the number of failures to tolerate in the vSAN cluster. **FTM** is the failure tolerance method; we can choose RAID-1 (Mirroring) or RAID-5/-6 (Erasure Coding). If we set FTM as RAID-1 (Mirroring), then we can set FTT to 1, 2, or 3. In *Figure 3.10*, there is a four-node vSAN cluster and a virtual machine configured by a virtual machine storage policy with FTT set to 1 and FTM set to RAID-1 (Mirroring). You can see three vSAN components across three nodes: two copies of the data component and one witness component. In the scenario in *Figure 3.10*, the virtual machine consists of one VMDK. Each vSAN object has three components: two copies of the data component and one witness component:

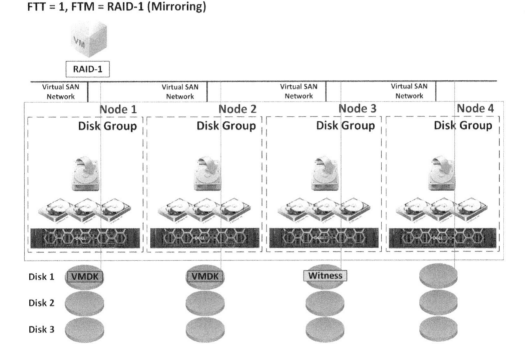

Figure 3.10 – Virtual machine storage policy with FTT = 1 and FTM = RAID-1 (Mirroring)

VMware vSAN uses voting algorithms to resolve the split-brain scenario; each component has 33% of the vote if both FTT is 1 and FTM is RAID-1, and the total number of votes is 100% (the virtual machine has three vSAN components, two are data and one is witness). If there's voting of more than 50% of the components, the vSAN components still can be accessed. In *Figure 3.11*, if one of the components fails, two of the three components can still be accessed because the vote of two components combined is 66% (more than 50%). The faulted component will start to rebuild into the standby vSAN node if there are free standby nodes available in the vSAN cluster. When two of the three components are faulted, the data cannot be accessed:

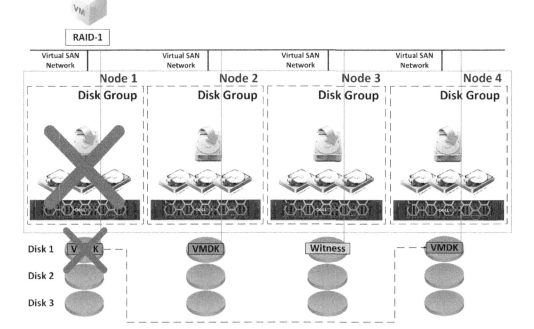

Figure 3.11 – Virtual machine storage policy with FTT = 1 and FTM = RAID-1 (Mirroring)

The recommended number of nodes is four in a vSAN cluster when setting FTT to 1 and FTM to RAID-1 (Mirroring).

When we set FTM to Erasure Coding in a virtual machine storage policy, the protection behavior is different with RAID-1. If we set FTM to RAID-5 (Erasure Coding), then we must set FTT to 1. In RAID-5 (Erasure Coding), there are four components, which are three data components and one parity component, and each component has 25% of the vote. The witness component only exists in RAID-1 (Mirroring); it does not exist in erasure coding. In *Figure 3.12*, you can see that there are five nodes in a vSAN cluster and a virtual machine is configured by a virtual machine storage policy with FTT set to 1 and FTM set to RAID-5 (Erasure Coding). You can see four vSAN components across four nodes: three copies of the data component and one parity component:

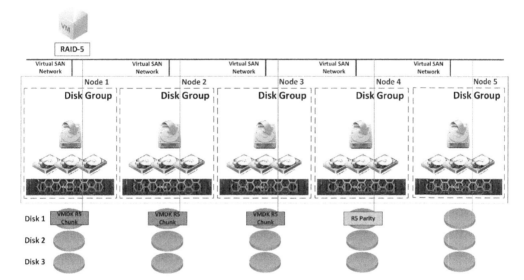

Figure 3.12 – Virtual machine storage policy with FTT = 1 and FTM = RAID-5 (Erasure Coding)

> **Important note**
>
> Erasure coding only supports the vSAN All-Flash configuration and requires vSAN Advanced Edition or above.

In *Figure 3.13*, if one of the components fails, three of the four components can still be accessed because the combined vote of the three components is 75% (more than 50%). The faulted component will start to rebuild into the standby vSAN node if there are free standby nodes available in the vSAN cluster. If two of the four components are faulted, the data cannot be accessed. This virtual machine storage policy can only allow one component to be faulted:

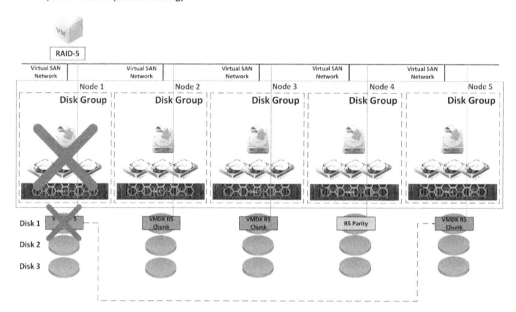

Figure 3.13 – Virtual machine storage policy with FTT = 1 and FTM = RAID-5 (Erasure Coding)

The recommended number of nodes is five in a vSAN cluster when setting FTT to 1 and FTM to RAID-5 (Erasure Coding). The minimum number of nodes is four when FTM is set to RAID-5 (Erasure Coding).

In *Figure 3.14*, there is a six-node vSAN cluster, and a virtual machine is configured by a virtual machine storage policy with FTT set to 2 and FTM set to RAID-6 (Erasure Coding). When we set FTM to RAID-6 (Erasure Coding), we must set FTT to 2. In RAID-6 (Erasure Coding), there are six components, which are four data components and two parity components, and each component has 16.6% of the vote:

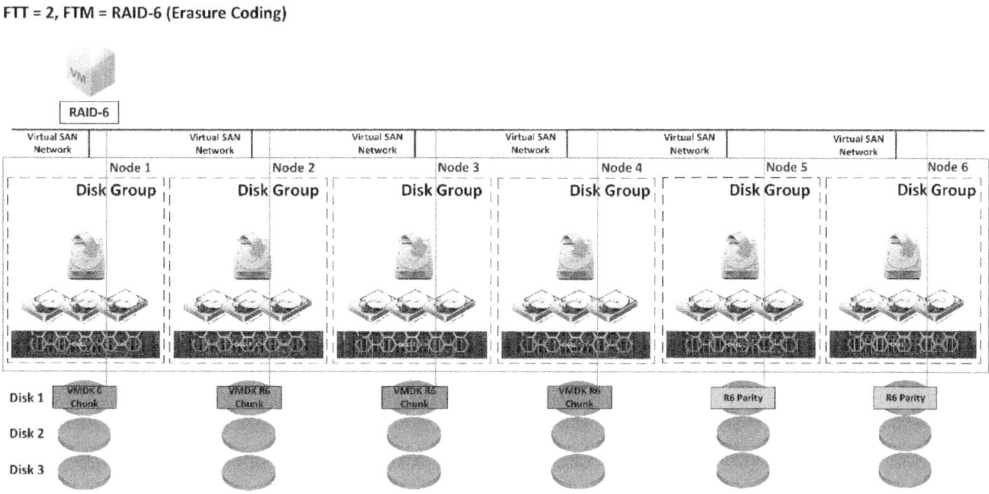

Figure 3.14 – Virtual machine storage policy with FTT = 1 and FTM = RAID-6 (Erasure Coding)

> **Important note**
>
> When you apply a virtual machine storage policy with FTM set to RAID-6 (Erasure Coding) in the virtual machine, the required storage capacity of a virtual machine is more than RAID-5 (Erasure Coding).

In *Figure 3.15*, if two of the components fail, four of the six components can still be accessed because the combined vote of the four components is 66.4% (more than 50%). The faulted component will start to rebuild into the standby vSAN node if there are free standby nodes available in the vSAN cluster. If three of the six components are faulted, the data cannot be accessed. In this VM storage policy, only two components can be faulted:

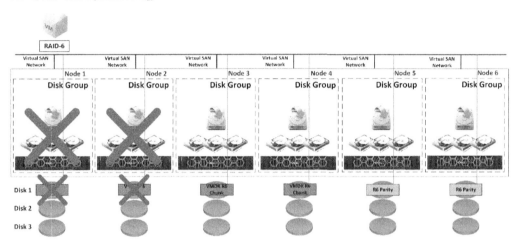

Figure 3.15 – Virtual machine storage policy with FTT = 1 and FTM = RAID-6 (Erasure Coding)

Based on the preceding scenarios, we will summarize the combinations of FTT and FTM. You can refer to the following for more details:

Number of Failures to Tolerate	FTT	FTM	Minimum Number of Nodes	Recommended Number of Nodes
1	1	RAID-1 (Mirroring)	3 nodes	4 nodes
2	2	RAID-1 (Mirroring)	5 nodes	6 nodes
3	3	RAID-1 (Mirroring)	7 nodes	8 nodes
1	1	RAID-5 (Erasure Coding)	4 nodes	5 nodes
2	2	RAID-6 (Erasure Coding)	6 nodes	7 nodes

In this section, we understood what VMware vSAN is, and the different options for FTT and FTM in the virtual machine storage policies. Now, we will go on to the next section to discuss what the core components and configuration of the VxRail cluster are.

VxRail cluster configuration

In this section, we will discuss an overview of VxRail system virtual machines, vDS and port groups, VxRail disk groups, and vSAN storage policies.

VxRail system virtual machines

When you log in to a VxRail cluster with vSphere Web Client for the first time, you can see some VxRail system virtual machines. In the VxRail initialization, we can choose the option for deploying VMware vCenter Server. You can check out *Chapter 2*, *VxRail Installation*, for more details. When the VxRail deployment is completed, you can see that some VxRail system virtual machines are ready in the VxRail cluster. In *Figure 3.16*, if you choose VxRail deployments with the embedded vCenter Server, you can see four virtual machines, consisting of the following:

- **VMware vCenter Server Appliance**
- **VMware vCenter Server Platform Services Controller**
- **VMware vRealize Log Insight**
- **VxRail Manager**

If you choose VxRail deployments with the external vCenter Server, you can see only one virtual machine, **VxRail Manager**:

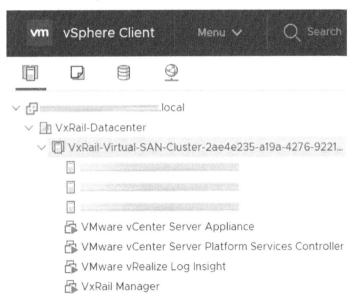

Figure 3.16 – VxRail system virtual machine with embedded vCenter

In the next section, we will discuss the vDS and network port groups on a VxRail cluster.

vDS and port groups

VxRail initialization will automatically create a VxRail cluster and a **VMware HCIA Distributed Switch** vDS in this cluster. Then, it will create some distributed port groups on this vDS, which include **Management Network**, **vCenter Server Network**, **Virtual SAN**, **vSphere vMotion**, **VxRail Management**, and **VM**. You cannot modify or remove these distributed port groups except the **VM** network. Refer to the following for more details:

- **Management Network**: This is the management network between each VxRail node.

- **vCenter Server Network**: This is the management network between vCenter Server and the VxRail Manager virtual machine.

- **Virtual SAN**: This is the vSAN network between each VxRail node.

- **vSphere vMotion**: This is the vSphere vMotion network between each VxRail node.

- **VxRail Management**: This is the management network between a VxRail node and a VxRail Manager virtual machine. The default internal VLAN is 3939.

- **VM**: This is the production network for virtual machines; you can define this port group based on your network requirements:

Figure 3.17 – vDS

> **Important note**
> We cannot change the display name of each distributed port group in a vDS because all configurations are stored in VxRail Manager and vCenter Server.

In this section, we understood the pre-defined distributed port groups and network settings in the VxRail cluster. We will discuss VxRail disk groups in the next section.

VxRail disk groups

Each VxRail node creates at least a disk group automatically after the VxRail initialization. In each group, there is a Flash device and a capacity device. You can refer to *Chapter 1, Overview of VxRail HCI*, for more details. In *Figure 3.18*, you can see that there is a disk group in a VxRail cluster. The first node consists of a 20.00 GB Flash device and an 80.00 GB capacity device in the disk group. In a VxRail cluster, the number of Flash devices and capacity devices is the same because it offers the best configuration for performance across each node:

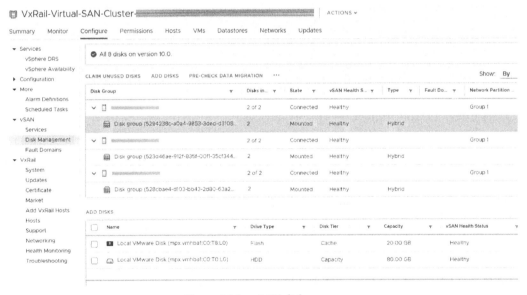

Figure 3.18 – vSAN disk groups

The following is the recommended configuration of a VxRail cluster. You can see that there are two disk groups in each node, each disk group including a 400 GB flash device and three 2 TB capacity devices. In this vSAN configuration, we can make sure the vSAN objects are across two disk groups and balance the disk IOPS in a VxRail cluster. For the high availability of disk groups and network configuration, this configuration should meet these requirements:

VxRail Node	Number of Flash Devices	Number of Capacity Devices	Number of Disk Groups	vSAN Network Uplinks
Node 1	2 x 400 GB	3 or above (2 TB)	2	2
Node 2	2 x 400 GB	3 or above (2 TB)	2	2
Node 3	2 x 400 GB	3 or above (2 TB)	2	2
Node 4	2 x 400 GB	3 or above (2 TB)	2	2

> **Important note**
>
> The maximum number of capacity devices that can be supported on a VxRail appliance depends on the model of the VxRail series.

The following is a not-recommended configuration of a VxRail cluster. You can see that there is one disk group in the first three nodes that includes one 400 GB flash device and three 2 TB capacity devices. In Node 4, there is one 800 GB flash device and five 3 TB capacity devices. The number of capacity devices is more than the first three nodes, and the usable capacity of both devices is different from the first three nodes. In this vSAN configuration, if the usable capacity of both tier devices and the number of capacity devices are different in the first three nodes, there may be a performance problem across the four nodes in this VxRail cluster. For the high availability of disk groups, the following table shows a vSAN configuration that is *not* suggested:

VxRail Node	Number of Flash Devices	Number of Capacity Devices	Number of Disk Groups	vSAN Network Uplinks
Node 1	1 x 400 GB	3 or above (2 TB)	1	2
Node 2	1 x 400 GB	3 or above (2 TB)	1	2
Node 3	1 x 400 GB	3 or above (2 TB)	1	2
Node 4	1 x 800 GB	5 x 3 TB	1	2

Based on the preceding configuration, we make sure that the usable capacity and the number of both Flash and capacity devices is the same in each disk group.

vSAN services

Some VMware vSAN services are disabled in VxRail clusters after the VxRail initialization; you need to enable these services manually if you need them. This includes the following services:

- **Deduplication and compression**: This can be enabled on an All-Flash VxRail cluster; hybrid VxRail clusters are not supported.

- **Encryption**: vSAN encryption is available on VxRail 4.5 or above; it requires an external **Key Management Server** (**KMS**) outside of the VxRail cluster.

- **Performance Service**: This service is used to monitor all vSAN services in the VxRail cluster.

- **vSAN iSCSI Target Service**: VxRail supports presenting iSCSI shared/non-shared disks in external hosts. If you need this feature, you must enable this service:

Figure 3.19 – vSAN services

In the next section, we will discuss the vSAN storage policy in the VxRail cluster.

VxRail storage policy

The VxRail cluster creates a **vSAN Default Storage Policy** virtual machine storage policy automatically after the VxRail initialization. This vSAN storage policy sets FTT to 1 and FTM to RAID-1 (Mirroring), and it is applied to the VxRail vSAN datastore in the VxRail cluster. You can refer to *Chapter 5, Managing VMware vSAN*, for more details. In *Figure 3.20*, we can see the default vSAN storage policies after the VxRail initialization:

Figure 3.20 – vSAN SPBM

By default, all virtual machines are configured with this virtual machine storage policy; you can change the virtual machine storage policy. When the virtual machine is compliant with the virtual machine storage policy, it shows the compliance status as **Compliant**:

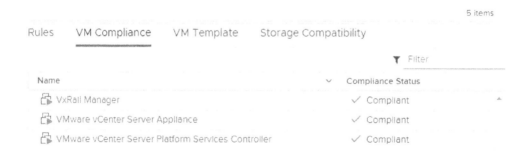

Figure 3.21 – Compliance status of the virtual machine storage policy

In *Figure 3.21*, we can see that the compliance status of the VxRail system virtual machines is **Compliant**. If the compliance status of each virtual machine shows non-compliance, it may be a vSAN data protection problem exists, for example, the vSAN node faulted, or the vSAN usable capacity is low, and so on.

Summary

In this chapter, you learned about the VxRail management interface and VxRail system virtual machines. Compared to the architecture of a traditional server and storage, you now know how VMware vSAN is different. Up to now, we have covered the overview and installation of a VxRail appliance in *Chapters 1* to *3*. In the rest of the book, we will learn about the configuration of and daily operations in the VxRail cluster.

In the next chapter, we will cover an overview of VxRail management. The content includes the VxRail Manager plugin for vCenter, VxRail monitoring, and permission management.

Questions

1. Which of these is not a VxRail management interface?

   a. VxRail Manager plugin for vCenter

   b. VMware vCenter Server

   c. VMware vRealize Operation Manager

   d. VMware vSphere Web Client

   e. Dell iDRAC

2. Which VxRail software supports the VxRail Manager plugin for vCenter?

   a. VxRail 4.0.xxx

   b. VxRail 4.5.xxx

   c. VxRail 4.7.000

   d. VxRail 4.7.100

   e. All the above

3. Which management interface is used for monitoring the VxRail hardware status?

   a. VxRail Manager plugin for vCenter

   b. VMware vCenter Server

   c. VMware vRealize Operation Manager

   d. VMware vSphere Web Client

   e. iDRAC

4. How many types does the VxRail vSAN configuration have?

    a. 2

    b. 3

    c. 4

    d. 5

    e. 6

5. What components does a vSAN disk group have?

    a. Both cache and capacity tiers

    b. A cache or capacity tier

    c. Only the cache tier

    d. Only the capacity tier

    e. All the above

6. What component does not exist in vSAN objects?

    a. VM home

    b. VM VMDK

    c. VM storage

    d. VM snapshot

    e. VM swap

7. Which configuration does not support a virtual machine storage policy?

    a. FTM = RAID-1 (Mirroring)

    b. FTM = RAID-10 (Mirroring)

    c. FTM = RAID-5 (Erasure Coding)

    d. FTM = RAID-6 (Erasure Coding)

    e. All the above

8. Which configurations support FTM set to RAID-1 (Mirroring)?

    a. FTT = 1

    b. FTT = 2

    c. FTT = 3

d. FTT = 4

e. FTT = 5

9. What is the minimum number of nodes that supports a virtual machine storage policy with FTT = 1 and FTM = RAID-1 (Mirroring)?

   a. 2

   b. 3

   c. 4

   d. 5

   e. 6

10. Which service exists in a VxRail vSAN cluster?

    a. Performance Service

    b. Deduplication and compression

    c. Encryption

    d. vSAN iSCSI Target Service

    e. All the above

11. What are the VLAN IDs for a VxRail internal management network?

    a. 3900

    b. 3929

    c. 3939

    d. 3949

    e. All the above

12. Which distributed port groups will be created on a VMware HCIA Distributed Switch after the VxRail initialization?

    a. Management Network

    b. vSphere vMotion

    c. vSAN Network

    d. VxRail Management Network

    e. vCenter Server Network

    f. All the above

4
VxRail Management Overview

The previous chapter provided an overview of VxRail administration. You learned about all the administration interfaces that are used to manage Dell EMC VxRail appliances, including VxRail Manager, the VxRail Manager plugin for vCenter, vCenter Server, and iDRAC. VxRail appliances can deliver a central management dashboard for managing virtual machines. They also understand the architecture of VMware **Virtual SAN (vSAN)** and the differences vis-à-vis traditional storage. Lastly, we listed a number of vSAN cluster scenarios based on the different settings of FTT and FTM.

In this chapter, we will provide an overview of VxRail management. We will learn about the functions of the VxRail Manager plugin for vCenter. We will become familiar with how to monitor the status of VxRail appliances with the VxRail Manager plugin for vCenter, how to manage vCenter roles and permissions in the VxRail cluster, and which roles and permissions are required to manage the VxRail appliance.

In this chapter, we are going to cover the following main topics:

- VxRail Manager overview
- VxRail monitoring
- VxRail roles and permission management

Technical requirements

In this chapter, we need to make sure that our workstation is a Windows platform, with a web browser installed. The latest versions of Firefox, Google Chrome, and Microsoft Internet Explorer 10 or above are all supported. The VxRail software running is version 4.7.300 or above.

VxRail Manager overview

Chapter 2, VxRail Installation, already mentioned the fact that the VxRail Manager plugin for vCenter is available on VxRail software 4.7.100 or higher. This plugin is installed automatically following VxRail initialization. We perform the daily operations of the VxRail cluster through the VxRail Manager plugin for vCenter. When you log in to vCenter Server, you will see that **VxRail HTML5 Client Plugin** is enabled under **Client Plug-Ins** in vCenter Server:

Client Plug-Ins

ENABLE　DISABLE

	Name	Vendor	Version	Description	Plugin ID
○	VMware vRops Client Plugin	VMware, Inc	6.7.0.40000	VMware vRops Client Plugin	com.vmware.vrops.install
○	VMware vSAN H5 Client Plugin	VMware, Inc	6.7.0.40000	VMware vSAN H5 Client Plugin	com.vmware.vsphere.client.h5vsan
○	VMware Update Manager	VMware	6.7.0.41905	VMware Update Manager HTML client	com.vmware.vum.client
○	VxRail HTML5 Client Plugin	VMware Inc	4.7.300	vSphere Client Extension for VxRail Clusters	com.vmware.vxrail
○	VMware Update Manager	VMware	6.7.0.41905	Update Manager client	com.vmware.vcIntegrity.vcIntegrity
○	VMware vSAN Web Client Plugin	VMware, Inc	6.7.0.40000	VMware vSAN Web Client Plugin	com.vmware.vsan.health

Figure 4.1 – VxRail Manager plugin for vCenter

Now, let's discuss the function of the VxRail Manager plugin for vCenter.

The VxRail Manager plugin at the cluster level

The functions of the VxRail Manager plugin are only available at the VxRail cluster level and VxRail host level. At the VxRail cluster level, all functions are available under the **Monitor** and **Configure** tabs. In *Figure 4.2*, you can see the **Monitor** and **Configure** tabs in the cluster-level **VxRail-Virtual-SAN-Cluster-8596e7aa-99**. The following table is a summary of each function for the **Monitor** and **Configure** tabs:

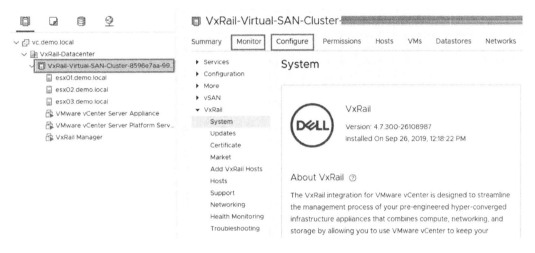

Figure 4.2 – VxRail Manager plugin at the cluster level

Now we will discuss each function in turn:

VxRail Manager plugin at the cluster level	Monitor tab	Configure tab
	Appliances	System
	Last Configuration Data Sent	Updates
		Certificate
		Market
		Add VxRail Hosts
		Hosts
		Support
		Networking
		Health Monitoring
		Troubleshooting

We will now discuss the VxRail Manager plugin features under the **Configure** tab.

In **System**, you can find the installed software information relating to the VxRail cluster and a link to the VxRail production documentation:

Figure 4.3 – System information on the VxRail Manager plugin

In **Updates**, you can see the installed version of each VxRail component, including Dell PTAgent, VMware ESXi, VxRail Manager, VMware vCenter Server Appliance, and VxRail Manager VIB. If we plan to upgrade the VxRail software, there are two options, **INTERNET UPDATES** and **LOCAL UPDATES**. You can go to *Chapter 6, VxRail Upgrade*, for further details:

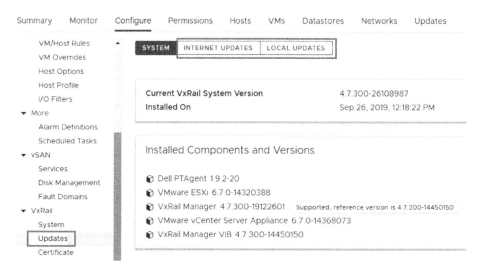

Figure 4.4 – Installed components and versions of the VxRail cluster

In **Certificate**, you can replace the VxRail SSL certificate if you want to apply a third-party certificate to the VxRail cluster:

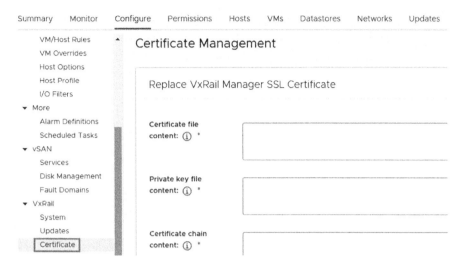

Figure 4.5 – Certificate Management of the VxRail cluster

In **Market**, you can download the qualified software products for the VxRail appliance that are installed in the VxRail cluster, for example, Dell EMC RecoverPoint for Virtual Machines:

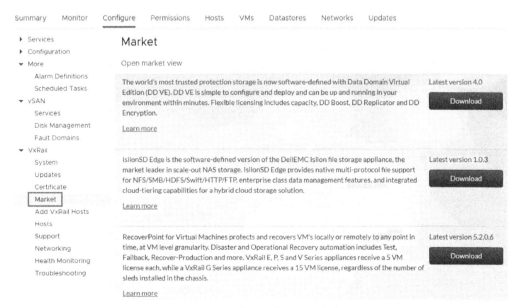

Figure 4.6 – Market in the VxRail cluster

In **Add VxRail Hosts**, we can add new VxRail nodes to the VxRail cluster in this wizard. Refer to *Chapter 7, VxRail Scale-Out Operations*, for more details:

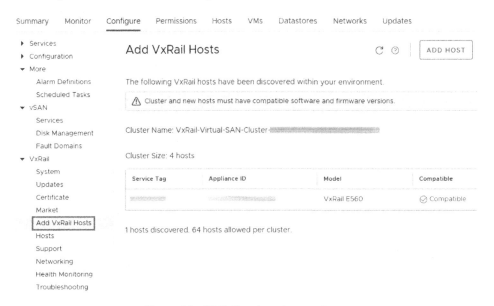

Figure 4.7 – VxRail scale-out operations

In **Hosts**, the number of VxRail nodes in the VxRail cluster is indicated. We can ascertain the hostname and management IP address of each node:

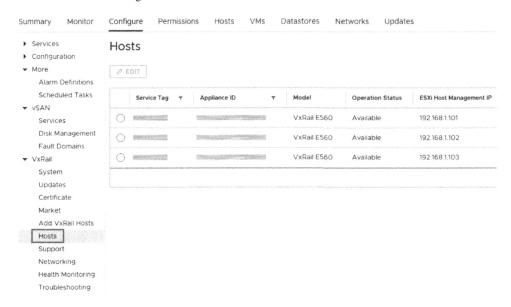

Figure 4.8 – Node information in the VxRail cluster

In **Support**, we can configure **Dell EMC Support Account** and **Dell EMC Secure Remote Service (SRS)**. If you wish to enable **Dell EMC Secure Remote Service (SRS)**, this requires a Dell support account, which you can register on the Dell EMC website:

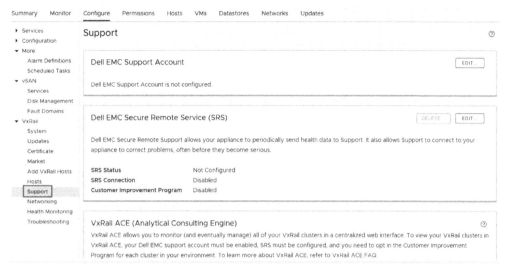

Figure 4.9 – Dell EMC support configuration in the VxRail cluster

In **Networking**, we can set up an internet connection for VxRail Manager. This enables us to configure the connections to an external network through an internal network's proxy server. This network configuration must be enabled if we want to access the VxRail market and perform an internet upgrade of the VxRail software:

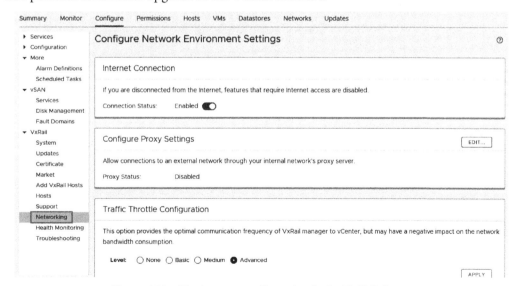

Figure 4.10 – The internet configuration in the VxRail cluster

Health Monitoring is used to monitor the VxRail cluster's health status when this setting is enabled:

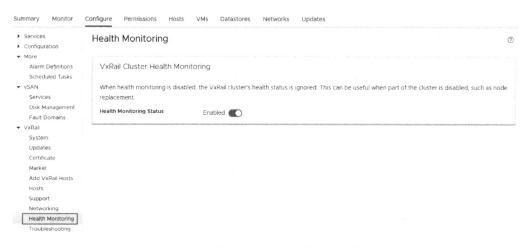

Figure 4.11 – Health monitoring in the VxRail cluster

Troubleshooting allows a new log bundle file to be generated for the VxRail cluster. We must send this log bundle file to the Dell EMC support team to diagnose issues:

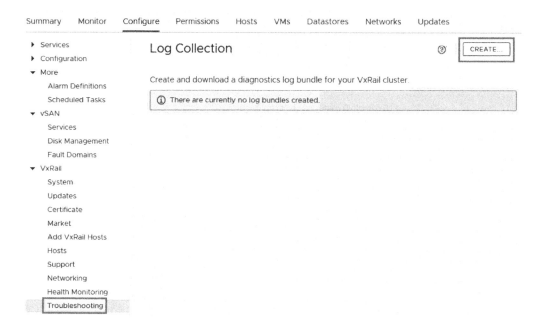

Figure 4.12 – Log Collection in the VxRail cluster

When we create a log bundle file, this includes the **VxRail Manager**, **vCenter**, **ESXi**, **iDRAC**, and **PTAgent** logs:

Figure 4.13 – Creating a log bundle in the log collection wizard

All of the above features are available under the **Configure** tab at the VxRail cluster level. Now, let's discuss the features under the **Monitor** tab at the VxRail cluster level.

Appliances shows the physical view of each VxRail appliance. We can find the **Service Tag**, **Appliance ID**, **Appliance PSNT**, **Model**, **ESXi IP Address**, and **iDRAC IP Address** fields. In *Figure 4.14*, there are four **VxRail E560** nodes in this VxRail cluster:

Figure 4.14 – Monitoring in the VxRail cluster

In **Last Configuration Data Sent**, you can view and download the most recent configuration data sent to the Dell EMC support team using SRS:

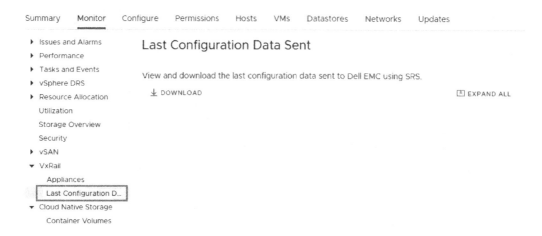

Figure 4.15 – The most recent configuration dataset in the VxRail cluster

All of the above features are available on the VxRail Manager plugin at the cluster level. Now we will discuss the features that are available on the VxRail Manager plugin at the host level.

The VxRail Manager plugin at the host level

In the VxRail Manager plugin at the host level, there is only one menu item available, **Physical View**, under the **Monitor** tab of the VxRail cluster. We can see the **System Health**, **Appliance PSNT**, **Service Tag**, **Appliance ID**, **ESXi IP Address**, and **iDRAC IP Address** fields:

Figure 4.16 – The physical view of the VxRail node

In **Physical View**, we can also see the details of the firmware version of each hardware and software component on the VxRail node, as demonstrated in *Figure 4.17*. Examples include **BIOS** (Basic Input/Output System), **BMC** (Baseboard Management Controller), **HBA** (Host Bus Adapter), **BOSS** (Boot Optimized Storage Solution), **Dell PtAgent**, and **HBA Driver**:

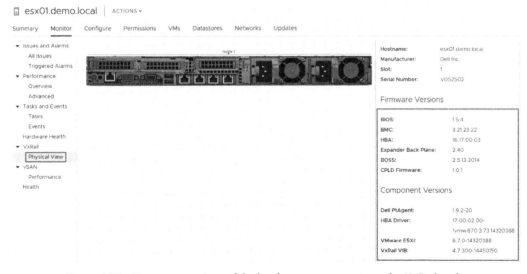

Figure 4.17 – Firmware versions of the hardware components on the VxRail node

It also supports the displaying of information pertaining to each independent hardware component, for example, disk drive, network adapter, and power supply. In *Figure 4.18*, we click the SSD on the VxRail E560 and this displays all the information relating to this hardware component, including **Health**, **Serial Number**, **Model**, and **Firmware**:

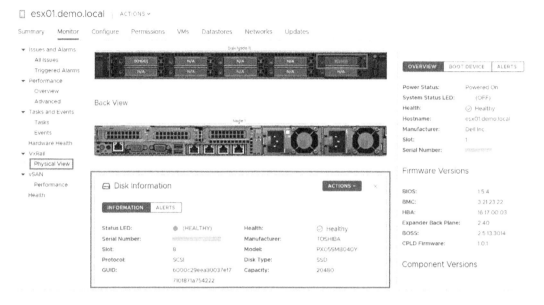

Figure 4.18 – Component information on the VxRail E560

In the next section, we will discuss which components can be monitored with the VxRail Manager plugin for vCenter.

VxRail monitoring

In this section, we will discuss the monitoring of the hardware and software status of the VxRail appliance. The VxRail Manager plugin for vCenter can provide hardware monitoring of each VxRail appliance, including the VxRail node, network connection interface, power supply, and disk drive. In *Figure 4.19*, we make sure that **Health Monitoring Status** is **Enabled**, and then this provides proactive hardware monitoring of the VxRail appliance:

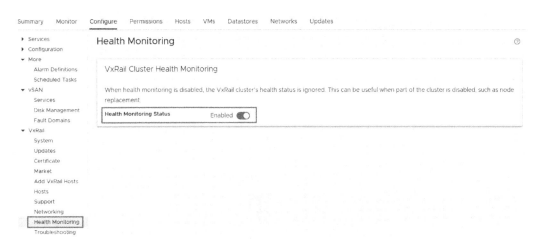

Figure 4.19 – VxRail cluster health monitoring

> **Important note**
> When the health monitoring status is disabled, any hardware issue and health system event/warning associated with the VxRail node cannot be displayed.

Let's now discuss how to monitor VxRail with the VxRail Manager plugin for vCenter.

The VxRail Manager plugin for vCenter

Now we will view the details of the VxRail node, a network connection interface, power supply, and disk drive. In this section, we will go to the physical view of a VxRail E50 node.

When we click the **Physical View** tab of the VxRail node, this shows the **Front View** and **Back View** views of the VxRail E560, along with **System Health**, **Service Tag**, **Appliance PSNT**, **Software versions**, **Firmware versions**, and **BOOT DEVICE** information:

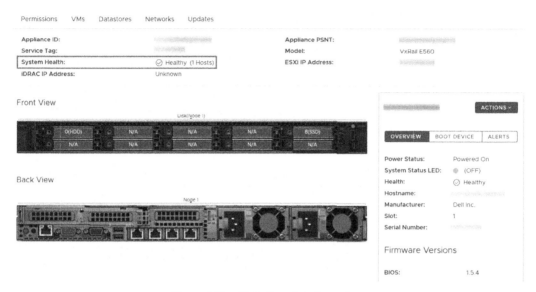

Figure 4.20 – VxRail node information

In **Back View**, we can click on the network interface controller and power supply of the VxRail E560 node to view the details information, and it can monitor the **Link Status** of each network port, **Firmware Family Version**, and **DRIVER VERSION**:

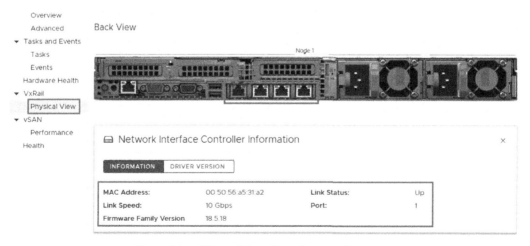

Figure 4.21 – Network interface adapter information

When we click on **Power Supply Information** of the VxRail E560 node to view the details information, it can monitor the health and display **Part Number** and **Revision Number** for any hardware replacement:

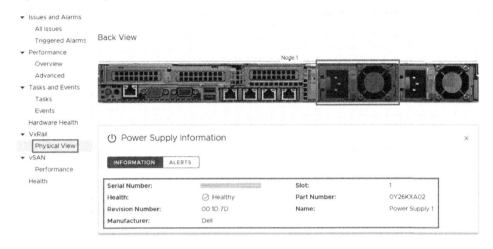

Figure 4.22 – The power supply information on VxRail

In **Front View**, we can click on **HDD** (**Hard Disk Drive**) and **SSD** (**Solid-State Drive**) of the VxRail E560 node to view the details information, for example, **Health**, **Serial Number**, and **Model**:

Figure 4.23 – The disk drive information on VxRail

In the following section, we will learn how to monitor the VxRail cluster status at the hardware level.

VxRail events in vCenter

For software monitoring of the VxRail cluster, we can view all VxRail events and triggered alarms in VMware vCenter Server. The alarms include VxRail node, vSAN datastore, CPU usage, memory usage, VxRail system virtual machines, and VxRail Manager. We go to the **Monitor** tab of the VxRail cluster and choose **Triggered Alarms**. This displays the related alarm if it triggers any VxRail issue. In *Figure 4.24*, we can trigger an alarm, **Host memory usage**, on the VxRail node, **esx02.demo.local**:

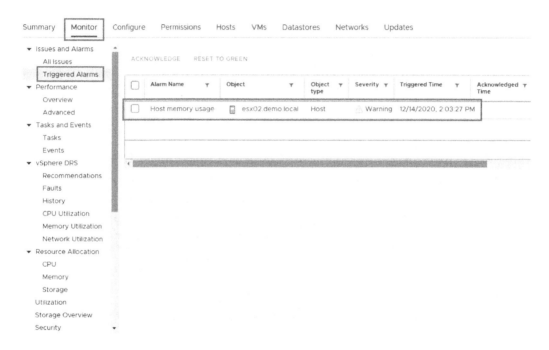

Figure 4.24 – Triggered alarm in the VxRail cluster

The alarm has two **severity** types – **Warning** and **Critical**. As soon as the related issue is fixed, the alarm disappears immediately. All VxRail operations and configuration events are stored in VMware vCenter Server. We can go to the **Monitor** tab of the VxRail cluster and choose **Events**, and this will display the history of VxRail operations, configurations, and issues:

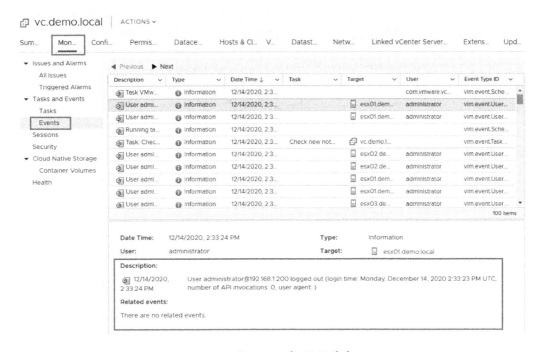

Figure 4.25 – Events in the VxRail cluster

In this section, we learned how to perform hardware and software monitoring on the VxRail cluster. Now we can move on to the next section – VxRail roles and permission management.

VxRail roles and permission management

In this section, we will discuss the roles and permission management of the VxRail cluster. VMware vCenter permission management is controlled by the user account, user group, and permission roles in VMware vCenter Server. VxRail permission management (the VxRail Manager plugin for vCenter) is only accessed by a vCenter user with the roles of **Administrator** or **VMware HCIA Management**. When we go to the **Administrator** menu of vCenter Server and choose **Roles**, there are many roles predefined for user management, including **Administrator**, **Network administrator (sample)**, **Virtual machine power user (sample)**, and **VMware HCIA Management**:

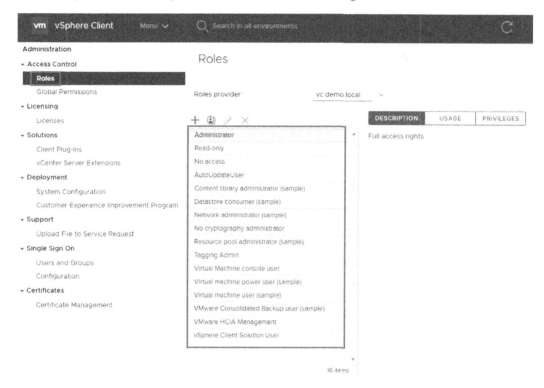

Figure 4.26 – The roles and permission management on vCenter Server

When defining the user account for managing the VxRail cluster, we need to follow up on the role-based access control architecture in *Figure 4.27*. **Administrator Role** must be assigned to **Root Folder**. **HCIA Role** must be assigned to **Data Center** (vCenter Server). The user account with either an administrator role or HCIA role can manage and control the VxRail cluster. By default, an account, **administrator@vsphere.local**, with an administrator role is created in the root folder:

VxRail Role Based Access Control

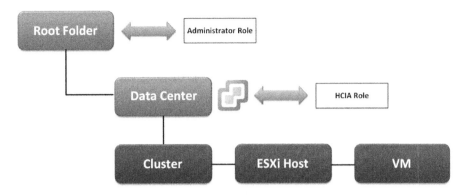

Figure 4.27 – VxRail role-based access control architecture

For example, if you want to create a user account to manage a VxRail cluster, its permission includes software upgrades, as well as management and expansion of the cluster. You can add the **Administrator** or **VMware HCIA Management** roles to this user account:

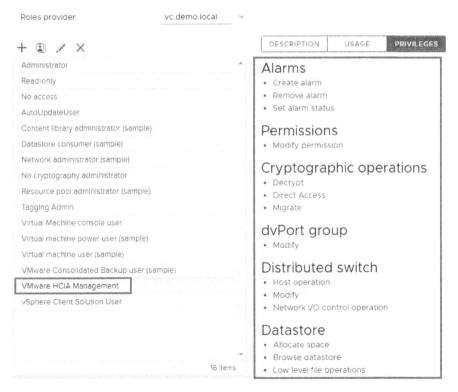

Figure 4.28 – VMware HCIA Management privileges

In the next section, we will show how to create a user account for VxRail management.

Creating a user account with an HCIA Management role

Now we will create a user account with an HCIA Management role by performing the following steps:

1. Go to the **Administration** menu of vCenter Server, choose **Users and Groups** under **Single Sign On**, and then click **ADD USER**:

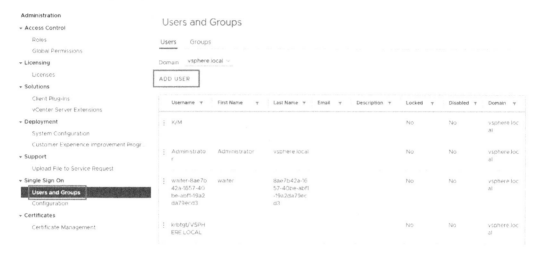

Figure 4.29 – Users and Groups on vCenter Server

2. Complete the **Username** and **Password** fields and then click the **ADD** button. In this example, we will create an account, with `user1` as the username:

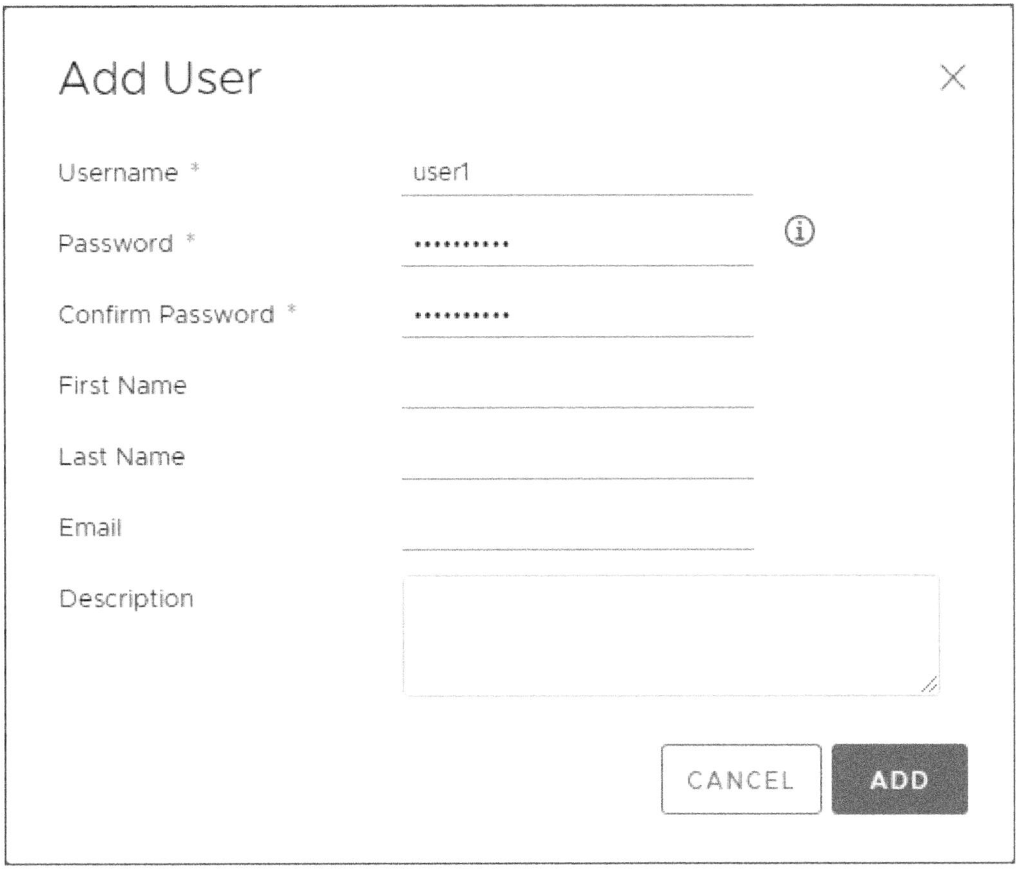

Add User

Username *   user1

Password *   ••••••••••   ⓘ

Confirm Password *   ••••••••••

First Name

Last Name

Email

Description

CANCEL   ADD

Figure 4.30 – Add User management on vCenter Server

3. Go to the **Permission** tab of the VxRail cluster, and then click the + button:

Figure 4.31 – Permission tab on the root folder

4. Search for `user1`, which you created an account for in *step 2*, choose **VMware HCIA Management** in the **Role** menu, and then select **Propagate to children**. Then, click the **OK** button:

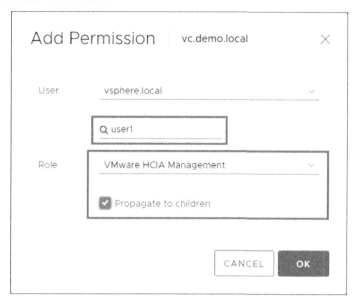

Figure 4.32 – Adding a permission to an account in vCenter Server

5. Finally, we can see that a new account, **user1**, is created, and its role is **VMware HCIA Management**:

Figure 4.33 – The user and group in vCenter Server

By following the procedures detailed above, we are able to create a user account with different roles and permissions.

Summary

In this chapter, we covered the VxRail Manager plugin functions that can deliver a central management dashboard for hardware and software monitoring in the VxRail cluster. We also learned how to define the VxRail roles and permissions for managing the VxRail cluster.

In the next chapter, we will learn about the day-to-day operation of VMware vSAN. We will see how to define the vSAN storage policy to protect virtual machines, and discuss the FTT, FTM, and Fault Domain in different scenarios.

Questions

1. The VxRail Manager plugin for vCenter is available on what version of VxRail software?

   a. VxRail software 4.5.100

   b. VxRail software 4.5.300

   c. VxRail software 4.7.000

   d. VxRail software 4.7.100

   e. All the above

2. Which functions are available on the VxRail Manager plugin at the cluster level?

   a. Add VxRail Hosts

   b. Updates

   c. Support

   d. Market

   e. All the above

3. Which log files are not included in the VxRail log bundle?

   a. VxRail

   b. vCenter

   c. ESXi

   d. Virtual machines

   e. All the above

4. Which VxRail function can download the qualified software products for the VxRail appliance?

    a. vCenter Server

    b. VxRail Manager

    c. Market

    d. VxRail Scale-out

    e. VxRail Lifecycle Management

5. Which service must be enabled to monitor the hardware status in the VxRail cluster?

    a. VxRail Manager Service

    b. SSH Service

    c. Health Monitoring Status

    d. vCenter Server Services

    e. None of the above

6. Which upgrade option is available on the VxRail cluster?

    a. Local upgrade

    b. Download upgrade

    c. Internet upgrade

    d. Manual upgrade

    e. All the above

7. Which role and permission need to be added to your user account if you want to manage the VxRail cluster?

    a. Administrator

    b. Power User

    c. VMware HCIA Management

    d. Power User and VMware HCIA Management

    e. Administrator and VMware HCIA Management

8. Which hardware component can be monitored with the VxRail Manager plugin for vCenter?

    a. VxRail nodes

    b. Network adapter

    c. Power supply

    d. HDD and SSD

    e. All the above

9. What role and permission must be added to the root folder?

    a. Power User

    b. Administrator

    c. VMware HCIA Management

    d. Root

    e. Network User

10. What are the requirements for the Dell EMC Secure Remote Service?

    a. A Dell support account

    b. A VMware support account

    c. Root

    d. VMware HCIA Management

    e. All the above

11. Which role and permission need to be added to your user account if the management of a VxRail cluster is not required?

    a. Administrator

    b. VMware HCIA Management

    c. Administrator or VMware HCIA Management

    d. Administrator and VMware HCIA Management

    e. Power User

    f. All the above

12. By default, which account is available in the root folder in the VxRail cluster?

    a. Administrator

    b. Administrator@vsphere.local

    c. Root

    d. administrator@vmware.com

    e. Power User

5
Managing VMware vSAN

Chapter 4, VxRail Management Overview, described the VxRail Manager plugin's functions and how to deliver a central management dashboard for hardware and software monitoring in a VxRail cluster, such as what components can be monitored at the cluster level and host level. We learned how to define VxRail roles and permissions for managing a VxRail cluster and gained an understanding of the architecture of VxRail role-based access control.

In this chapter, we'll describe an overview of VMware vSAN configuration and operations in a VxRail cluster. This includes different vSAN services, management of vSAN storage policies, monitoring vSAN objects in a VxRail cluster, and vSAN availability. We will also list some of the best practices for vSAN configuration in a VxRail cluster. After this chapter, you'll understand the day-to-day operations of VMs in a VxRail cluster.

In this chapter, we're going to cover the following main topics:

- VMware vSAN service configuration
- Defining vSAN storage policies
- Monitoring a vSAN cluster
- vSAN availability
- Building VMs

Technical requirements

In this chapter, you'll need to make sure your workstation (laptop) is running on the Windows platform, and a web browser is installed on your laptop. The latest versions of Firefox, Google Chrome, and Microsoft Internet Explorer 10 or above are all supported. You need to run the VxRail software at version 4.7.300 or above.

VMware vSAN service configuration

In this section, we will discuss vSAN service configuration in a VxRail cluster, including the following:

- vSAN Deduplication and Compression
- vSAN Encryption
- vSAN Performance Service
- The vSAN iSCSI target service
- Advanced options

These features can be enabled during deployment, if we specify in the PEQ, or can be enabled manually after deployment; we need to enable these features manually if we want to use them. If we go to the **Configure** tab of the VxRail cluster and choose **Services** under the **vSAN** menu, we can enable these features:

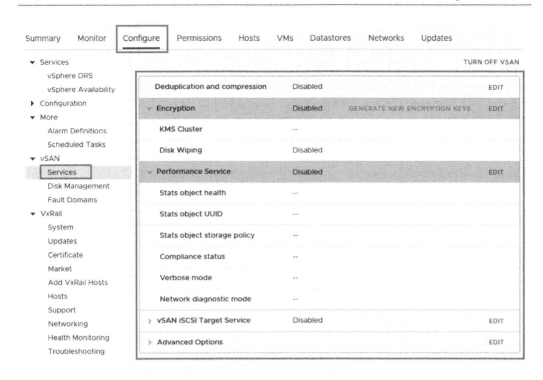

Figure 5.1 – vSAN service configuration

Now we will discuss each vSAN feature one by one.

vSAN Deduplication and Compression

vSAN Deduplication and Compression is only supported on VxRail all-flash clusters; VxRail hybrid clusters are not supported. It also requires a VMware vSAN license edition of Advanced or above. When vSAN deduplication is enabled, it will trigger inline deduplication when the data is de-staged from the cache tier to the capacity tier in the VxRail vSAN cluster. VxRail all-flash systems can provide more benefits than VxRail hybrid systems; for example, the vSAN deduplication feature can minimize the network overhead and CPU utilization, and save the usable capacity. The vSAN compression feature can provide further data deduction. If the data is text or **JPEG (Joint Photographic Experts Group)** files, the OS files will be compressed. The compression ratio is often 2:1 or higher.

If we plan to enable vSAN Deduplication and Compression on a VxRail cluster, it is highly recommended to enable it during VxRail initialization because the performance impact would only be during enabling deduplication and compression, when it is performing a rolling update on -disk format on disk groups. After enabling, it would work normally without performance impact.

To enable vSAN Deduplication and Compression, click the **EDIT** button in **Services** under the **vSAN** menu, then move the **Deduplication and Compression** toggle to the right and click the **APPLY** button. There is an optional setting called **Allow Reduced Redundancy** for vSAN Deduplication and Compression; it is used to enable the process of a vSAN cluster with limited resources. For example, if there is a four-node vSAN cluster with FTT set to 1 that does not have enough resource capacity to evacuate data for disk group reformatting, this option will allow the VMs to keep running. In the same scenario, the VMs still have failure-level protection when the **Allow Reduced Redundancy** option is enabled. This option is used for temporary configuration; it is not advisable to use it in a production environment:

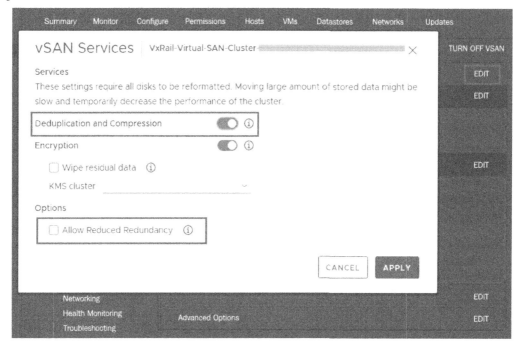

Figure 5.2 – Enabling vSAN Deduplication and Compression

This feature is used to save the vSAN cluster's usable capacity. Now we will discuss vSAN Encryption in the next section.

vSAN Encryption

VMware **vSAN Encryption** can deliver data-at-rest encryption in vSphere's datastore; it can be applied at the vSphere cluster level. When we enable this feature, it can encrypt the data in both the cache tier and the capacity tier of the vSAN cluster. This feature can work together with vSAN Deduplication and Compression; it can save the encrypted data's capacity when enabling deduplication and compression.

There is a requirement for vSAN data-at-rest encryption; it requires an external **Key Management Server** (**KMS**). The KMS cluster's and server's configurations need to be done at the vCenter level, only then can you pick the KMS cluster while enabling vSAN Encryption. For supported KMS, we can find all compatible KMS vendors at `https://core.vmware.com/`.

To enable vSAN data-at-rest encryption, click the **EDIT** button in **Services** under the **vSAN** menu, then move the **Encryption** toggle to the right and click the **APPLY** button. We need to specify the KMS cluster before enabling vSAN Encryption, and it also has an optional setting, **Wipe residual data** (formerly **Erase disks before use**). It is highly recommended to enable this during VxRail initialization because it can avoid the potential performance impact of enabling encryption on existing data:

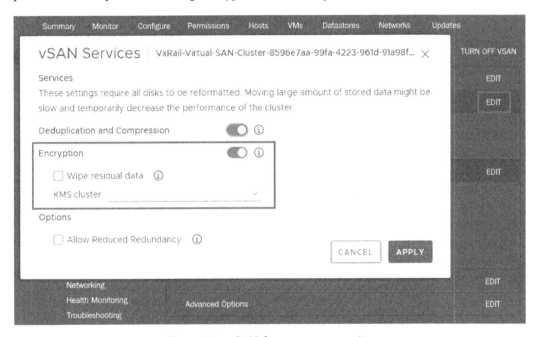

Figure 5.3 – vSAN data-at-rest encryption

VMware vSphere also supports the VM encryption feature. In a VxRail vSAN cluster, vSAN data-at-rest encryption and VM encryption are mutually compatible. The encryption architectures are different; the differences are shown in the following table:

Features	VM Encryption	vSAN Encryption
Requires an external KMS	Yes	Yes
Per-VM-level encryption	Yes	No
Datastore encryption	No	Yes
Deduplication and compression	No	Yes
Data-at-rest encryption	Yes	Yes
VMs encrypted by:	Storage policy	On datastore
Licensing	vSphere Enterprise Plus	vSAN Enterprise or above
Encryption occurs:	Before deduplication	After deduplication

With the preceding table, you should understand the differences between the two encryption options.

> **Important note**
> The KMS must be placed outside of the encrypted vSphere cluster.

This feature is used to encrypt vSAN cluster data. Now we will discuss vSAN Performance Service in the next section.

vSAN Performance Service

vSAN Performance Service is disabled by default. It is used to deliver vSAN performance monitoring and a statistical performance chart that includes information about the vSAN **Input/Output Operations Per Second** (**IOPS**), latency, network throughput, vSAN clusters, the vSAN host, the disk group, disk, VMs, and so on. To enable vSAN Performance Service, click the **EDIT** button in **Services** under the **vSAN** menu, then move the **Enable vSAN Performance Service** toggle to the right and click the **APPLY** button. The vSAN performance history database is stored as a vSAN object. The storage policy controls the availability, space consumption, and performance of that object. If the object is unavailable, the vSAN performance history for the cluster will also be unavailable:

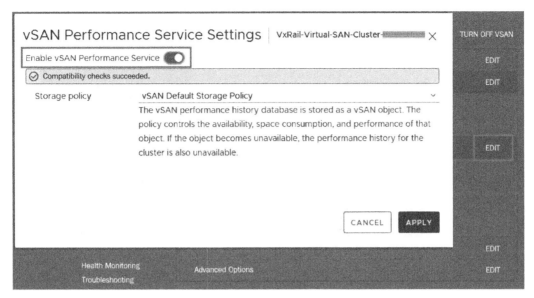

Figure 5.4 – vSAN Performance Service Settings

This feature is used to monitor vSAN performance objects. Now we will discuss the vSAN iSCSI target service in the next section.

The vSAN iSCSI target service

The **vSAN iSCSI target service** is available on vSAN 6.5 and above. If we want to enable this service, we must define a VMkernel network for the iSCSI network and authentication. It supports authentication and can be enabled without authentication as well.

This service is used to present a vSAN iSCSI volume to the physical or virtual servers. When we enable the vSAN iSCSI target service, vSAN creates a home object that stores metadata for the iSCSI target service, similar to the VM home object of a VM:

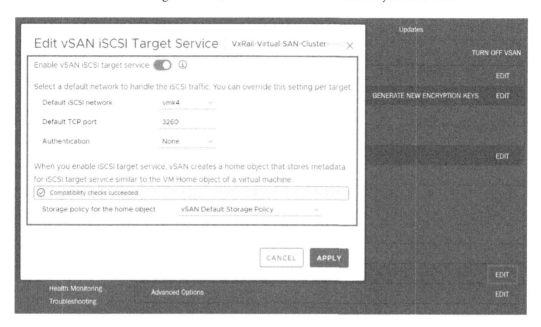

Figure 5.5 – vSAN iSCSI target service configuration

To enable the vSAN iSCSI target service, click the **EDIT** button in **Services** under the **vSAN** menu, then move the **Enable vSAN iSCSI target service** toggle to the right. We need to choose the pre-defined iSCSI network, TCP port (the default is 3260), and authentication.

Advanced options

In the vSAN cluster, there are some advanced parameters: **Object Repair Timer**, **Site Read Locality**, **Thin Swap**, **Large Cluster Support**, and **Automatic Re balance**. Now we will explain each parameter:

- **Object Repair Timer**: This parameter specifies how long vSAN will wait before rebuilding the vSAN components that have entered an **ABSENT** state when any vSAN node or disk has faulted in the cluster. By default, this parameter is set to 60 minutes. We do recommend keeping the default value for most normal vSAN operations.

- **Site Read Locality**: This parameter specifies the read approach in a vSAN cluster. In a vSAN standard cluster, the VM reads the data locally from only the replica. In a vSAN stretched cluster, the read approach is different. By default, this parameter is disabled. This option is only enabled for a vSAN stretched cluster.

- **Thin Swap**: This parameter specifies VM swap objects as thick or thin. In order to save the space capacity of each VM, by default, this value is set to thin.

- **Large Cluster Support**: By default, a vSAN cluster can support up to 32 nodes. When we enable this parameter, a vSAN cluster can support up to 64 nodes. If we change this parameter, it requires a manual reboot of each vSAN node.

- **Automatic Rebalance**: This parameter specifies whether any vSAN nodes are overloaded. When this option is enabled, if the performance of a vSAN cluster is unbalanced, it will start rebalancing automatically:

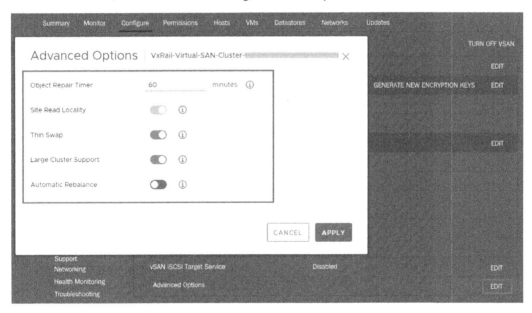

Figure 5.6 – vSAN Advanced Options

> **Important note**
>
> The **Large Cluster Support** and **Automatic Rebalance** advanced options are available on VMware vSAN 6.7 Update 3 or above.

Having reached the end of this section, *VMware vSAN service configuration*, we've now had an overview of the vSAN services and we understand their functions. In the next section, we will discuss what VM storage policies are.

Defining vSAN storage policies

In this section, we will discuss an overview of VM storage policy rules and the configuration of VM storage policies. This includes storage providers, VM storage policy rules, and creating and monitoring VM storage policies in vCenter Server.

Overview of VM storage policies

Storage providers are software **Application Programming Interfaces** (**APIs**) that are available from VMware or other storage vendors to enable **vSphere APIs for Storage Awareness** (**VASA**). Storage providers can integrate with different storage and software-defined storage (for example, VMware vSAN and virtual volumes).

When we initially set up a VxRail cluster, it will automatically configure the vSAN storage provider for each VxRail node in the cluster. We can find the vSAN storage provider information in the **Configure** tab of vCenter Server and select **Storage Providers**. The operation of the VM storage policy depends on the storage provider in vCenter Server. In **Storage Providers**, we can get the storage provider information, for example, **Provider name**, **Provider version**, **VASA API version**, and **Supported profiles**:

Figure 5.7 – vSAN Storage Providers

Now we will discuss VM storage policies. Go to **VM Storage Policies** on the **Policies and Profiles** page in vCenter Server. There are four default vSAN storage policies and one VxRail vSAN storage policy.

In *Figure 5.8*, we can see there are four vSAN default storage policies. **VXRAIL-SYSTEM-STORAGE-PROFILE** is the VxRail vSAN storage policy, which is available after VxRail initialization. This policy has been defined with **Failures to tolerate** set to **1** with **RAID-1 (Mirroring)** and uses **Thin provisioning**. We can create a new VM storage policy with different rules; we will discuss this in the next section, *Creating VM storage policies*:

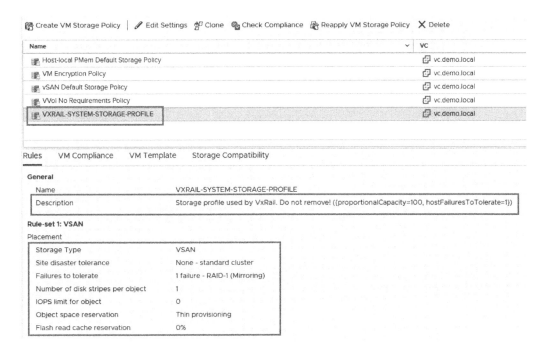

Figure 5.8 – VM storage policies

Important note

We do not delete the **VXRAIL-SYSTEM-STORAGE-PROFILE** VM storage policy because it is required for the normal operation of the VxRail system.

To monitor the VM storage policy, we select the following options to monitor the default policies and the VM storage policies we defined, that is, **Rules**, **VM Compliance**, **VM Template**, and **Storage Compatibility**:

- **Rules**: This shows the configuration of availability and advanced policy rules in the selected VM storage policy.

- **VM Compliance**: This shows the number of VMs that are compliant with the VM storage policy. In *Figure 5.9*, there are three VMs assigned to the **VXRAIL-SYSTEM-STORAGE-PROFILE** VM storage policy:

Figure 5.9 – The monitoring options in the VM storage policy

- **VM Template**: This shows the templates associated with the selected VM storage policy.

- **Storage Compatibility**: This shows the compatible storage resources with the selected VM storage policy.

We now understand what VM storage policies are. Now we will go on to discuss how to create a VM storage policy.

Creating VM storage policies

In this section, we discuss how to create a new VM storage policy with the following rules:

Policy Name	New VM Storage Policy
Site disaster tolerance	None - standard cluster
Failures to tolerate	1 failure - RAID-1 (Mirroring)
Number of disk stripes per object	1
IOPS limit for object	0
Object space reservation	Thin provisioning
Flash read cache reservation	5
Disable object checksum	Default
Force provisioning	Default

Now we will create a new VM storage policy with the following procedure based on the preceding requirements:

1. Click **Create VM Storage Policy** on the **VM Storage Policies** page.

2. Specific the policy name, then click the **NEXT** button:

Figure 5.10 – Specifying the VM storage policy name

3. Select the **Enable rules for "vSAN" storage** option, then click the **NEXT** button:

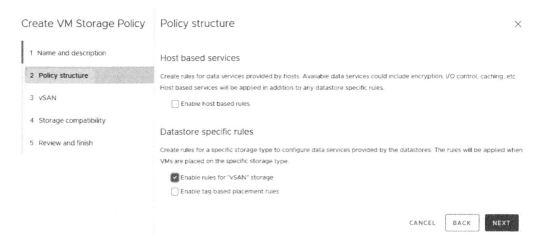

Figure 5.11 – Enabling the VM storage policy rules

4. In the **Site disaster tolerance** menu, we can select the following options:

Site Disaster Tolerance	Description
None - standard cluster	This policy only keeps the data on one site.
None - standard cluster with nested fault domains	This policy keeps the data across the fault domains.
Dual site mirroring (stretched cluster)	This policy keeps replicas of each component on both the preferred and non-preferred sites. If one of the sites is down, the replicas on the other site will still be running.
None - Keep data on Preferred (stretched cluster)	This policy keeps all components of the vSAN object and the VM compute resources with DRS rules on the preferred site.
None - Keep data on Non-preferred (stretched cluster)	This policy keeps all components of the vSAN object and the VM compute resources with DRS rules on the non-preferred site.
None - stretched cluster	This policy keeps all components of the vSAN object on the preferred site or non-preferred site.

We'll select **None - standard cluster** from the **Site disaster tolerance** menu:

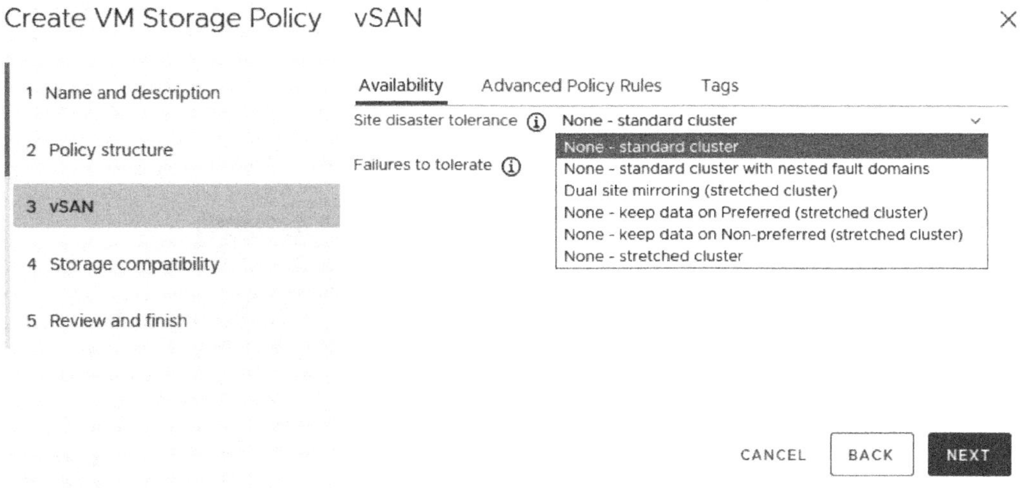

Create VM Storage Policy   vSAN   ✕

1 Name and description	Availability Advanced Policy Rules Tags
2 Policy structure	Site disaster tolerance ⓘ None - standard cluster ⌄
3 vSAN	Failures to tolerate ⓘ
4 Storage compatibility	
5 Review and finish	

- None - standard cluster
- None - standard cluster with nested fault domains
- Dual site mirroring (stretched cluster)
- None - keep data on Preferred (stretched cluster)
- None - keep data on Non-preferred (stretched cluster)
- None - stretched cluster

CANCEL   BACK   NEXT

Figure 5.12 – Site disaster tolerance options

5. From the **Failures to tolerate** menu, we can select the following options:

Failures to Tolerate	Description	Minimum Hosts
No data redundancy	No protection in this policy. **Failures to Tolerate** (**FTT**) is set to 0.	N/A
1 failure - RAID-1 (Mirroring)	Keeps the data with RAID-1 protection and allows one replica to be faulted. FTT is set to 1.	3
1 failure - RAID-5 (Erasure Coding)	Keeps the data with RAID-5 protection and allows one replica to be faulted. It is only supported on vSAN All-Flash configuration. FTT is set to 1.	4
2 failures - RAID-1 (Mirroring)	Keeps the data with RAID-1 protection and allows two replicas to be faulted. FTT is set to 2.	5
2 failures - RAID-6 (Erasure Coding)	Keeps the data with RAID-6 protection and allows two replicas to be faulted. It is only supported on vSAN All-Flash configuration. FTT is set to 2.	6
3 failures - RAID-1 (Mirroring)	Keeps the data with RAID-1 protection and allows three replicas to be faulted. FTT is set to 3.	7

We'll select **1 failure - RAID-1 (Mirroring)** from the **Failures to tolerate** menu, then click the **NEXT** button:

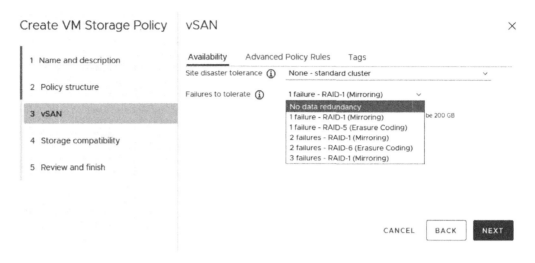

Figure 5.13 – Failures to tolerate options

6. In **Advanced Policy Rules**, we can define the following settings:

Number of disk stripes per object: Define the number of drives across which each replica of a storage object is striped.

IOPS limit for object: Define the IOPS for the disk.

Object space reservation: Define the space type of the storage object as thick provisioning or thin provisioning.

Flash read cache reservation: Define the flash read cache for each storage object.

Disable object checksum: If this option is enabled, the storage object will not calculate the checksum information.

Force provisioning: If this option is enabled, the storage object will be provisioned even if the policy specified in the storage policy cannot satisfy the resources available in the cluster.

We'll select **Thin provisioning** for **Object space reservation** and set **Flash read cache reservation** to 5, then click the **NEXT** button:

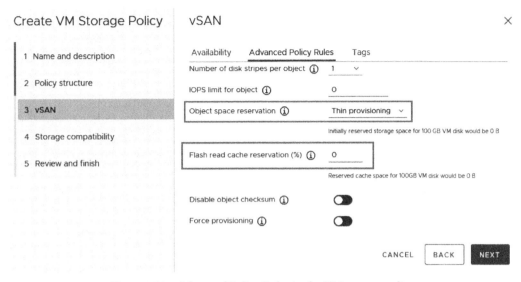

Figure 5.14 – Advanced Policy Rules in the VM storage policy

7. In **Storage compatibility**, we choose the supported vSAN datastore and click the **NEXT** button:

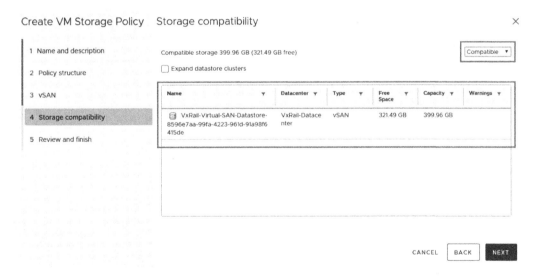

Figure 5.15 – Storage compatibility in the VM storage policy

8. In the final stage, we review all the configuration to confirm the VM storage policy and click the **FINISH** button to create the policy:

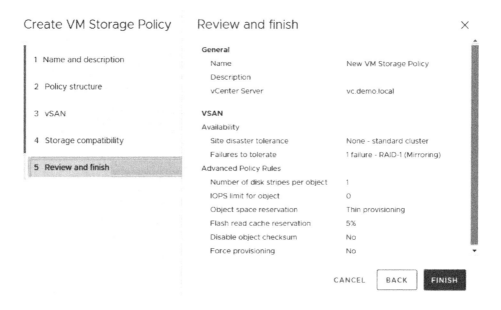

Figure 5.16 – Reviewing to confirm the VM storage policy

9. We can see the new policy, **New VM Storage Policy**, is ready:

Figure 5.17 – The VM Storage Policies page

> **Important note**
> It's best practice for **Object space reservation** to be set to thin or thick provisioning when using RAID-5 or RAID-6 (Erasure Coding) with deduplication and compression.

Based on the preceding procedures, we now understand how to create VM storage policies. In the next section, we will discuss how to apply them to VMs.

Applying VM storage policies

We can apply a VM storage policy to a VM anytime; the vSAN objects must fulfill the requirement of the number of hosts and the capacity space in the VM storage policy. In this example, we will change the default VM storage policy, **vSAN Default Storage Policy**, to a new policy, **New VM Storage Policy**:

1. Select your VM and go to **Policies** on the **Configure** tab:

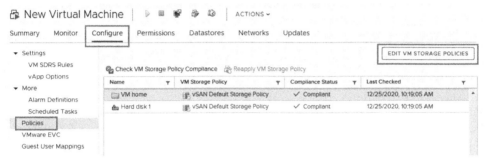

Figure 5.18 – Viewing the storage policy of the VM

2. In the **VM storage policy** menu, we can select the new policy, **New VM Storage Policy**, and then click the **OK** button to confirm this configuration:

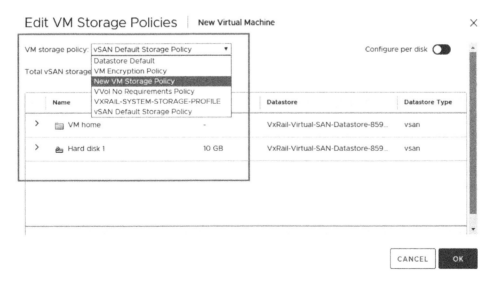

Figure 5.19 – Editing the VM storage policy

When we confirm the new storage policy, the VM storage policy will execute the new configuration on this VM immediately. The compliance status of this VM displays **Compliant** when the new confirmation is done successfully:

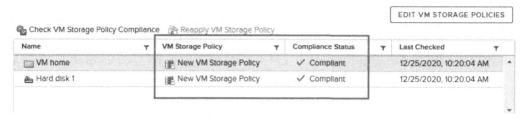

Figure 5.20 – The compliance status of the VM storage policy

Important note

The execution time of the VM storage policy depends on the number of copies and the capacity of each virtual disk.

Having reached the end of this section, *Defining vSAN storage policies*, we've now had an overview of the configuration of VM storage policies. In the next section, we will discuss how to monitor VM storage policies.

Monitoring a vSAN cluster

In this section, we will discuss the monitoring of a VxRail vSAN cluster. This includes the monitoring of vSAN health, vSAN virtual objects, vSAN resyncing objects, vSAN capacity, and vSAN performance. Now we will discuss each one.

vSAN health

vSAN health checks can provide the overall status of a VxRail vSAN cluster; this includes the vSAN hardware compatibility, vSAN network configuration, vSAN build recommendation, vSAN performance, storage device health, VM objects, and so on. We can see the status of each component in a vSAN health check. It will display a warning or an error message if any issues exist on each component. In *Figure 5.21*, we can see the status of each component on the **Health** page in this VxRail vSAN cluster:

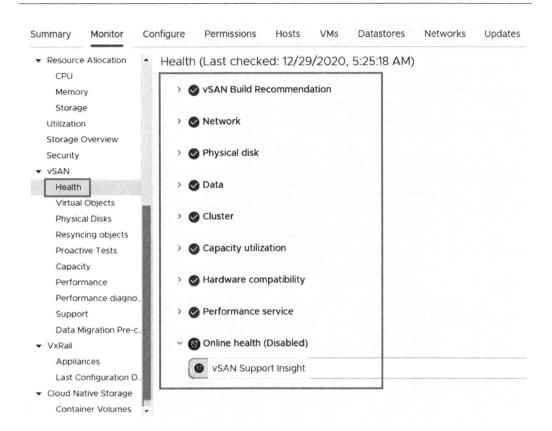

Figure 5.21 – vSAN Health

The vSAN **Health** page is used to display the status of all vSAN components and objects. Now we will discuss vSAN virtual objects in the next section.

vSAN virtual objects

On the **Virtual Objects** page, we can see the number of vSAN objects in each VM. In *Figure 5.22*, there are three VMs: **VMware vCenter Server Appliance**, **VMware vCenter Server Platform Service Controller**, and **VxRail Manager**. In total, there are 38 virtual objects in this vSAN cluster. We can also drill into each VM; it will display the number of virtual objects that exist in a VM:

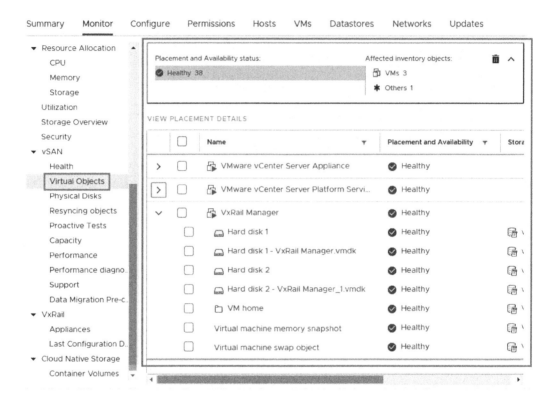

Figure 5.22 – vSAN Virtual Objects

Virtual Objects is used to display the vSAN objects of each VM. Now we will discuss vSAN resyncing objects in the next section.

vSAN resyncing objects

When any hardware device, network connection, or vSAN host faults, or if any vSAN host is placed into maintenance mode, it initiates the object's resynchronization in the VxRail vSAN cluster. By default, **Object repair timer** is set to 60 minutes; this means that it initiates an object's resynchronization after 60 minutes when any hardware fault occurs or a vSAN host is placed into maintenance mode. Then we can see **Total resyncing objects**, **Bytes left to resync**, and **Total resyncing ETA**:

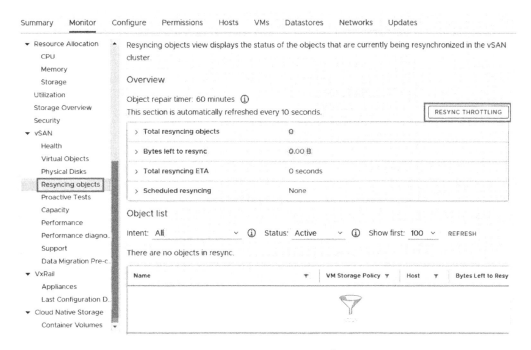

Figure 5.23 – vSAN resyncing objects

You can see a **RESYNC THROTTLING** button at the top, and we can use it to reduce the vSAN network bandwidth and resynchronize the disk groups in a VxRail vSAN cluster.

vSAN capacity

We can monitor the capacity of a vSAN datastore in a VxRail vSAN cluster; this includes **Capacity Overview**, **Usable capacity analysis**, and **Usage breakdown before dedup and compression**. **Capacity Overview** displays the usable and free capacity of storage on a vSAN datastore. **Usable capacity analysis** displays the effective free space if deploying a new workload with the selected storage policy:

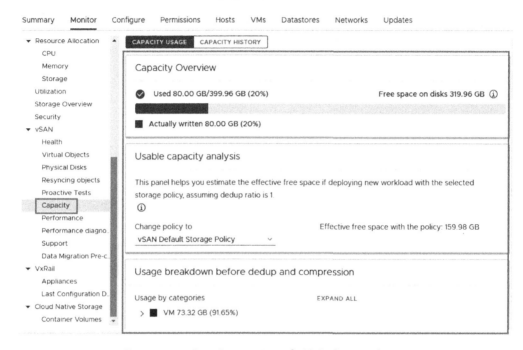

Figure 5.24 – Capacity overview of a VxRail vSAN cluster

Usage breakdown before dedup and compression displays the capacity percentage of each vSAN object; it includes the virtual disks, VM home objects, swap objects, and so on.

vSAN cluster level

We can use performance metrics to monitor the performance of a VxRail vSAN cluster if any performance problems exist. When we click the **VM** button, we can get the performance metrics for IOPS, throughput latency, congestion, and outstanding I/O:

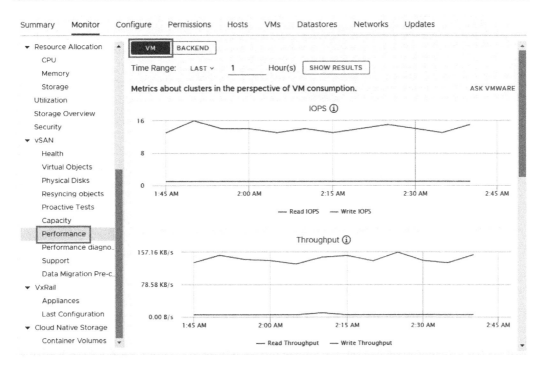

Figure 5.25 – The performance monitor at the vSAN cluster level

When we click the **BACKEND** button, we can get the performance metrics for the cluster backend operations, including IOPS, throughput, latency, congestion, and outstanding I/O.

vSAN host level

We can monitor the performance metrics at the VxRail host level; select the VxRail host and go to **Performance** under the **Monitor** tab. At the host level, we can view detailed performance charts for **VM**, **BACKEND**, **DISKS**, **PHYSICAL ADAPTERS**, and **HOST NETWORK**:

- **VM**: This provides the VM performance chart for this host.

- **BACKEND**: This provides the vSAN backend performance chart for this host.

- **DISKS**: This provides the vSAN disk group performance chart for this host.

- **PHYSICAL ADAPTERS**: This provides the network adapters performance chart for this host.

- **HOST NETWORK**: This provides the vSAN network performance chart for this host:

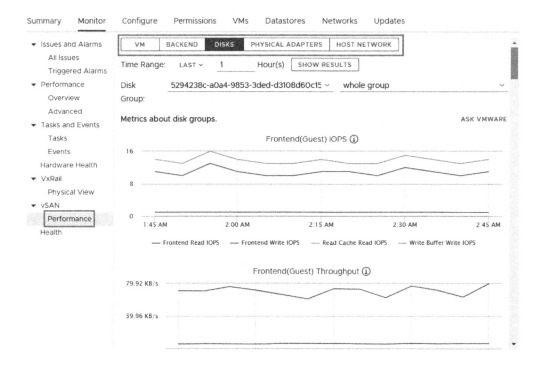

Figure 5.26 – Performance monitoring at the VxRail host level

This feature is used to display the vSAN performance at the vSAN host level. Now we will discuss how to monitor vSAN performance at the VM level in the next section.

vSAN VM level

We can monitor the performance metrics at the VM level; select the VM and go to **Performance** under the **Monitor** tab. At the VM level, we can view detailed performance charts for **VM** and **VIRTUAL DISKS**:

- **VM**: This provides the selected VM's performance chart.

- **VIRTUAL DISKS**: This provides the performance chart of the selected VM's virtual disks:

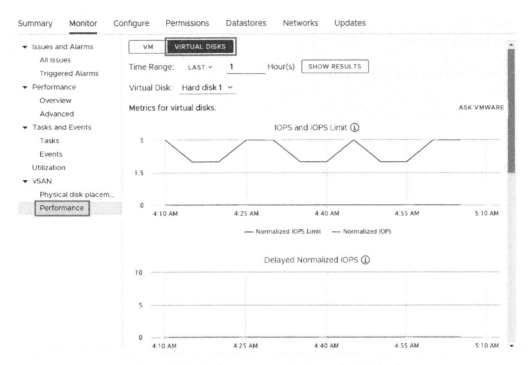

Figure 5.27 – Performance monitoring at the VM level

If we need to collect the performance figures for a VxRail vSAN cluster, we go to the preceding performance charts.

Having reached the end of this section, *Monitoring the vSAN cluster*, we understand how to monitor vSAN performance at different cluster levels. Now we will discuss vSAN high availability in the next section, *vSAN availability*.

vSAN availability

In this section, we will discuss high availability in a VxRail vSAN cluster. This includes the vSAN fault domains and maintenance mode. Now we will discuss these aspects.

Overview of vSAN fault domains

vSAN fault domains are used to ensure protection against rack or room failure, and we can create fault domains for vSAN high availability. A fault domain consists of a vSAN host or more vSAN hosts in a physical location, for example, racks or data centers. When we define fault domains, it depends on the vSAN tolerate failures of entire physical racks, a single host, disk devices, the network switch, and so on.

Now we will discuss an example. *Figure 5.28* shows an example of fault domains in a VxRail vSAN cluster:

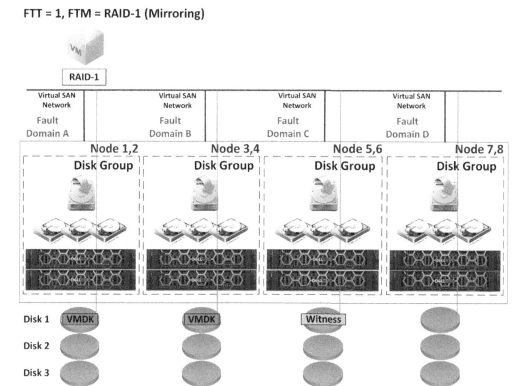

Figure 5.28 – vSAN fault domain example

The minimum requirement for fault domains is three domains. In best practice, four or more fault domains is the recommended configuration. In *Figure 5.28*, there are eight nodes running in the VxRail vSAN cluster; there are four fault domains in this cluster, **Fault Domain A**, **Fault Domain B**, **Fault Domain C**, and **Fault Domain D**, and each domain has two nodes. The VM storage policy is defined with FTT set to 1 and FTM set to **RAID-1 (Mirroring)**, and any vSAN objects are stored on three of the four fault domains that are based on this VM storage policy.

When we define the number of fault domains with VM storage policies, the failure tolerance method is the minimum requirement for the fault domain. The following table shows the minimum number of fault domains based on different FTT and FTM settings. If the fault domain is enabled in the VxRail vSAN cluster, vSAN will apply the VM storage policies to fault domains instead of individual hosts:

Number of Failures to Tolerate	Failure Tolerance Method	Witness	Minimum Number of Fault Domains
1	RAID-1 (Mirroring)	1	3
2	RAID-1 (Mirroring)	2	5
3	RAID-1 (Mirroring)	3	7
1	RAID-5 (Erase Coding)	N/A	4
2	RAID-6 (Erase Coding)	N/A	6

> **Important note**
> We must assign the same number of hosts to each fault domain, and each host must have the same hardware configuration.

In the next section, we will discuss how to create fault domains in a VxRail vSAN cluster.

Creating vSAN fault domains

In this section, we will create a new fault domain in the VxRail vSAN cluster. To manage the fault domain, we select the VxRail vSAN cluster and go to **Fault Domains** under **vSAN** on the **Configure** tab. In *Figure 5.29*, there are three standalone hosts in this cluster:

Figure 5.29 – The vSAN fault domains

> **Important note**
>
> A VxRail cluster does not create any fault domains automatically after the VxRail initialization; we need to create the fault domains manually.

Now we will create three fault domains and assign a host to each fault domain. Click the plus icon to create a fault domain. We need to specify the fault domain name and assign a host to each domain:

New Fault Domain ✕

Fault domain name: Fault Domain A

☐	Host ▼	Current fault domain ▼
☑	📱 esx01.demo.local	
☐	📱 esx02.demo.local	
☐	📱 esx03.demo.local	

☑ 1	3 hosts

CANCEL   **CREATE**

Figure 5.30 – Creating a fault domain

In *Figure 5.31*, we can see three fault domains: **Fault Domain A**, **Fault Domain B**, and **Fault Domain C**. Each domain has one host:

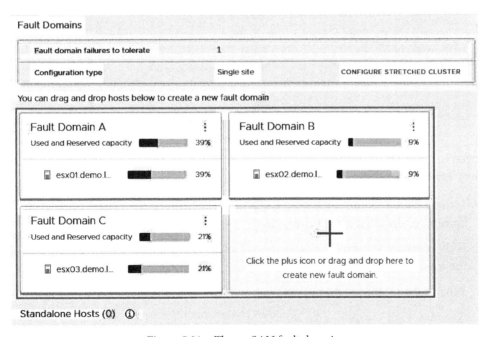

Figure 5.31 – Three vSAN fault domains

We've had an overview of vSAN fault domains and their functions. Now we will discuss how to create a vSAN fault domain in the next section.

vSAN maintenance mode

vSAN maintenance mode is used for remedial operations on a host. We right-click the VxRail node and select **Enter Maintenance Mode** from the available menu. When we place a host into maintenance mode, the total capacity of the VxRail vSAN cluster will reduce automatically because this host does not contribute storage to the VxRail vSAN cluster:

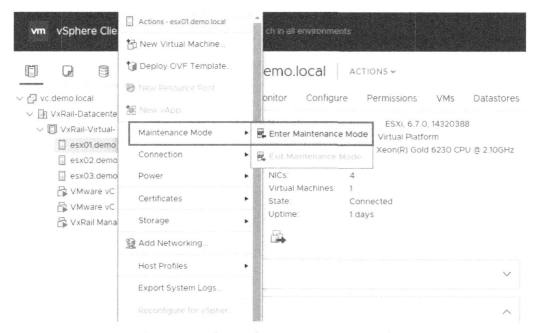

Figure 5.32 – Placing a host into maintenance mode

We need to consider the following conditions before we place a host into maintenance mode:

- Is there enough total capacity on the remaining hosts in the cluster to store the amount of data that must be migrated?

- Is there enough flash cache capacity on the remaining hosts in the cluster to handle the total flash read cache?

- What is the minimum number of hosts in the cluster that meets the FTT requirement?

Once the host is placed in maintenance mode, all the VMs must migrate to other hosts or be powered off. The vSAN maintenance mode has three options for vSAN data migration: **Ensure accessibility**, **Full data migration**, and **No data migration**. We can also see it has a default option, **Move powered-off and suspended virtual machines to other hosts in the cluster**. We can enable or disable this option before placing a host into maintenance mode:

- **Ensure accessibility**: Only partial data transfer is required. All VMs on this host will remain accessible.

- **Full data migration**: All data on this host will be transferred to other hosts in the cluster to ensure availability compliance. This option results in the largest amount of data transfer and consumes the most time and resources.

- **No data migration**: No data from this host will be transferred. Some objects might become inaccessible:

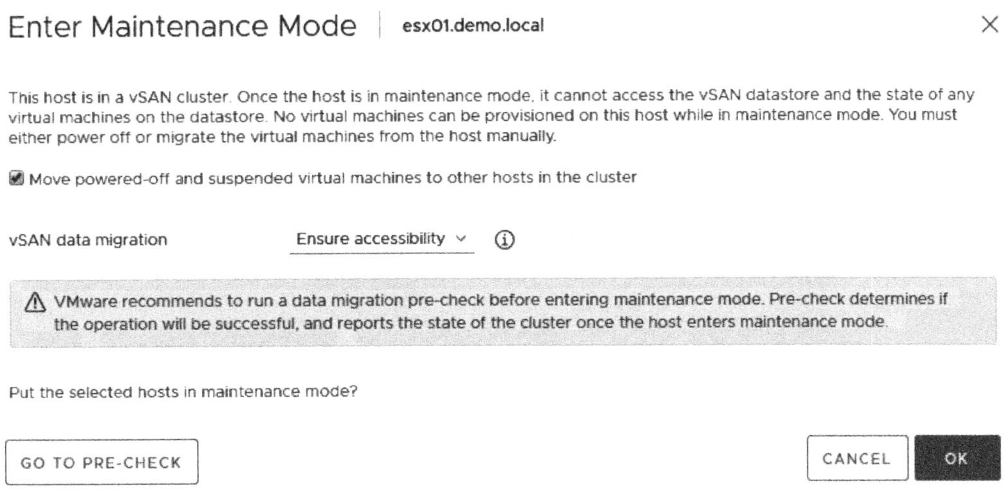

Figure 5.33 – vSAN data migration options

Now we will discuss the result when we select each option with a scenario.

This scenario includes a VxRail vSAN cluster with four nodes, and two VMs are running in this cluster: the VM storage policy with FTT set to 1 and FTM set to RAID-1 (Mirroring), which are assigned to **VM 1** and **VM 2**. Each VM has three vSAN components: two **VMDK** components and one **Witness** component. Each vSAN component is allowed into the dedicated host:

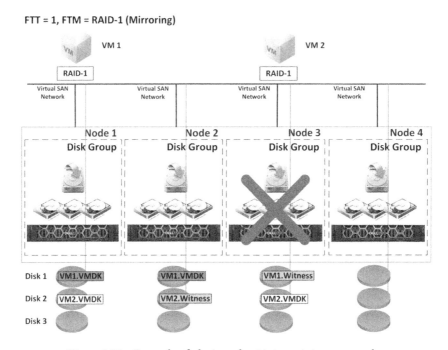

Figure 5.34 – Example of placing a host into maintenance mode

If we plan to place a host (**Node 3**) into maintenance mode with the **Ensure accessibility** option, the VM (**VM 2**) will migrate to the other host (**Node 4**), and all vSAN components not needed remain allocated. In the example in *Figure 5.34*, if **Node 3** is put into maintenance mode with the **Ensure accessibility** option, the final result is as displayed in *Figure 5.35*:

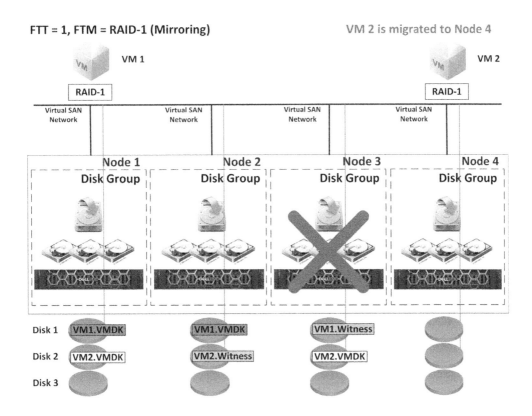

Figure 5.35 – Maintenance mode result with the Ensure accessibility option

If we plan to place a host (**Node 3**) in maintenance mode with the **Full data migration** option, the VM (**VM 2**) will migrate to the other host (**Node 4**), and all vSAN components will migrate to **Node 4**.

Now we will discuss the other scenario. In the example in *Figure 5.34*, if **Node 3** is put into maintenance mode with the **Full data migration** option, the final result is as displayed in *Figure 5.36*:

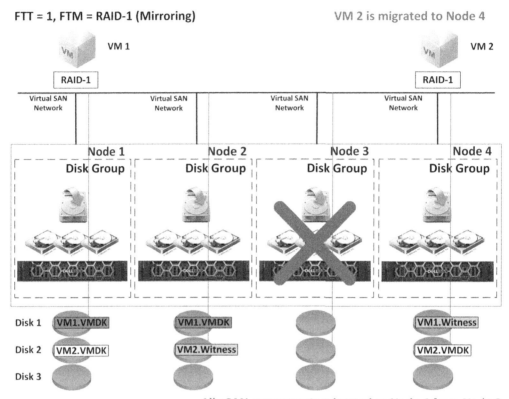

Figure 5.36 – The maintenance mode result with the Full data migration option

If we plan to place a host (**Node 3**) into maintenance mode with the **No data migration** option, the VM (**VM 2**) will be migrated into **Node 4** from **Node 3**, and all vSAN components will still remain allocated to **Node 3**.

In the example in *Figure 5.34*, if **Node 3** is put into maintenance mode with the **No data migration** option, the final result is as displayed in *Figure 5.37*:

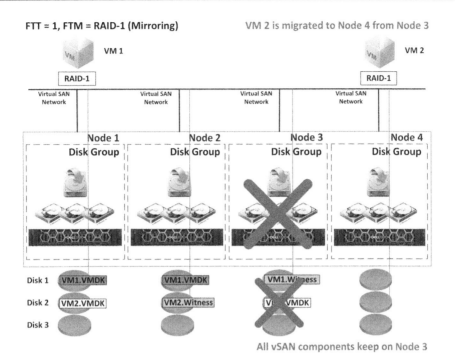

Figure 5.37 – All vSAN components remain on Node 3

This table shows the advantages and disadvantages of each vSAN maintenance mode:

Maintenance Mode	Advantages	Disadvantages
Ensure accessibility	Minimal data migration is needed compared to full data migration.	This option will not re-protect the data during the failure and may cause unexpected data loss.
Full data migration	This option will re-protect the data during the failure and ensure availability compliance.	This option requires a large amount of time for vSAN data migration and consumes the extra resources in the other hosts.
No data migration	The vSAN cluster does not evacuate any data from the host	Based on FTT and RAID configurations, first data will be non-compliant and if it satisfies the minimum requirements of FTT and FTM, it will rebuild on the next available node.

According to the preceding scenarios, we can now understand the results when we place a host into vSAN maintenance mode with each option.

We can click the **PRE-CHECK** button to show the number of vSAN objects that become non-compliant if each option is used before placing a host into maintenance mode:

Figure 5.38 – The PRE-CHECK result before placing a host into maintenance mode

Having reached the end of this section, *vSAN availability*, we've now had an overview of the functions of vSAN availability. In the next section, we will discuss how to build VMs with VM storage policies.

Building VMs

In this section, we will discuss how to create VMs with vSAN storage policies on a VxRail cluster. We can build VMs with the following deployment methods:

- **Building a VM**: Create a VM and install a guest OS (the Windows or Linux platforms) on the VM.

- **Deploying from a template**: Deploy a VM from the VM template that was pre-defined by the OS configuration and customization by the system administrator on day 1.

- **Cloning from a VM**: Make a copy of a VM, then perform OS customization.

- **Importing a virtual appliance**: Import a virtual appliance from **Open Virtualization Format (OVF)** into vCenter Server. We only define the management network for this VM, then it can start up.

Now we will show how to create a VM with a vSAN storage policy on a VxRail cluster:

1. Right-click the host and select **New Virtual Machine**, and then choose **Create a new virtual machine**. Then, click the **NEXT** button:

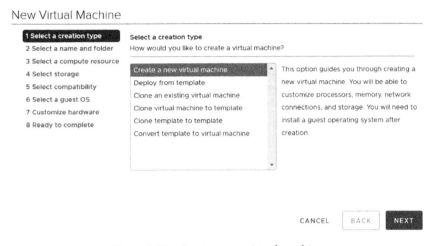

Figure 5.39 – Create a new virtual machine

2. Specify the VM name and folder, then click the **NEXT** button:

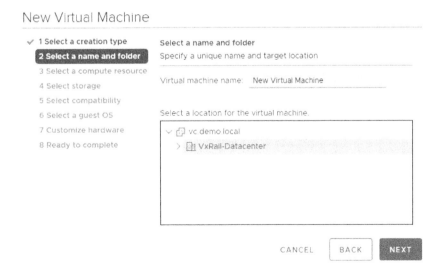

Figure 5.40 – Specifying the VM name

3. Select the target VxRail host, then click the **NEXT** button:

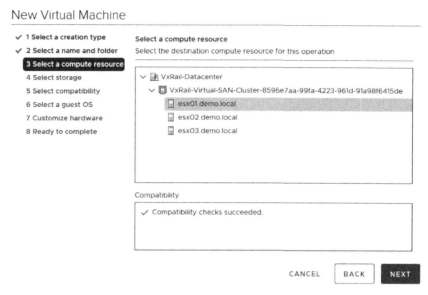

Figure 5.41 – Selecting the target VxRail host

4. Select the vSAN datastore and vSAN storage policy, then click the **NEXT** button:

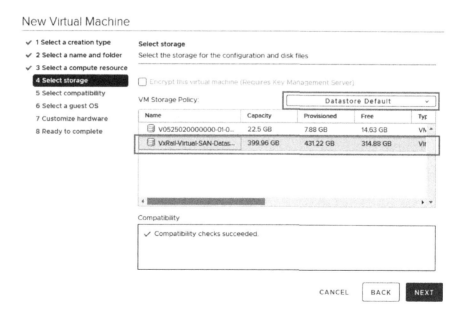

Figure 5.42 – Selecting the vSAN datastore

5. Select **ESXi 6.7 and later** from the **Compatible with** menu, then click the **NEXT** button. If we ever need to migrate VMs to older versions, it's a better idea to deploy VMs compatible with them:

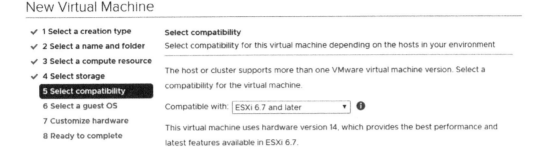

Figure 5.43 – Selecting the ESXi compatibility

6. Select a guest OS family and version – for example, Windows Server 2016 – then click the **NEXT** button:

Figure 5.44 – Selecting a guest OS

7. Specify the hardware configuration on the VM, then click the **NEXT** button:

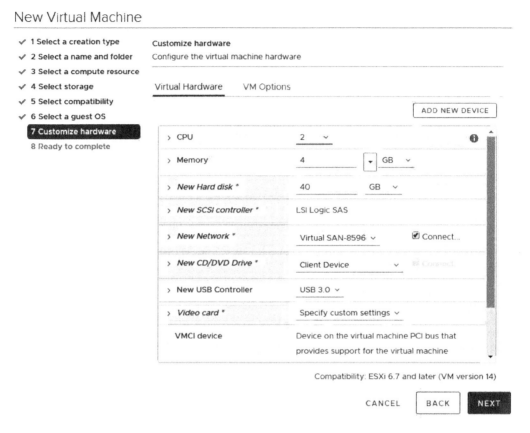

Figure 5.45 – Customizing the hardware on the guest OS

8. Review the configuration and click the **FINISH** button to confirm and build the VM:

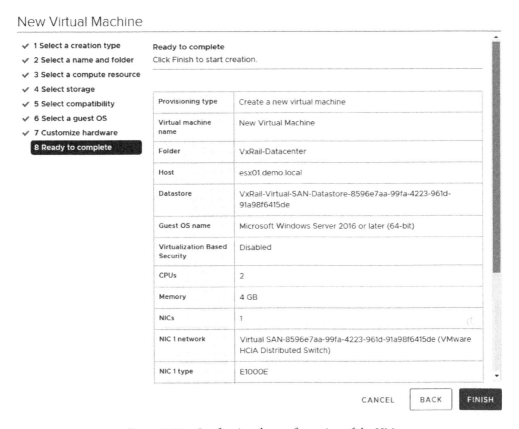

Figure 5.46 – Confirming the configuration of the VM

We can follow the preceding procedure to deploy a VM in a VxRail cluster.

Having reached the end of this section, *Building VMs*, we now understand the procedure for building VMs with VM storage policies.

Summary

This chapter has given you an understanding of the advantages of vSAN storage policies. With them, we can easily define different FTT methods to protect VMs and change the RAID protection level of a VM without any service interruption. Finally, you now understand the difference between vSAN storage provisioning and traditional storage provisioning.

In the next chapter, we will learn about **Life Cycle Management** (**LCM**) on a VxRail cluster, and we will look at the advantages of LCM compared with a traditional server and storage.

Questions

1. Which service is not available in a vSAN service configuration?

   a. vSAN Encryption

   b. vSAN Performance Service

   c. vSAN iSCSI target service

   d. vSAN Deduplication and Compression

   e. vSAN VM Storage Policy

2. Which service is available in the vSAN advanced options?

   a. Object Repair Timer

   b. Site Read Locality

   c. Thin Swap

   d. Large Cluster Support

   e. Automatic Rebalance

   f. All the above

3. Which default VxRail VM storage policy is pre-defined after VxRail initialization?

   a. VXRAIL-STORAGE-POLICY

   b. VXRAIL-SYSTEM-STORAGE-PROFILE

   c. vSAN Default Storage Policy

   d. vSAN Storage Policy

   e. None of the above

4. What is the minimum number of hosts for applying a VM storage policy with FTT set to 1 and FTM set to RAID-5 (Erasure Coding)?

   a. 3

   b. 4

   c. 5

   d. 6

   e. 7

5. Which FTM option is not available in a VM storage policy?

    a. 3 failures - RAID-1 (Mirroring)

    b. 2 failures - RAID-1 (Mirroring)

    c. 1 failure - RAID-5 (Erasure Coding)

    d. 4 failures - RAID-1 (Mirroring)

    e. 2 failures - RAID-6 (Erasure Coding)

6. Which site disaster tolerance option is available in a VM storage policy?

    a. None - standard cluster

    b. Dual site mirroring (stretched cluster)

    c. None - Keep data on Preferred (stretched cluster)

    d. None - stretched cluster

    e. All the above

7. Which settings are disabled (by default) in advanced policy rules? (Choose two)

    a. Force provisioning

    b. Flash read cache reservation

    c. Disable object checksum

    d. Number of disk stripes per object

    e. IOPS limit for object

8. Where can we find the relevant information if we want to monitor vSAN virtual objects?

    a. vSAN Health

    b. vSAN Capacity

    c. vSAN Performance

    d. vSAN Resyncing objects

    e. vSAN Virtual Objects

9.　What is the minimum number of hosts for a fault domain configuration?

a. 2

b. 3

c. 4

d. 5

e. 6

10.　Which option is available for vSAN data migration?

a. No data migration

b. Full data migration

c. Ensure accessibility

d. Only A and C

e. A, B, and C

11.　Which option is not a VM deployment method?

a. Cloning from VMs

b. Backup and restore

c. Creating VMs

d. Importing the OVA file

e. Deploying from the VM template

12.　What is the default port for the vSAN iSCSI target service?

a. 1000

b. 8080

c. 3260

d. 5480

e. None of the above

6
VxRail Upgrade

In *Chapter 5*, *Managing VMware vSAN*, we described the advantages of the vSAN storage policy. The advantage is that we can easily define the different failure tolerance methods to protect the virtual machine and change the RAID protection level of the virtual machine without any service interruption.

In this chapter, we will provide an overview of VxRail drive expansion and software upgrade procedures. We can easily upgrade the vSAN capacity in the VxRail cluster based on the disk group configuration rules. The life cycle management of VxRail can help us to minimize the service interruption in the maintenance window.

In this chapter, we're going to cover the following main topics:

- VxRail disk group upgrade
- VxRail software upgrade

Technical requirements

In this chapter, we need to ensure that our workstation is a Windows platform and that a web browser is installed. The latest versions of Firefox, Google Chrome, and Microsoft Internet Explorer 10 or above are all supported. The VxRail software is running in version 4.7.300 or above.

As regards the disk group upgrade, there is a free, available capacity drive installed in the VxRail node.

For the VxRail software upgrade, we downloaded the VxRail composite 7.0.010 upgrade package from the Dell support website, and then we prepared the VMware licenses of vSphere 7, vCenter Server 7, and vSAN 7.

VxRail disk group upgrade

In this section, we will learn the disk group configuration rules and the drive expansion procedure in the VxRail cluster. When we plan to upgrade the vSAN capacity in the VxRail cluster, we must consider the following disk group configuration rules:

- Mixing SAS/SATA/NVMe SSD drives in the same disk group is not supported.
- All capacity drives must be the same size in the same disk group.
- Mixing capacity drives with capacity SSD drives in the same disk group is not supported.
- Each VxRail Appliance supports the different capacity drive sizes and types in the different disk groups.
- Each VxRail Appliance supports the different cache drive sizes and types in the different disk groups.

The following table shows a summary of the disk group configurations in each VxRail model:

VxRail Appliance model	Number of flash drives per disk group	Number of capacity drives per disk group	Number of disk groups (maximum)
E560/E560F/ E560N	1	1 to 4	2
P570/P570F	1	1 to 5	4
V570/V570F	1	1 to 5	4
D560/D560F	1	1 to 3	2
S570	1	1 to 6	2
G560/G560F	1	1 to 5	1
P580N	1	1 to 5	4

In the following sub-sections, we will discuss how to access the drive expansion procedures and upgrade the number of drives in the disk group.

Drive expansion procedures

We can access the VxRail drive expansion procedures in the Dell EMC SolVe Desktop application or SolVe Online. You can refer to *Chapter 1, Overview of VxRail HCI*, for more details. In SolVe Online, we choose the **VxRail Appliance** product and then select **Hardware Upgrade/Expansion Procedures**:

Figure 6.1 – Dell Technologies SolVe Online

Then, select **Capacity Drive (HDD/SSD) Expansion**:

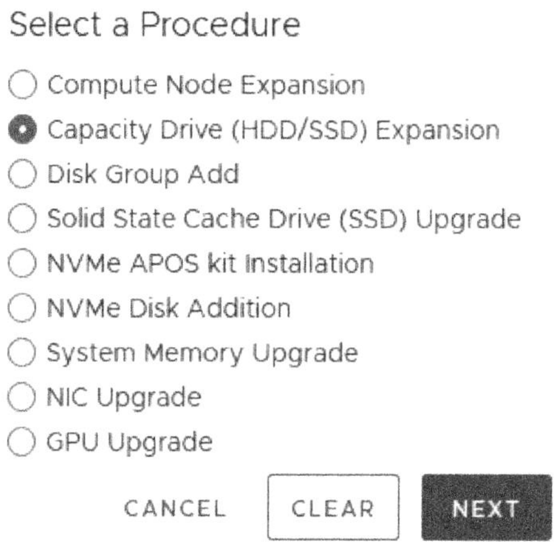

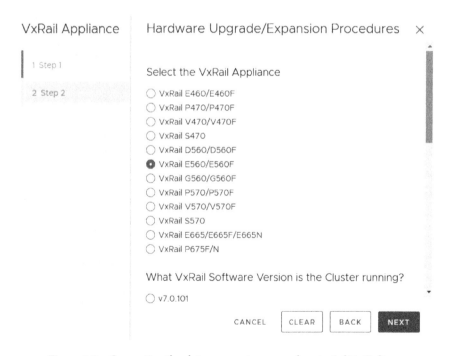

Figure 6.2 – Selecting the Capacity Drive (HDD/SDD) Expansion procedure

Finally, we select the VxRail model and the VxRail software version that is running, and then we can generate the VxRail drive expansion procedure:

Figure 6.3 – Generating the drive expansion procedure in SolVe Online

In the next section, we will discuss a disk group upgrade example and demonstrate how to upgrade the capacity drive in the disk group.

Drive upgrade in the disk group

In *Figure 6.4*, there is a VxRail cluster with three nodes. Each VxRail node has a disk group with one SSD drive as a cache tier and three capacity drives as a capacity tier. If the usable capacity on the vSAN datastore is almost full, we should increase the usable capacity in a VxRail cluster. We can upgrade the number of capacity drives on each VxRail node. For example, we will upgrade the capacity tier of **Disk Group** in Node 2. We will assume that there is a free drive available in Node 2, and we will add this drive to the disk group:

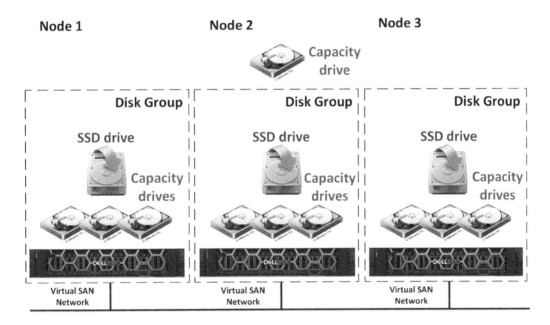

Figure 6.4 – The disk group upgrade example

After adding the capacity drives to the disk group, the number of capacity drives will change to four:

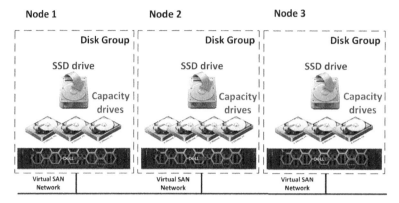

Figure 6.5 – The new capacity drives have been added into the Disk Group on Node 2

In this scenario, there is a VxRail cluster with three E560 nodes. One E560 node, `esx02.demo.local`, has a disk group with one SSD drive as the cache tier and three capacity drives as the capacity tier. We will add one capacity drive to the existing disk group in this node. The capacity drive upgrade procedure in the VxRail cluster is as follows:

1. First, we select the VxRail node and then select **Disk Management** on the **Configure** tab:

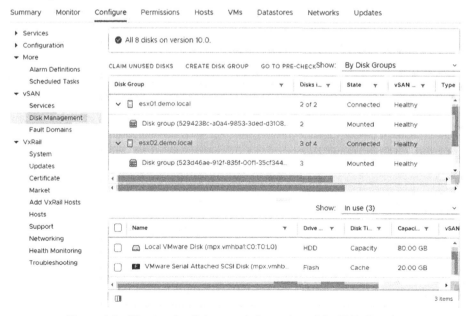

Figure 6.6 – Viewing the disk group information of the VxRail node

2. Select the disk group and then click the **ADD DISKS** button:

Figure 6.7 – Adding disks to the vSAN disk group

3. We can see one available capacity drive (80 GB SAS drive). Select this drive and then click the **ADD** button:

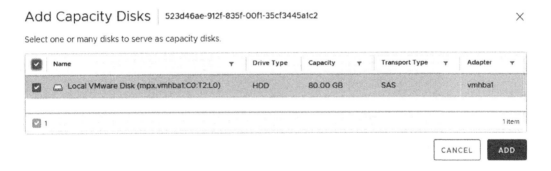

Figure 6.8 – Adding the capacity disk wizard to the VxRail cluster

4. Once the addition of the capacity drive is confirmed, the disk group will increase vSAN's usable capacity in this VxRail node. Now we can see that there are four drives in this disk group:

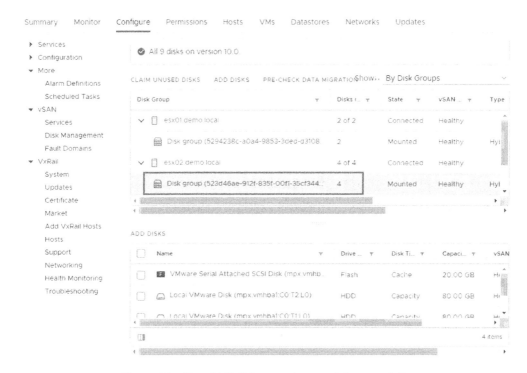

Figure 6.9 – The vSAN disk group is upgraded successfully

According to the aforementioned procedures, we understand how to upgrade the disk group in the VxRail cluster. In the next section, we will discuss the software upgrade in the VxRail Appliance.

VxRail software upgrade

In this section, we will discuss the VxRail software and understand what components comprise the VxRail software package. The VxRail software package includes four main components. The following table provides a summary of each component:

Main component	Subcomponent
VxRail Software	VxRail Manager
VMware Software	VMware ESXi Service Patch
	VMware vCenter Server Virtual Appliance
	VMware vSAN Service Patch
	VMware vRealize Log Insight
Dell EMC Software	Dell Secure Remote Services
Dell PowerEdge platform component	PTAgent
	BIOS (Basic Input/Output System)
	ISM (iDRAC Service Module)
	iDRAC (Integrated Dell Remote Access Controller)

Let's review each component in the VxRail cluster. The following components will upgrade the software version during the software upgrade process:

- **VxRail Manager** is a virtual appliance that performs all VxRail operation tasks with the VxRail Manager plugin for vCenter.

- **VMware ESXi Service Patch** is the version upgrade patch for a vSphere host; for example, upgrading vSphere 6.7 to 7.0.

- **VMware vCenter Server Virtual Appliance** is optimized Linux server, runs all vCenter services, and also provides a centralized dashboard.

- **VMware vSAN Service Patch** is the version upgrade patch for a vSAN cluster; for example, upgrading vSAN 6.7 to 7.0.

- **VMware vRealize Log Insight** is a virtual appliance that delivers log management for the VxRail cluster.

- **Dell Secure Remote Services** perform 24x7 remote monitoring support on the VxRail cluster; it is also called **EMC Secure Remote Services** (**ESRS**).

- **Power Tools Agent (PTAgent)** is hardware-related and runs on each cluster level not specific to VxRails or not at the cluster level; it runs on Dell hardware and other hypervisors as well, such as Hyper-V and Nutanix.

- **BIOS** is used to perform hardware initialization during the VxRail node bootup.

- **iDRAC Service Module (iSM)** also a each Dell node hardware level, it provides an additional level of hardware management and integration with operating systems.

- **iDRAC** is used for secure local and remote server management, and it delivers deployment, software updates, and monitoring on Dell EMC PowerEdge servers.

When we upgrade the software package in the VxRail cluster, it will automatically upgrade the preceding components one by one.

Accessing the VxRail upgrade procedure

This section will show how to access the VxRail software upgrade procedures. We can access the VxRail software upgrade procedures in the Dell EMC SolVe Desktop application or SolVe Online.

In SolVe Online, we select **VxRail Procedures**, followed by **Software Upgrade Procedures**, under **Upgrade**:

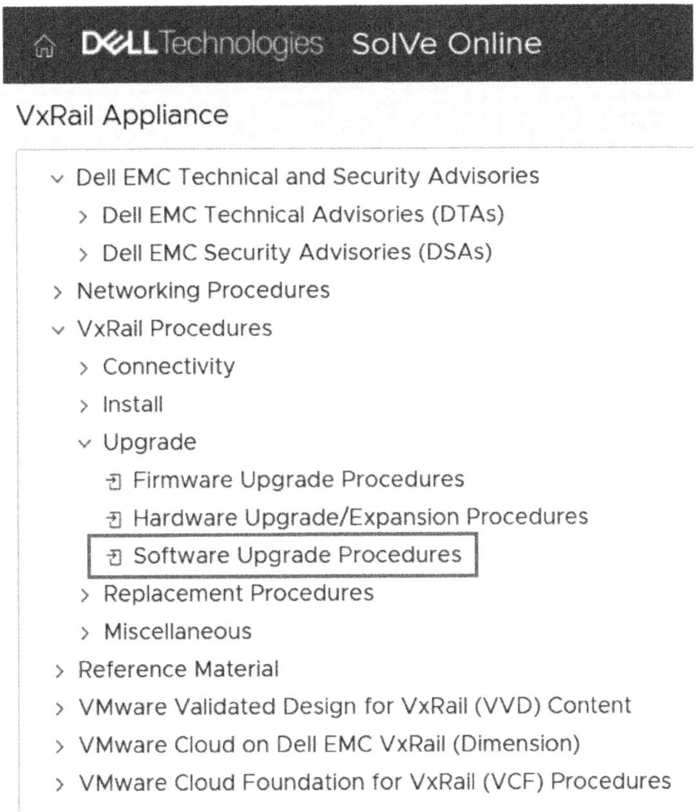

Figure 6.10 – Choosing Software Upgrade Procedures in SolVe Online

When we choose **Software Upgrade Procedures**, we need to perform the following steps to access the procedures:

1. We select the model of the VxRail appliance, for example, **VxRail P570/P570F**, and then click the **NEXT** button:

Figure 6.11 – Selecting the VxRail appliance model in Software Upgrade Procedures

2. Select the installed software version and target version, then click the **NEXT** button:

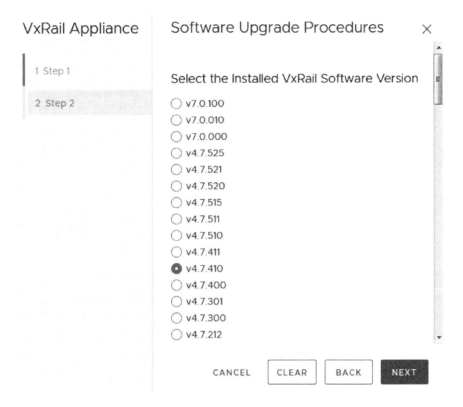

VxRail Appliance

Software Upgrade Procedures   ✕

1 Step 1

2 Step 2

Select the Installed VxRail Software Version

○ v7.0.100
○ v7.0.010
○ v7.0.000
○ v4.7.525
○ v4.7.521
○ v4.7.520
○ v4.7.515
○ v4.7.511
○ v4.7.510
○ v4.7.411
● v4.7.410
○ v4.7.400
○ v4.7.301
○ v4.7.300
○ v4.7.212

CANCEL   CLEAR   BACK   NEXT

Figure 6.12 – Selecting the installed VxRail software version

3. Then, select the running VxRail configuration, **non-vSAN Stretched Cluster** or **VxRail vSAN Stretched Cluster**.

Non-vSAN Stretched Cluster is a standalone vSAN cluster in a location.

VxRail vSAN Stretched Cluster is the active-active vSAN cluster running across two separate locations. You can refer to *Chapter 9, Active-Active Solution for VxRail,* of this book for further details.

If VMware Horizon VDI is installed, select **Yes** or **No**. Then, click the **NEXT** button to access the procedures:

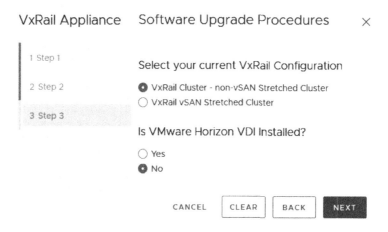

Figure 6.13 – Selecting the current VxRail configuration

According to the aforementioned procedures, SolVe Online will generate the procedure in PDF format automatically after we click the **NEXT** button. Then, we can access the VxRail software upgrade procedures for each VxRail appliance model. In the next section, we will demonstrate how to upgrade from VxRail software version 4.7 to 7.0.

Downloading the VxRail software

To download the VxRail composite 7.0.010 upgrade package, you have to access the Dell support website (`https://www.dell.com/support`) with your Dell partner account. Select **VxRail Appliance Series** and then choose the **DRIVERS & DOWNLOADS** menu:

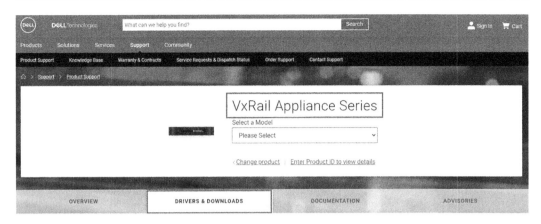

Figure 6.14 – The Dell support website

We can then search all the VxRail composite upgrade packages and download the package required:

Find a download for your VxRail Appliance Series

Keyword

| Keyword |

Category

| Full Release ⌄ |

⬤ Only show downloads I have access to. ⓘ   ⬤ Show recommended downloads only.

	NAME ⬍	CATEGORY ⬍	PUBLISH DATE ⬍	ACTION	
☐	VxRail 4.7.526 Composite Upgrade Package for 4.7.x	Full Release	17 Dec 2020	Download	⌄
☐	VxRail 4.5.452 Composite Upgrade Package for 4.0.x	Full Release	03 Dec 2020	Download	⌄
☐	VxRail 4.5.452 Composite Upgrade Package for 4.5.x	Full Release	03 Dec 2020	Download	⌄
☐	VxRail 4.7.525 Composite Upgrade Package for 4.0.x	Full Release	03 Dec 2020	Download	⌄
☐	VxRail 4.7.525 Composite Upgrade Package for 4.5.x	Full Release	03 Dec 2020	Download	⌄
☐	VxRail 4.7.525 Composite Upgrade Package for 4.7.x	Full Release	03 Dec 2020	Download	⌄
☐	VxRail 7.0.101 Composite Upgrade Package for 4.5.x	Full Release	03 Dec 2020	Download	⌄
☐	VxRail 7.0.101 Composite Upgrade Package for 4.7.x	Full Release	03 Dec 2020	Download	⌄

Figure 6.15 – VxRail software upgrade packages

If we want to know what new features are to be found in the VxRail update package, we can download the VxRail 7.0 release notes from the documentation menu:

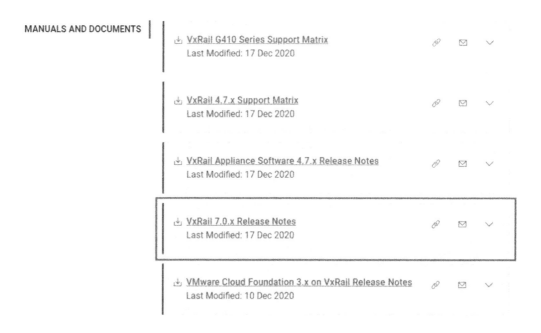

Figure 6.16 – The Dell support website documentation

Once we have checked the VxRail update procedure and downloaded the VxRail update package, then we can start the VxRail software update. In the next section, we will discuss the upgrade procedure.

Upgrading the VxRail software from version 4.7 to version 7.0

In this section, we will upgrade the VxRail software from version 4.7 to version 7.0. In this demonstration environment, there is a VxRail cluster with three nodes and four VxRail system virtual machines, in other words, **VMware vCenter Server Appliance**, **VMware vCenter Server Platform Services Controller**, **VMware vRealize Log Insight**, and **VxRail Manager**:

Figure 6.17 – In the demonstration environment of the VxRail cluster

We have to download the VxRail composite 7.0.010 upgrade package from the Dell support website (`http://support.emc.com`) before upgrading the VxRail software. In this demonstration, we upgrade VxRail version 4.7.410 to version 7.0.010. The VxRail software upgrade procedure is detailed here:

1.   As a first step, we have to create a VM snapshot of the VxRail Manager virtual machine as a backup copy. Right-click on **VxRail Manager** and then select **Take Snapshot…**:

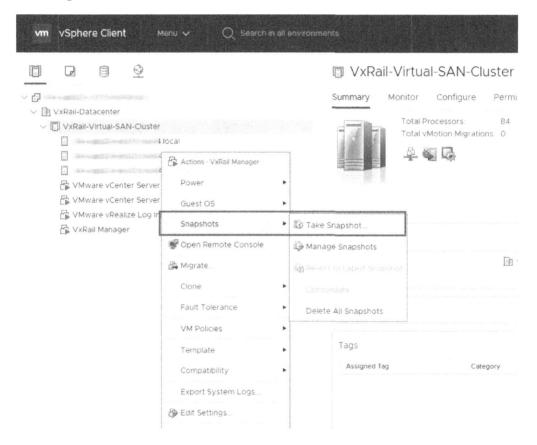

Figure 6.18 – Taking a VM snapshot of VxRail Manager

2. Specify the snapshot name of **VxRail Manager** and then click the **OK** button:

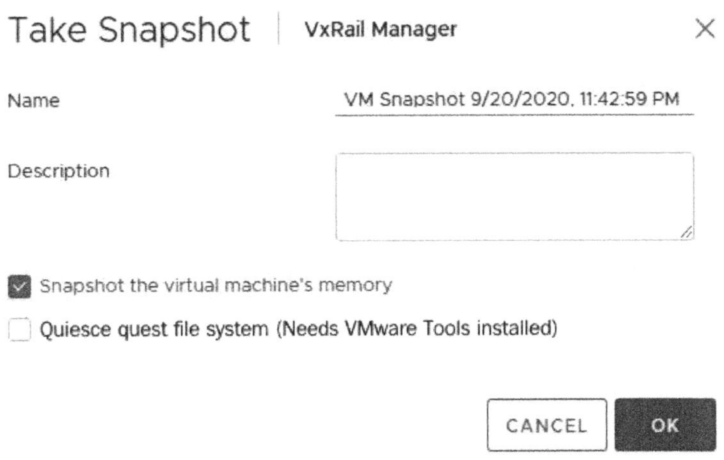

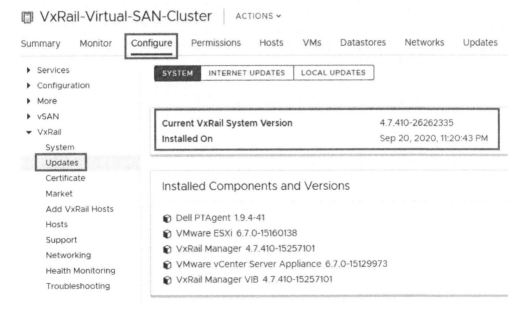

Figure 6.19 – Specifying the VM snapshot name

3. Once the VM snapshot has been completed successfully, we can go to the **Configure** tab and select **Updates** under the VxRail menu. We can see that the installed VxRail system version is **4.7.410-26262335**:

Figure 6.20 – The VxRail Updates dashboard

4. We can choose either **INTERNET UPDATES** or **LOCAL UPDATES** to upgrade the VxRail software. In this demonstration, we will use **LOCAL UPDATES** to upgrade the VxRail cluster. We choose the **LOCAL UPDATES** button and then select the **BROWSE…** button to upload the VxRail composite 7.0.010 upgrade package from your workstation. Then, click the **OK** button:

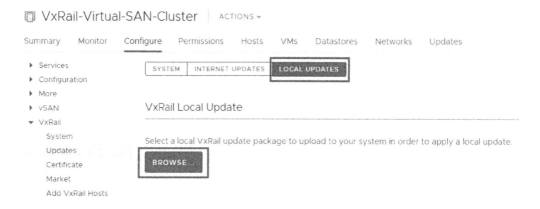

Figure 6.21 – Choosing LOCAL UPDATES in the VxRail cluster

5. The upgrade package can be uploaded in a few minutes. We will see that the status changes to 100%:

Figure 6.22 – Uploading the VxRail update package

6. Once uploading is complete, we can obtain a summary of this VxRail upgrade package. We need to review the following information before clicking the **CONTINUE UPDATE** button:

The version of the VxRail update package is **7.0.010-26590399**.

The estimated minimum update time is **5.1 hours**.

Under the important information reminder (highlighted in yellow), we must review all the reminder information and make sure that the VxRail cluster does not exhibit any issues.

- The software components will be changed by this VxRail update package; for example, VxRail Manager, vCenter Server Appliance, VxRail Platform Service, and the NIC driver:

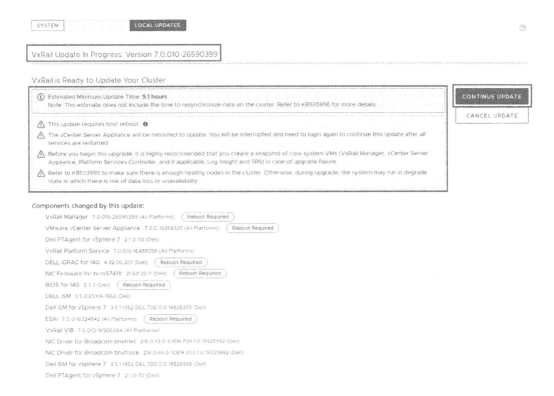

Figure 6.23 – A summary of the VxRail upgrade package

7. Select **Update Now** and then click the **NEXT** button:

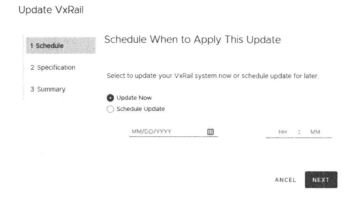

Figure 6.24 – Setting the schedule to apply the update to the VxRail cluster

8. Input the related account username and password. This includes the VxRail Manager root account, the VxRail Manager service account, the vCenter administrator account, the VCSA root account, and the PSC root cause. These accounts are defined during VxRail initialization:

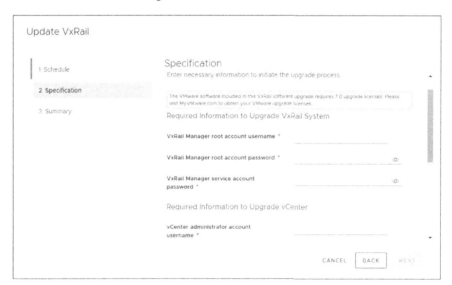

Figure 6.25 – Inputting the related VxRail account username and password

> **Important note**
> We must add the licenses of VMware vCenter Server 7, vSphere 7, and vSAN 7 to the VxRail cluster after upgrading the VxRail software to version 7.

9. Input a temporary IP address, netmask, and gateway, and then click the **NEXT** button. This temporary IP address must be the same subnet of the vCenter Server appliance that is running in the VxRail cluster:

Update VxRail

Specification

1 Schedule	
2 Specification	vCenter administrator account password *
3 Summary	VCSA upgrade root account username *
	VCSA upgrade root account password *
	PSC upgrade root account username *
	PSC upgrade root account password *

Temporary IP settings *

Netmask   255.255.255.0

Gateway

CANCEL   BACK   NEXT

Figure 6.26 – Inputting the related VxRail account username and password

10. On the summary page, we can see the target version and required uptime. Click the **FINISH** button to confirm this update:

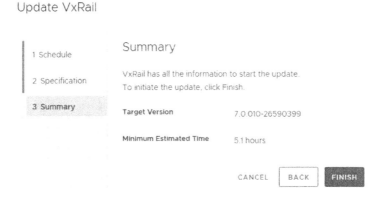

Update VxRail

Summary

1 Schedule

2 Specification   VxRail has all the information to start the update.
                       To initiate the update, click Finish.

3 Summary   Target Version   7.0.010-26590399

                       Minimum Estimated Time 5.1 hours

CANCEL   BACK   FINISH

Figure 6.27 – A summary of the VxRail update operation

11. Once we confirm the upgrade, this will begin the update process of the VxRail cluster:

Figure 6.28 – VxRail cluster update processing

12. The update process will conclude after about 5 hours. Once the update is complete, we can see that the installed version of the VxRail system has changed to **7.0.010-26590399**:

Figure 6.29 – The installed software version of the VxRail system

13. In the hosts and cluster of the VxRail system, we can see that three VxRail system virtual machines powered down after upgrading to VxRail software version 7.0, these being **VMware vCenter Server Appliance (legacy-6.7.0)**, **VMware vCenter Server Platform Services Controller (legacy-6.7.0)**, and **VxRail Manager (legacy-4.7.410)**. These virtual machines can be retired because the VxRail system created new VxRail system virtual machines (**VMware vCenter Server Appliance** and **VxRail Manager**) to replace these virtual machines during the process of updating to VxRail software version 7.0:

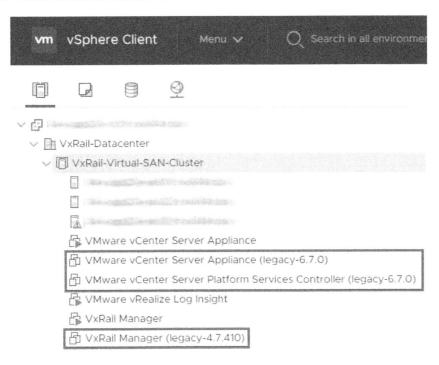

Figure 6.30 – The hosts and cluster of the VxRail system

14. In the final part of the procedure, we need to apply the licenses of vCenter Server 7, vSphere 7, and vSAN 7 to the VxRail system. Go to the **Administration** menu and select **Licensing**, then **Licenses**, and then click the **Add New Licenses** button to add the licenses:

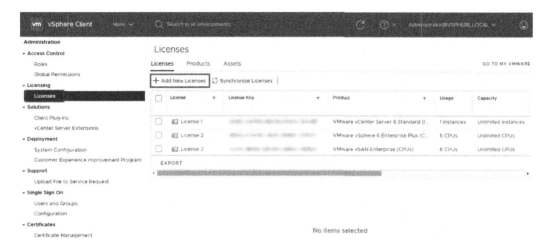

Figure 6.31 – Adding new VMware licenses to the VxRail cluster

15. Enter all the new VMware licenses and then click the **NEXT** button to confirm:

Figure 6.32 – Entering license keys in the New Licenses wizard

16. Once we have added new VMware licenses to the VxRail cluster, the VxRail software upgrade process is complete.

Having gone through the preceding *VxRail disk group upgrade* and *VxRail software upgrade* sections, we now understand how to access the upgrade procedures and execute them.

Summary

In this chapter, we covered the advantages of life cycle management in the VxRail system and saw how to upgrade the virtual environment and software-defined storage by using the one-click upgrade procedure. We can easily upgrade the usable capacity in software-defined storage by adding drives to the disk group in the VxRail system.

In the next chapter, you will learn about the advanced solution in the VxRail system and you will learn what the disaster recovery solutions for VxRail are. This includes the active-passive solution with VMware **Site Recovery Manager** (**SRM**). You will also learn how to plan and design for the solution in this coming chapter.

Questions

1. Which configuration is supported on the vSAN disk group?

    a. One flash drive only

    b. Two flash drives and two capacity drives

    c. One flash drive and two capacity drives

    d. Two capacity drives only

    e. All the above

2. What is the maximum number of drive groups in the VxRail P570/P570F?

    a. One

    b. Two

    c. Three

    d. Four

    e. Five

    f. None of the above

3. Which configuration rules are not supported in the vSAN disk group?

    a. All capacity drives must be the same size in the same disk group.

    b. The mixing of SAS/SATA/NVMe SSD drives in the same disk group is supported.

    c. Capacity drives cannot be mixed with capacity SSD drives in the same disk group.

d. Each VxRail appliance supports different capacity drive sizes and types in the different disk groups.

e. Each VxRail appliance supports different cache drive sizes and types in the different disk groups.

4. What is the maximum number of capacity drives in the VxRail S570?

   a. 3

   b. 4

   c. 5

   d. 6

   e. 7

5. How can we access the VxRail disk group procedures?

   a. Dell support website

   b. Dell online chat

   c. Dell EMC SolVe Online

   d. Dell documentation

   e. All the above

6. How can we access the VxRail software upgrade procedures?

   a. Dell support website

   b. Dell documentation

   c. Dell EMC SolVe Desktop application

   d. Dell online chat

   e. All the above

7. From where can we obtain the VxRail software update package?

   a. The VMware support website

   b. The Dell support website

   c. Dell online chat

   d. Dell Solve Online

   e. None of the above

8. Where can we find any new information relating to the VxRail software update package?

   a. VxRail administrator documentation

   b. VxRail installation documentation

   c. VMware vSphere documentation

   d. VMware vSphere release notes

   e. VxRail software release notes

9. Which two upgrade options are available on the VxRail system?

   a. Online updates

   b. Internet updates

   c. Local updates

   d. System updates

   e. vCenter updates

10. Which virtual machines will be upgraded when we upgrade the VxRail software?

    a. vCenter Server Appliance

    b. VxRail Manager

    c. vRealize Log Insight

    d. vRealize Operations Manager

    e. All the above

11. Which virtual machine do we require in order to create a VM snapshot manually before upgrading the VxRail software?

    a. vCenter Server Appliance

    b. VxRail Manager

    c. vRealize Log Insight

    d. vCenter Server Platform Services Controller

    e. None of the above

12. Which VMware licenses do we add to the VxRail system after upgrading the VxRail software version from 4.7 to 7.0?

a. VMware vCenter Server 7.0

b. VMware vSAN 7.0

c. VMware vRealize Operations 8.x

d. VMware vSphere 7.0

e. All the above

7
VxRail Scale-Out Operations

In an architecture of traditional servers and **Storage Area Network (SAN)** storage, a system scale-out is not an easy operation to configure. There are limitations in terms of system scale-outs in traditional servers and storage, such as the maximum number of CPU cores, system cache, and **input/output operations per second (IOPS)**. If your system is a hyper-converged infrastructure, you can efficiently perform scale-out operations on the VxRail system. A VxRail scale-out is an easy operation for the system administrator.

In this chapter, we will learn the process of adding a node to a VxRail cluster. The cluster expansion is performed with the VxRail Manager plugin in VMware vCenter Server. This is the core feature provided by VxRail; that is, to allow a configuration from three nodes (the minimum configuration).

In this chapter, we're going to cover the following main topics:

- VxRail scale-out rules
- VxRail cluster expansion

VxRail scale-out rules

When we seek to expand a VxRail cluster, we must stick to the following scale-out rules:

- The first three VxRail nodes in a cluster must be of identical models.

- Hybrid and all-flash modes, as well as an all-NVMe node, cannot mix in a VxRail cluster.

- All VxRail nodes in a cluster must run the same network speed, such as 25 GbE, 10 GbE, or 1 GbE.

- All VxRail nodes in a cluster must run software of the same version.

- All G Series VxRail nodes in a chassis must be of identical models.

- A 1 GbE network only supports the VxRail Hybrid system with a single CPU processor.

- The expansion node must have been physically added to the VxRail cluster, and the node connected to the VxRail network.

- The expansion node must be discovered with VxRail Manager. The external management network of a new node must be untagged on the native VLAN by default. The internal discovery network of a new node uses the default VLAN of 3939.

- A VMware vSphere license is ready for the new VxRail node.

We must follow these scale-out rules before expanding the VxRail cluster. Now we can move on to the next section.

Environment

In this chapter, the environment includes the following systems:

- 3 x VxRail E560 nodes

- 1 x VxRail E560 node for cluster expansion

- 1 x VxRail Manager virtual machine

- 1 x vCenter Server virtual machine

- 1 x vCenter Platform Service Controller virtual machine

- 1 x Microsoft Active Directory/Domain Controller server

- 1 x Windows workstation for managing the VxRail cluster

Let's take a look at the architecture of this system:

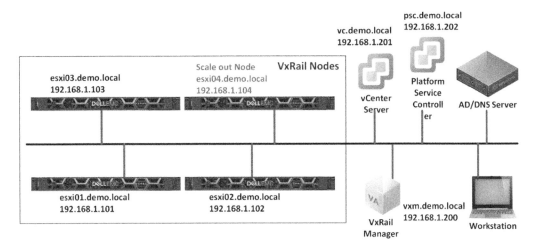

Figure 7.1 – VxRail scale-out architecture

In *Figure 7.1*, we can see that there are three VxRail nodes running in the cluster. Now we will add a new node to this VxRail cluster.

VxRail cluster expansion

In this chapter, we will learn the procedures for VxRail cluster expansion. According to *Figure 7.1*, we will add a new VxRail E560 node to the cluster to expand it. Finally, this VxRail cluster will become a four-node cluster. The cluster expansion operation is executed with vCenter Server, and we can start the wizard with the VxRail plugin that will guide us through the steps to add the node to the cluster. Now, let's start the VxRail cluster expansion based on the aforementioned environment configuration.

Preparation

For the preparation phase, follow these steps:

1. First, we open the web browser, go to the management IP address of the vCenter Server instance that is integrated with the VxRail Manager plugin, and then launch **vSphere Client (HTML5)**:

Figure 7.2 – Launching vSphere Client (HTML5)

Important note

VMware vSphere Web Client (**Flex**) has been deprecated and is no longer available in vSphere 7.0.

---

2. We use the VxRail administrator or an account with vCenter and VxRail
    administrator privileges to log in to vCenter:

Figure 7.3 – VMware vSphere Web Client login page

On the **Home** page, you can see the total resources available in this VxRail cluster –
a 25.14 GHz CPU, 63.99 GB of memory, and 467 GB of storage capacity:

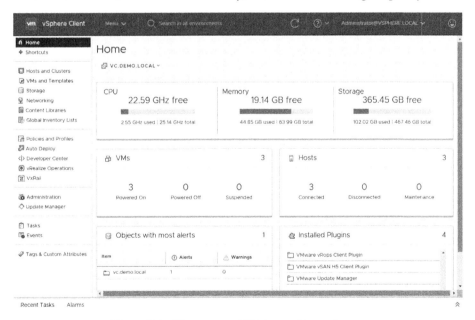

Figure 7.4 – Home page of VMware vCenter Server

3. Go to **Menu** and select **VxRail**. Make sure the system health shows **Healthy** and that the new E560 node can be detected on the **VxRail Dashboard**:

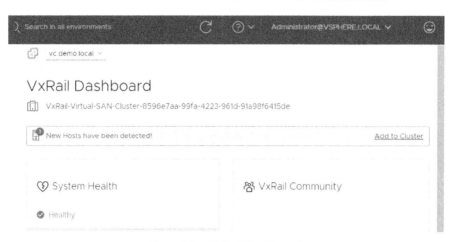

Figure 7.5 – VxRail Dashboard

Before cluster expansion, you can see that there are three VxRail E450 nodes running in the cluster:

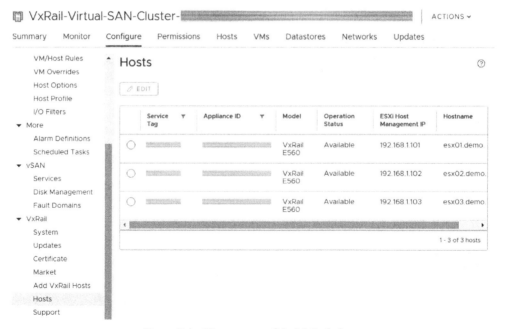

Figure 7.6 – Hosts menu of the VxRail cluster

Now we can start cluster expansion.

> **Important note**
> The VxRail cluster supports scale-out operations to a maximum of 64 nodes.

Scale-out operation

Before we execute the scale-out operation, we can generate the scale-out procedures in the Dell EMC SolVe Desktop application or SolVe Online. First, we choose the product **VxRail Appliance**, and then we select **Hardware Upgrade/Expansion Procedures** followed by **Compute Node Expansion** to generate the scale-out procedures. Let's begin the scale-out operation:

1. Select the **VxRail cluster**, click the **Configure** tab, select **VxRail**, and then click **Add VxRail Hosts**. We can see that **VxRail E560** has been discovered and shows as **Compatible**. Then, click the **ADD HOST** button:

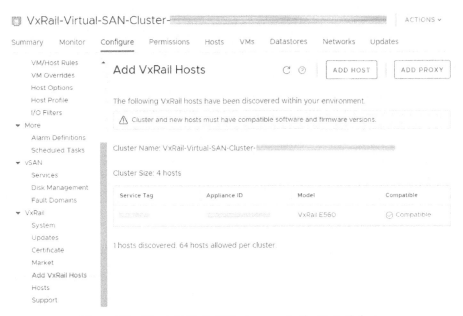

Figure 7.7 – The Add VxRail Hosts menu in the VxRail cluster

2. In the **Add Host** wizard, you need to select the discovered **VxRail E560** option:

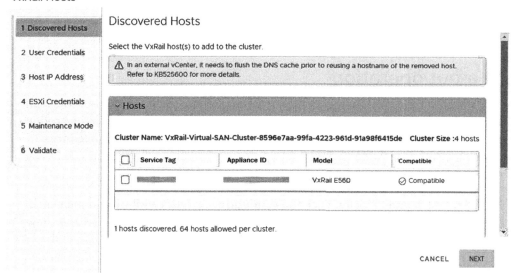

Figure 7.8 – The Discovered Hosts page in the Add Host wizard

Important note

If you are using an external vCenter instance, you need to flush the DNS cache prior to vCenter reusing the hostname of a removed VxRail node. Refer to **Dell Technologies Knowledge Base article 525600** for more details, available at `https://www.dell.com/support/kbdoc/en-us/525600`. A Dell Partner account is required to access Dell Technologies Knowledge Base articles.

3. Then, click the **NEXT** button:

VxRail Hosts

Figure 7.9 – The Discovered Hosts page in the Add Host wizard

4. Input the username and password of the VxRail or vCenter administrator with permissions to perform this configuration, and then click **NEXT**:

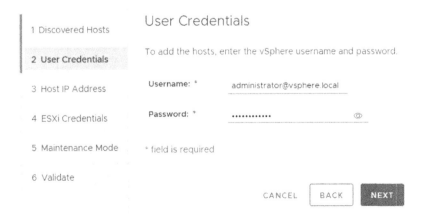

Figure 7.10 – The User Credentials page in the Add Host wizard

5. On the **Host IP Address** page of the wizard, you need to assign IP addresses to the new node. During VxRail system initialization, you defined three network IP pools: ESXi Management, vSphere vMotion, and vSAN (refer to *Chapter 2, VxRail Installation*, for more details). In this configuration, you can either get the new IP address from your existing IP pools or add a new IP address range. In this demonstration, we choose to get the new IP from our existing IP pools. ESXi Management is `192.168.1.104`, vMotion is `192.168.1.134`, and vSAN is `192.168.1.124`:

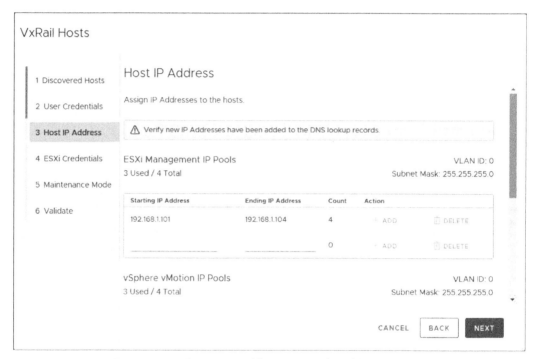

Figure 7.11 – The Host IP Address page in the Add Host wizard

> **Important note**
>
> If you choose to create new IP addresses for new VxRail nodes, these IP addresses need to be added to the DNS lookup records.

6. When you have finished the three network settings, click **NEXT**:

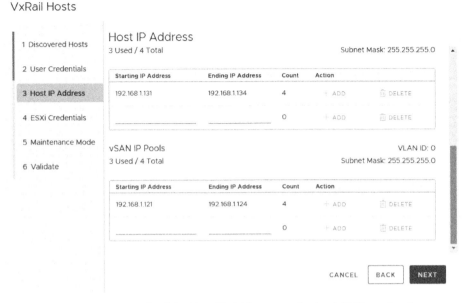

Figure 7.12 – Details of the Host IP Address page in the Add Host wizard

7. On the **ESXi Credentials** page of the wizard, you need to provide the credentials for the new E560 host. This includes the credentials of both the root account and the management account:

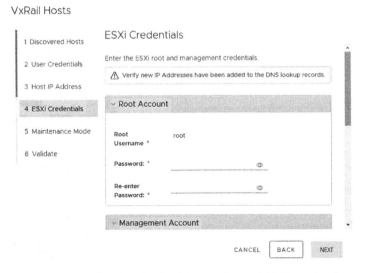

Figure 7.13 – The ESXi Credentials page in the Add Host wizard

> **Important note**
> Please note that the credentials are the same as the ones for the first three VxRail E560 hosts.

8. Keep the autofilled host configurations and then click **NEXT**:

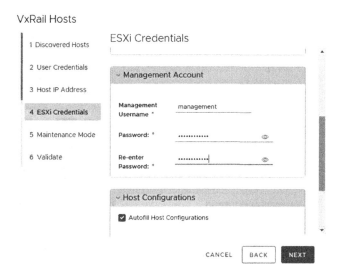

Figure 7.14 – The ESXi Credentials page in the Add Host wizard

9. On the **Maintenance Mode** page, you can set the new node to exit or enter maintenance mode when the cluster expansion is completed. In this configuration, we click to put the new node into maintenance mode, and then click **NEXT**:

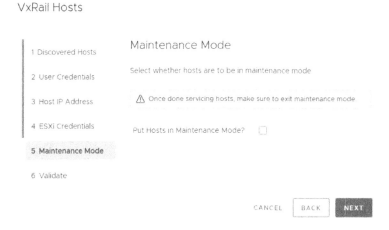

Figure 7.15 – The Maintenance Mode page in the Add Host wizard

10. For the final step, click the **VALIDATE** button to verify the configuration of the new node and its network:

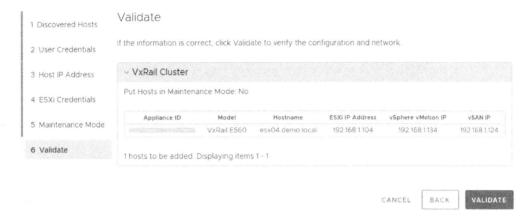

Figure 7.16 – The Validate page in the Add Host wizard

You can see the validation in progress. This ensures that all credentials, the host IP, and DNS/NSX are properly prepared for node expansion. You may have to wait a few minutes for this to complete:

Figure 7.17 – The validation process in the Add Host wizard

11. Once the validation has completed successfully, click **FINISH** to confirm the expansion request:

Figure 7.18 – Validation complete

Now you can monitor the expansion process in the **Add VxRail Hosts** tab. This process may take a few minutes to complete:

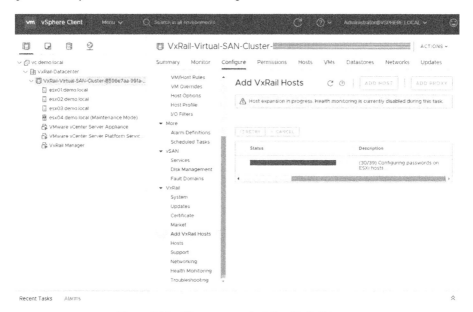

Figure 7.19 – The process of adding VxRail hosts

Once cluster expansion has completed successfully, the new E560 node is added to the VxRail cluster:

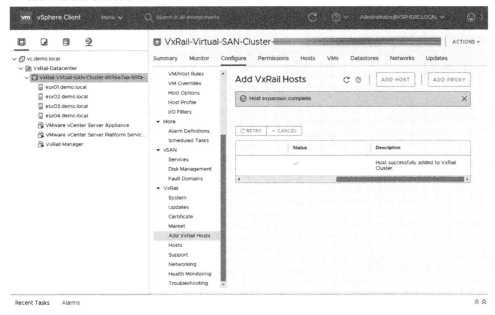

Figure 7.20 – The scale-out process has been completed successfully

12. Now, go to the **Configure** tab, select **VxRail**, and then click **Hosts**. There are now four E560 nodes in the cluster:

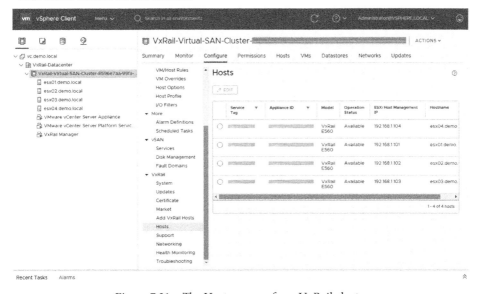

Figure 7.21 – The Hosts menu of our VxRail cluster

13. Go to the **Home** page again and you can see that the total resources of the VxRail cluster have increased. Now, the total CPU resource available is 33.52 GHz, the total memory available is 75.98 GB, and the total storage capacity is 489.96 GB:

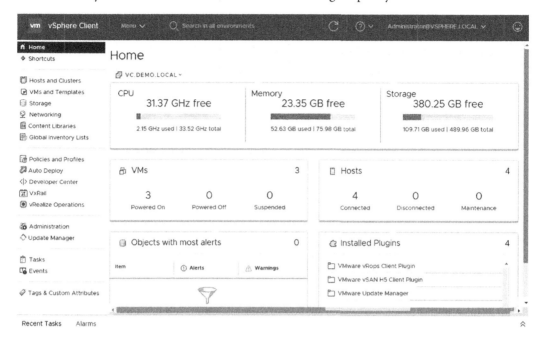

Figure 7.22 – The Home menu in VMware vCenter Server

14. Finally, you need to add your VMware vSphere license to the new E560 node. Go to the **Administration** menu and select **Licensing**, followed by **Licenses**, and then click the **Add New Licenses** button to add the license:

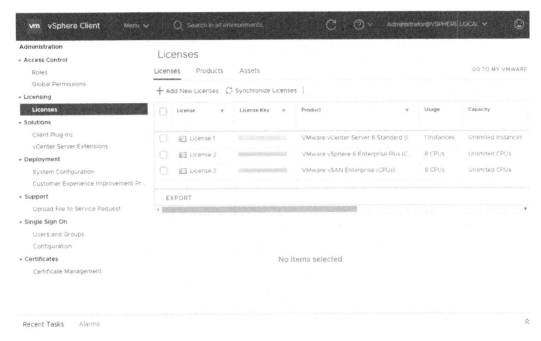

Figure 7.23 – The Licensing menu in vCenter Server

Once the license has been added to the new E560 node, VxRail cluster expansion has been completed successfully:

New Licenses   Enter license keys   ✕

    1 Enter license keys   License keys (one per line):

    2 Edit license names

    3 Ready to complete

                                                          CANCEL   **NEXT**

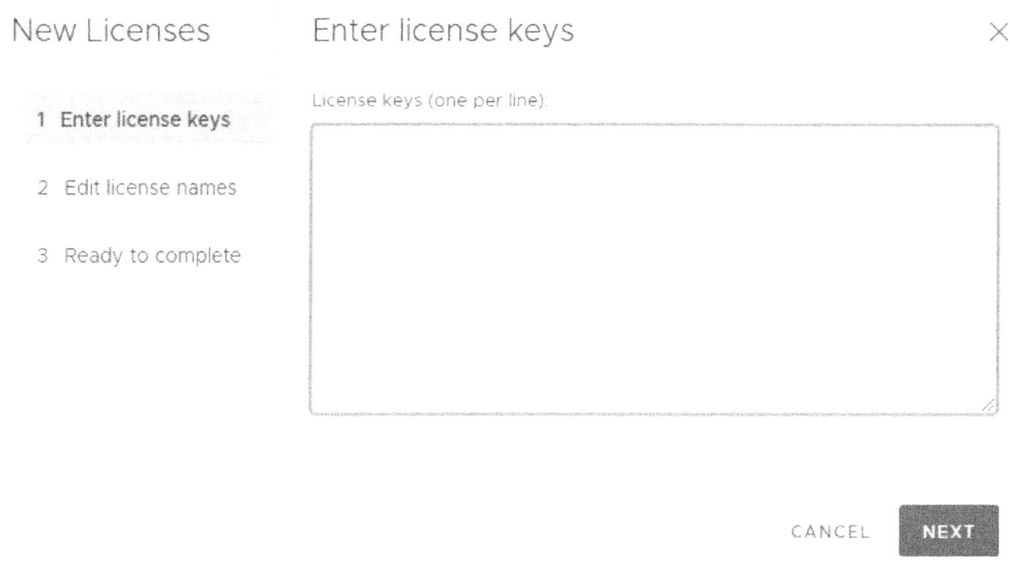

Figure 7.24 – The New Licenses wizard

Important note

VMware vSAN and vCenter Server licenses are bundled with VxRail appliances, and only VMware vSphere requires the license to be added manually to the VxRail cluster. Note that in the VxRail cluster, the vSphere licenses on each node must be of the same edition.

The VxRail cluster scale-out has been completed successfully after applying the vSphere license to the new VxRail node. You have now seen that the scale-out process is a simple operation for a system administrator.

Summary

This chapter described how we add a new node to an existing VxRail cluster with the VxRail Manager plugin in vCenter Server. You've learned how VxRail's scale-out feature supports organizations, starting small and growing only when needed.

In the next chapter, you will see the advanced solution for VxRail – the active-passive solution. This advanced solution is used to meet disaster recovery requirements.

Questions

Test the knowledge you've gained from this chapter by answering the following questions:

1. Which tool is used for VxRail cluster expansion?

   a. VxRail Manager

   b. VMware vCenter Server

   c. The VxRail Manager plugin

   d. VMware vSphere Client

2. What is the minimum number of nodes that can be run in a VxRail cluster? (A ROBO cluster configuration is not included.)

   a. Two nodes

   b. Three nodes

   c. Four nodes

   d. Five nodes

3. What is the maximum number of nodes that can be run in a VxRail cluster?

   a. 32 nodes

   b. 64 nodes

   c. 65 nodes

   d. 66 nodes

4. There are five E560F nodes running in a VxRail cluster. I will now add a new E560 node to this existing cluster. What is the final status?

   a. The new E560 node can be added to an existing cluster, changing it to a six-node cluster.

   b. The new E560 node can be added to an existing cluster, changing it to a five-node cluster.

   c. The new E560 node does not support cluster expansion.

   d. The new E560 node can be added to an existing cluster, changing it to a four-node cluster.

5. Which three network settings are available on new nodes during VxRail scale-out operations?

    a. A vCenter network, ESXi Management network, and vSAN network

    b. A vCenter network, ESXi Management network, and vSphere vMotion network

    c. An ESXi Management network, vSphere vMotion network, and vSAN network

    d. An ESXi Management network, vSphere vMotion network, and vCenter network

6. We should ensure that the VxRail cluster has which status before we commence with cluster expansion?

    a. Running

    b. Healthy

    c. Warring

    d. Stopping

7. For which user account do you need to define the username and password?

    a. Root

    b. vCenter Server administrator

    c. ESXi Management account

    d. VxRail Manager administrator

8. Which license is not bundled with the VxRail appliance?

    a. VMware vCenter Server

    b. The VMware ESXi hypervisor

    c. VMware Virtual SAN

    d. All the above

9. We have a VxRail cluster with four nodes running, and each VxRail is enabled with the VMware vSphere Enterprise Plus license. Which VMware license needs to be added to the new nodes following cluster expansion?

    a. VMware vCenter Standard

    b. VMware vSphere Standard

    c. VMware vSphere Enterprise Plus

    d. VMware vSAN Enterprise

10. Which of the following is not part of the VxRail scale-out rules?

    a. The first three VxRail nodes in a cluster must be of identical models.

    b. Hybrid and all-flash modes, as well as an all-NVMe node, can mix in a VxRail cluster.

    c. All VxRail nodes in a cluster must run software of the same version.

    d. The expansion node must be discovered with VxRail Manager.

11. Which of the following is a supported configuration in VxRail clusters?

    a. Five VxRail P series hybrid nodes are running in a cluster, with plans to add two P series all-flash nodes to the existing cluster.

    b. Three VxRail P series hybrid nodes are running in a cluster, with plans to add two P series hybrid nodes to the existing cluster.

    c. Five VxRail E series hybrid nodes are running on a 10 GB network in a cluster, with plans to add two E series hybrid nodes with a 1 GB network to the existing cluster.

    d. Five VxRail E series hybrid nodes are running on a 10 GB network in a cluster, with plans to add two E series all-flash nodes with a 10 GB network to the existing cluster.

12. During cluster expansion, how do we define the IP addresses for the new node?

    a. Define the new IP address only.

    b. Define the new IP address or get the IP address from the IP pools.

    c. It does not have this network configuration.

    d. Get the IP address from the IP pools only.

Section 3: Advanced Solutions for VxRail

In this section, we will have an overview of advanced solutions for VxRail, including the Active-Passive data center and Active-Active data center solutions. In the last chapter, we will discuss the different migration methodologies for VxRail.

This section of the book comprises the following chapters:

- *Chapter 8, Active-Passive Solution for VxRail*
- *Chapter 9, Active-Active Solution for VxRail*
- *Chapter 10, Migrating Virtual Machines into VxRail*

8
Active-Passive Solution for VxRail

In *Chapter 7*, *VxRail Scale-Out Operations*, we described how we add a new node to an existing VxRail cluster with the VxRail Manager plugin in vCenter Server. We learned how VxRail's scale-out feature supports organizations, starting small and growing only when needed.

In this chapter, you will learn what the disaster recovery solutions for VxRail are. This includes a solution with VMware **Site Recovery Manager** (**SRM**) and **vSphere Replication** (**VR**). You will learn how to plan and deploy an active-passive solution in this chapter.

In this chapter, we're going to cover the following main topics:

- Deploying an active-passive solution for VxRail
- SRM appliance deployment
- VR deployment
- Configuring SRM inventory mappings
- Protecting virtual machines
- Creating SRM recovery plans

Technical requirements

In this chapter, we need to make sure our workstation is a Windows platform, and that a web browser is installed. The latest versions of Firefox, Google Chrome, and Microsoft Internet Explorer 10 or above are all supported. The VxRail software should be running in version 4.7.300 or above.

For the deployment of disaster recovery solutions on VxRail, we must set up a replication network for virtual machine replication in each VxRail cluster across sites A and B. We require additional licenses for VMware SRM when defining the SRM recovery plan.

As regards the SRM appliance configuration, we must deploy an SRM appliance at each site. The version of the SRM appliance must be the same. The **Domain Name System (DNS)** name of the vCenter **Platform Service Controller (PSC)**, vCenter Server, and the SRM appliance have been configured to incorporate DNS with the relevant IP address.

For the VR configuration, we must deploy a VR appliance at each site. The VR is configured with a dual-core or quad-core CPU, a 13 GB and 9 GB hard disk, and 8 GB of memory. The DNS names of the vCenter PSC, vCenter Server, and the VR appliance have been configured to incorporate DNS with the relevant IP address.

Deploying an active-passive solution for VxRail

The disaster recovery solution is a core component of the system infrastructure environment. We must consider this factor when we plan and design the system infrastructure. What is disaster recovery? It is the process of restoring the system infrastructure when a problem suddenly occurs, for example, a data center outage, cyber attack, or service interruption.

In *Chapter 1*, *Overview of VxRail HCI*, we described how a VxRail appliance includes a data protection option, that is, VMware VR and Dell EMC **RecoverPoint for Virtual Machines (RP4VM)**. RP4VM can deliver the data protection of virtual machines with its point-in-time synchronization or asynchronization in a local VxRail cluster or across VxRail clusters between two separate locations, and these licenses are bundled on each VxRail appliance. VMware VR is the other data protection feature for VxRail, and its license is bundled on a VxRail appliance. In this chapter, we will discuss VMware VR as an active-passive solution for VxRail.

A VxRail appliance can also be integrated with additional software leveraging your existing environment; for example, with VMware VR and SRM, it can also extend the site-level protection to many other sites. VMware VR is a virtual appliance that can protect the data of virtual machines asynchronously in a local VxRail cluster or across VxRail clusters between two separate locations.

VMware SRM is a Windows-based platform or virtual appliance that can deliver a data recovery plan for the virtual machines when the data center is interrupted. This data recovery plan depends on the defined **Recovery Time Objective** (**RTO**).

In the next section, we will discuss the active-passive solutions for VxRail. These are solutions using both VMware SRM and VMware VR. We will also list out the deployment procedure of enabling this solution on VxRail.

Solution with VR and SRM

In this section, we will discuss an active-passive solution for VxRail. We will learn how to deploy VMware SRM and VR into a VxRail cluster across two locations.

In *Figure 8.1*, we can see that there are two locations (**Site A** and **Site B**) and a VxRail cluster (**HQ VxRail Cluster** and **DR VxRail Cluster**) with four E560 appliances running at each site. In each VxRail cluster, there are the VxRail system virtual machines (**vCenter Server Appliance**, **PSC**, **vRealize Log Insight**, and **VxRail Manager**). After enabling this active-passive solution on VxRail, the virtual machines can fail over to site B when site A has an outage:

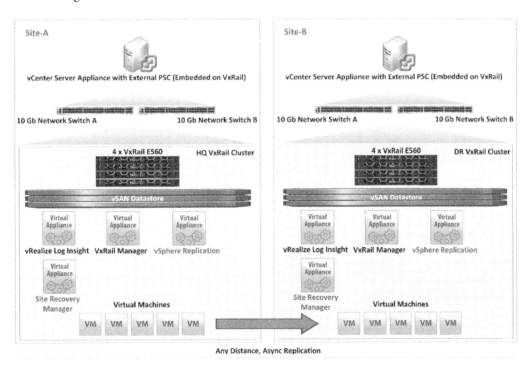

Figure 8.1 – A logical diagram of the active-passive solution with VR

In this active-passive solution, the virtual machines can be delivered at site A, and they can fail over to the **DR VxRail Cluster** at site B in the case of an event such as an outage at site A if the service of the **HQ VxRail Cluster** is stopped, or if some virtual machines at site A are corrupted. For example, if the **HQ VxRail Cluster** is faulted at site A, we can execute the SRM recovery plan to recover the protected virtual machine automatically into the **DR VxRail Cluster** at site B.

The following table shows a summary of each component for this solution:

Sites	Components	Version
A	2 x 10 GB network switches	N/A
	4 x VxRail E560	VxRail software 4.7.4xx or above
	1 x VxRail Manager	
	1 x vCenter Server	
	1 x vCenter PSC	
	1 x vRealize Log Insight	
	1 x VR appliance	8.2.x
	1 x SRM appliance	8.2.x
B	2 x 10 GB network switches	N/A
	4 x VxRail E560	VxRail software 4.7.4xx or above
	1 x VxRail Manager	
	1 x vCenter Server	
	1 x vCenter PSC	
	1 x vRealize Log Insight	
	1 x VR appliance	8.2.x
	1 x SRM appliance	8.2.x

Now we will discuss how to plan and design this solution in the next section.

Deployment procedures

In this section, we will discuss how to deploy the solution and list out the deployment procedures. First, we will see an overview of the deployment procedure of an active-passive solution for VxRail:

1. Deploy a set of VxRail clusters at sites A and B.

2. Download the installation file of the SRM appliance and the VR appliance from the VMware website.

3. Reserve four IP addresses for the SRM appliances, and the VR appliances, deployment – 1 at each location.

4. Deploy an SRM appliance and a VR appliance in the VxRail cluster at site A.

5. Deploy an SRM appliance and a VR appliance in the VxRail cluster at site B.

6. Pair two sites with SRM.

7. Add the licenses to each SRM appliance.

8. Set up the replication of virtual machines across two sites.

9. Create the SRM inventory mappings.

10. Create the virtual machine replication and protection groups.

11. Create the SRM recovery plan.

After reviewing the above procedures, we will discuss the deployment of the SRM appliance in the next section.

SRM appliance deployment

In this section, we will discuss the following procedure for deploying the SRM appliance:

1. First, we download the VMware SRM appliance from the VMware website (`https://www.vmware.com/`):

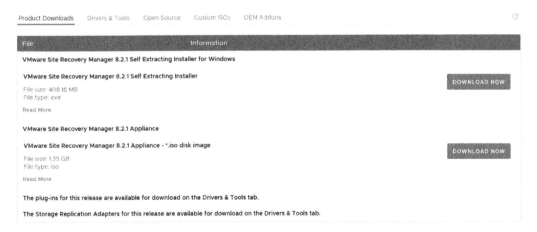

Figure 8.2 – Downloading SRM from the VMware website

2. Deploy the OVA file, and then connect to the VxRail cluster with the vSphere Web Client. Right-click on a data center, host, or cluster and select **Deploy OVF Template...**:

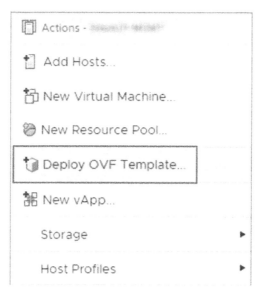

Figure 8.3 – Deploy OVF Template...

3. Select **Local file** and then click the **Choose Files** button to upload the OVF template:

Figure 8.4 – Selecting an OVF template

4. Specify the SRM name and select your HQ data center folder. Click the **NEXT** button:

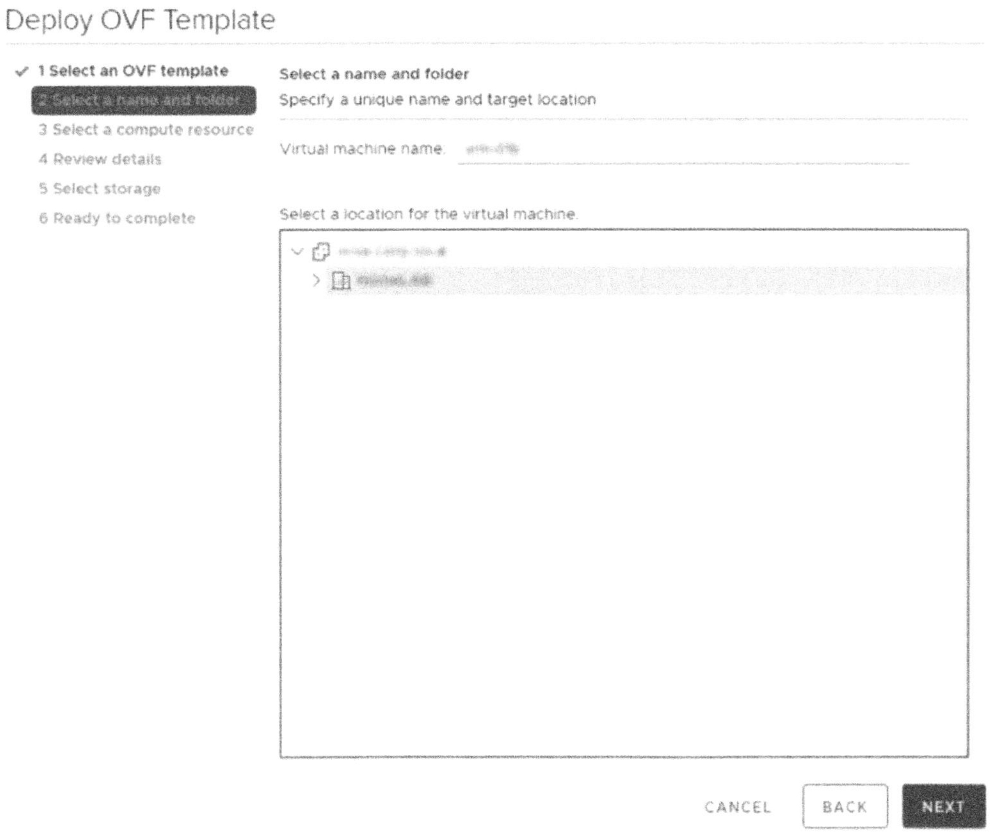

Figure 8.5 – Selecting a name and folder

5. Select a VxRail cluster, host, or resource pool where you want to run the deployed SRM appliance and then click the **NEXT** button:

Figure 8.6 – Selecting a compute resource

6. Review the virtual appliance's details and then click the **NEXT** button:

Figure 8.7 – Reviewing the details of the virtual appliance

7. Select to accept the **End User License Agreement (EULA)** and click the **NEXT** button:

Figure 8.8 – The license agreement of the SRM appliance

8. Select the number of vCPUs for the virtual appliance and then click the **NEXT** button:

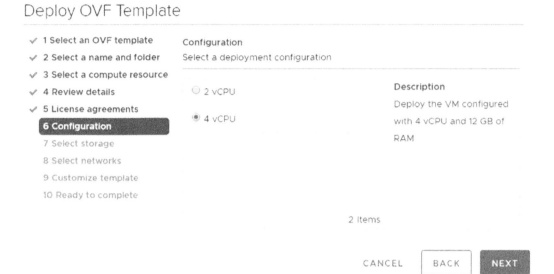

Figure 8.9 – Selecting the number of vCPUs for the SRM appliance

9. Choose a destination datastore and disk format (**Thick Provision**) for the virtual appliance and click the **NEXT** button:

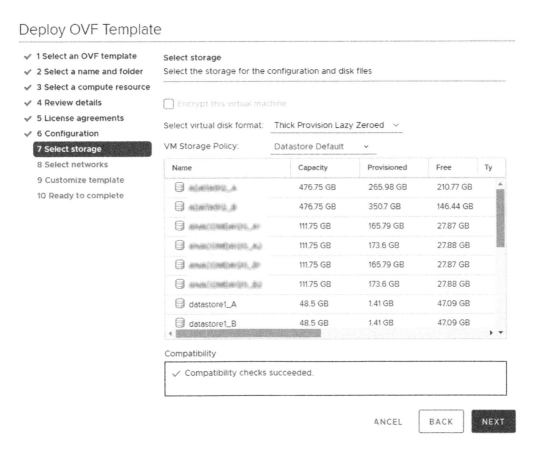

Figure 8.10 – Selecting a destination datastore and disk format

10. Select a network port group from the list of destination networks, set **IP allocation** to **Static - Manual**, **IP protocol** to **Ipv4**, and then click the **NEXT** button:

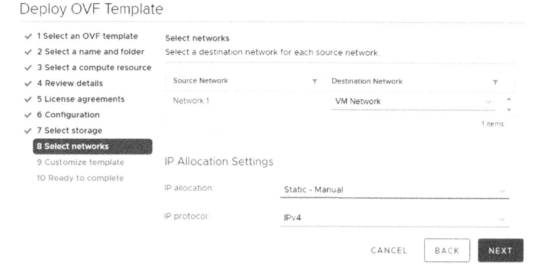

Figure 8.11 – Selecting a destination network for each source network

11. Specify passwords for the root account and the admin user account:

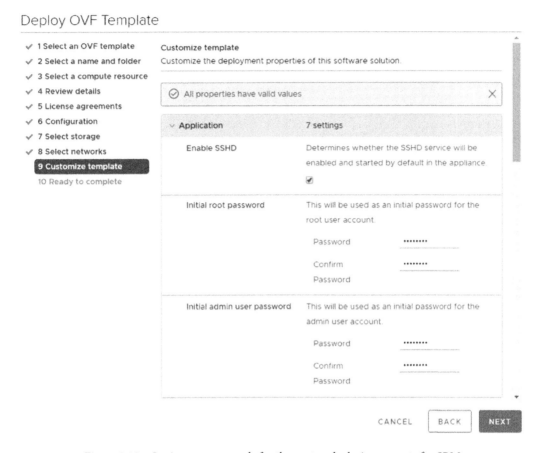

Figure 8.12 – Setting up passwords for the root and admin accounts for SRM

12. Specify the NTP servers, hostname, and password for the database user account:

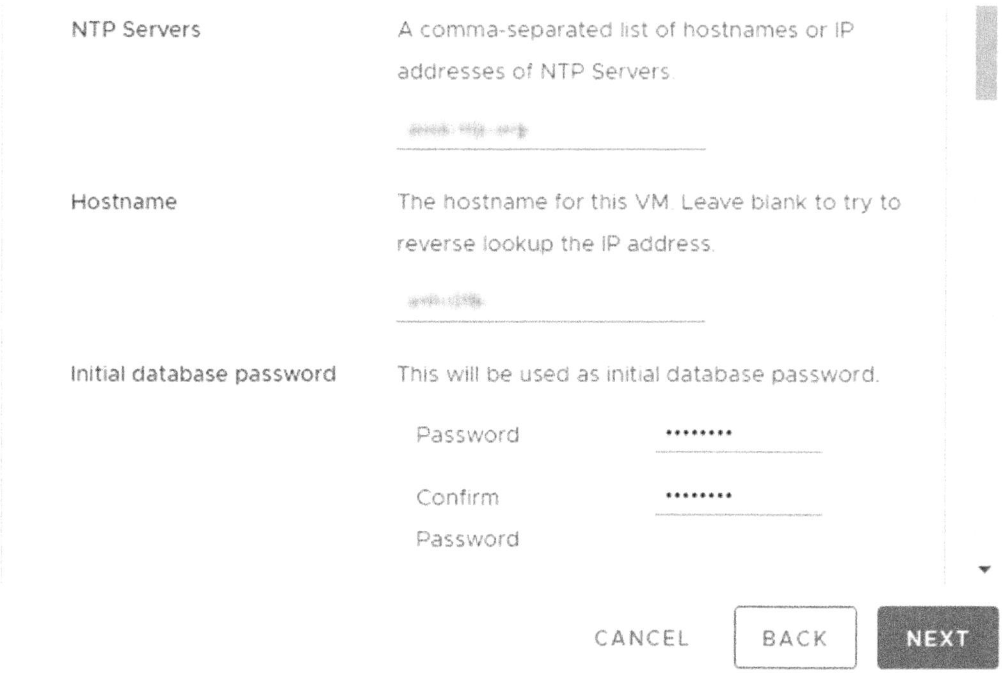

NTP Servers

A comma-separated list of hostnames or IP addresses of NTP Servers.

Hostname

The hostname for this VM. Leave blank to try to reverse lookup the IP address.

Initial database password

This will be used as initial database password.

Password   ••••••••

Confirm
Password   ••••••••

CANCEL   BACK   NEXT

Figure 8.13 – Setting up the NTP servers, hostname, and password for the database account for SRM

13. Specify the domain name, domain search path, domain name servers, network IP address, and network netmask. Click the **NEXT** button:

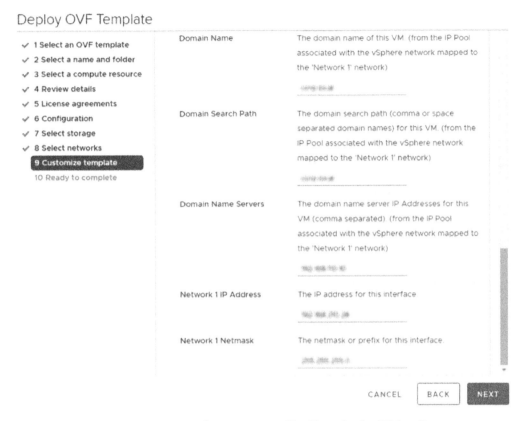

Figure 8.14 – Setting up the management IP address for the SRM appliance

14. Review the settings and then click the **FINISH** button to confirm deployment:

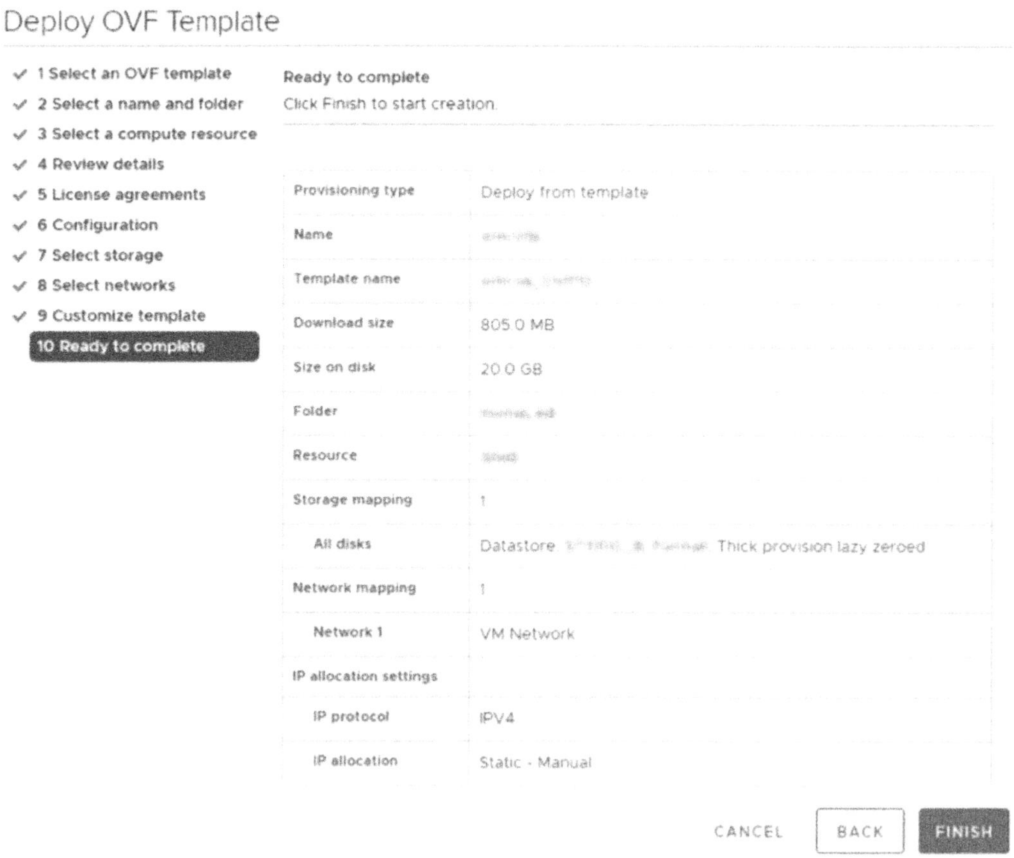

Deploy OVF Template

✓ 1 Select an OVF template
✓ 2 Select a name and folder
✓ 3 Select a compute resource
✓ 4 Review details
✓ 5 License agreements
✓ 6 Configuration
✓ 7 Select storage
✓ 8 Select networks
✓ 9 Customize template
10 Ready to complete

Ready to complete
Click Finish to start creation.

Provisioning type	Deploy from template
Name	
Template name	
Download size	805.0 MB
Size on disk	20.0 GB
Folder	
Resource	
Storage mapping	1
All disks	Datastore ... Thick provision lazy zeroed
Network mapping	1
Network 1	VM Network
IP allocation settings	
IP protocol	IPV4
IP allocation	Static · Manual

CANCEL   BACK   FINISH

Figure 8.15 – Reviewing the settings of the SRM appliance

15. We power on the SRM appliance once deployment is complete.

16. Go to the web browser and input the management IP address of SRM (set up in *step 13*). Then, click the **LAUNCH SRM APPLIANCE MANAGEMENT** button:

Figure 8.16 – Management page of SRM

17. Log in as an admin (the account that was set up in *step 11*).

18. Go to the **Summary** tab and then click the **CONFIGURE APPLIANCE** button:

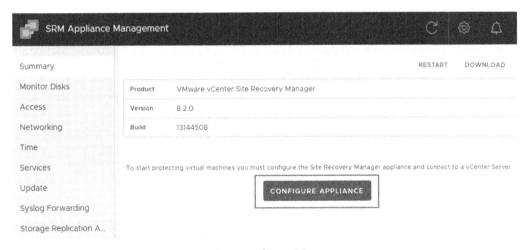

Figure 8.17 – SRM Appliance Management page

19. On the **Platform Services Controller** step, enter the hostname of PSC, which is running in the VxRail cluster, the username, and the password. Click the **NEXT** button:

Figure 8.18 – Configuring SRM

20. On the **vCenter Server** step, select the vCenter Server instance with which to register the SRM appliance and click the **NEXT** button.

21. On the **Name and extension** step, specify **Site name** (for example, Site A), **Administrator email**, and **Local host** (for example, the SRM IP address or FQDN).

    Select the default SRM extension identifier option or create a custom extension ID for this SRM pair and then click the **NEXT** button:

> **Important note**
> Both SRM instances in a site pair must use the same extension ID.

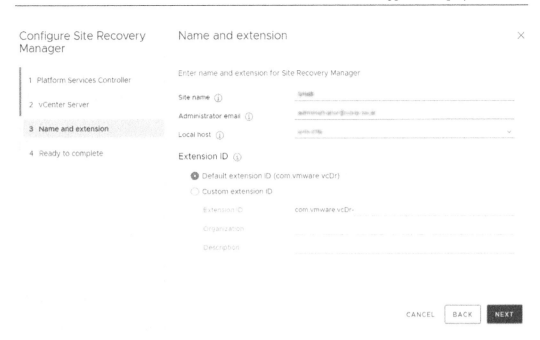

Figure 8.19 – Name and extension configuration in SRM

22. Review your settings and then click the **FINISH** button to confirm these settings:

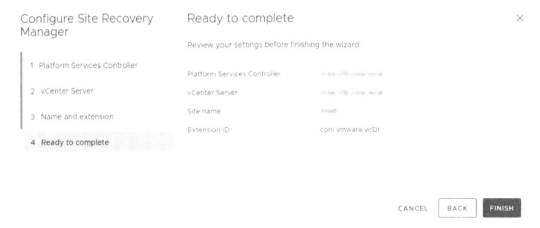

Figure 8.20 – Reviewing and confirming the SRM settings

23. Once the configuration has completed successfully, we can see that it shows all the SRM information, as follows:

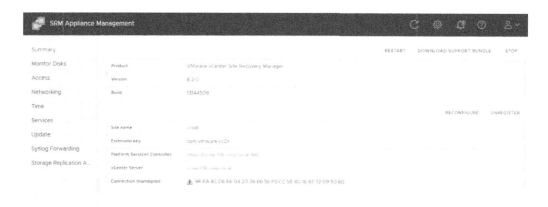

Figure 8.21 – The SRM configuration is complete

24. Go to the license page of vCenter Server and add the licenses to SRM.

25. Now, we can configure the SRM appliance on the other site (that is, site B), so repeat *steps 2* to *23*.

Once we have finished the SRM configuration on both sites, we can move on to the next section to deploy the VR appliance.

VR deployment

In this section, we will discuss the following procedures for deploying the VR appliance:

1. We download the VMware VR software (OVA file) from the VMware website (`https://www.vmware.com/`):

Figure 8.22 – Downloading VR from the VMware website

2. We need to deploy the OVA file and connect to the VxRail cluster with the vSphere Web Client. Right-click on a data center, host, or cluster and select **Deploy OVF Template…**:

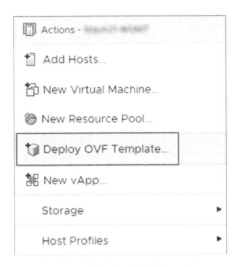

Figure 8.23 – Deploy OVF Template…

3. Select **Local file** and then click the **Choose Files** button to upload the OVF template:

Figure 8.24 – Selecting an OVF template

4. The VR software is an ISO image (downloaded in *step 1*). Mount this ISO image on a system in your workstation, navigate to the `\bin` directory in the ISO image, and then select the **vSphere_Replication-system.vmdk, vSphere_Replication-support. vmdk, vSphere_Replication_OVF10.ovf, vSphere_Replication_OVF10.mf**, and **vSphere_Replication_OVF10.cert** files:

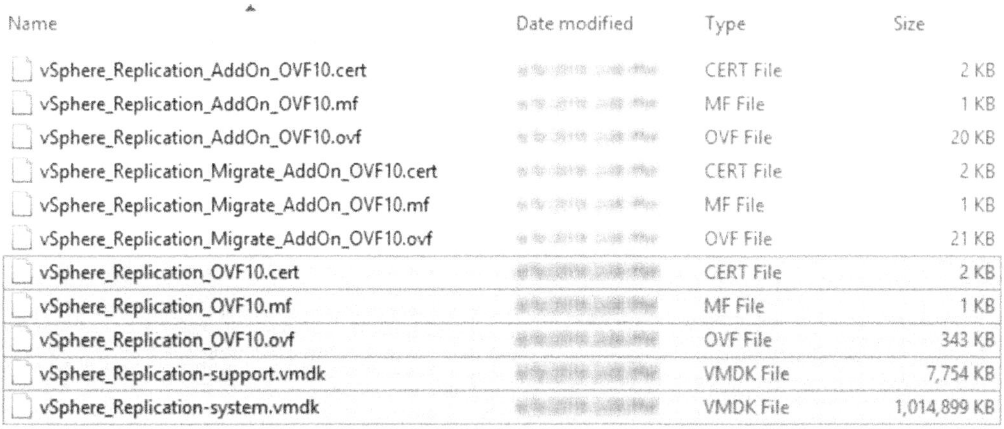

Name	Date modified	Type	Size
vSphere_Replication_AddOn_OVF10.cert		CERT File	2 KB
vSphere_Replication_AddOn_OVF10.mf		MF File	1 KB
vSphere_Replication_AddOn_OVF10.ovf		OVF File	20 KB
vSphere_Replication_Migrate_AddOn_OVF10.cert		CERT File	2 KB
vSphere_Replication_Migrate_AddOn_OVF10.mf		MF File	1 KB
vSphere_Replication_Migrate_AddOn_OVF10.ovf		OVF File	21 KB
vSphere_Replication_OVF10.cert		CERT File	2 KB
vSphere_Replication_OVF10.mf		MF File	1 KB
vSphere_Replication_OVF10.ovf		OVF File	343 KB
vSphere_Replication-support.vmdk		VMDK File	7,754 KB
vSphere_Replication-system.vmdk		VMDK File	1,014,899 KB

Figure 8.25 – VMware VR OVF files

5. Specify the VR name, select your HQ data center folder, and then click the **NEXT** button:

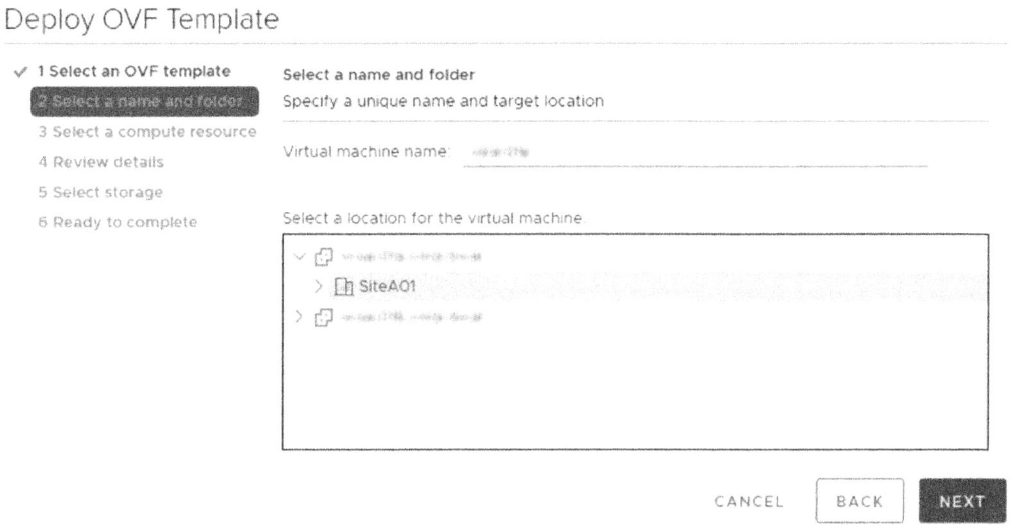

Deploy OVF Template

✓ 1 Select an OVF template

2 Select a name and folder

3 Select a compute resource

4 Review details

5 Select storage

6 Ready to complete

Select a name and folder
Specify a unique name and target location

Virtual machine name:

Select a location for the virtual machine

> SiteAO1

CANCEL   BACK   NEXT

Figure 8.26 – Selecting a name and folder

6. Review the virtual appliance's details and click the **NEXT** button:

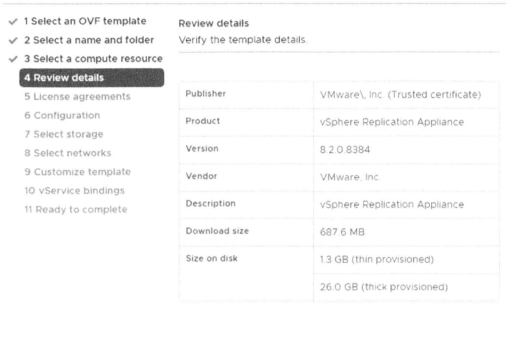

Figure 8.27 – Reviewing the details of the virtual appliance

7.   Select to accept the EULA and then click the **NEXT** button:

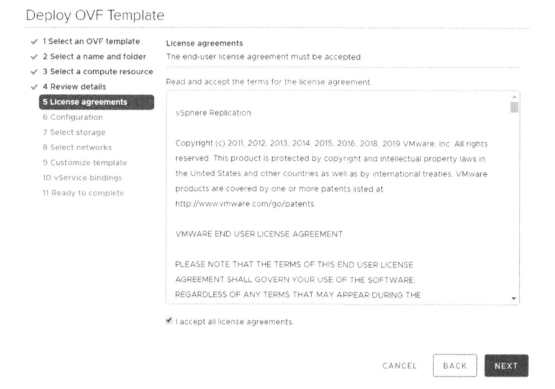

Figure 8.28 – The license agreement of VR

8.   Select the number of vCPUs for the VR virtual appliance and click the **NEXT** button:

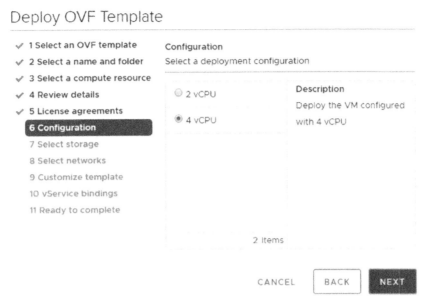

Figure 8.29 – Selecting the number of vCPUs for VR

9. Choose a destination datastore and disk format (**Thin Provision**) for the virtual appliance and then click the **NEXT** button:

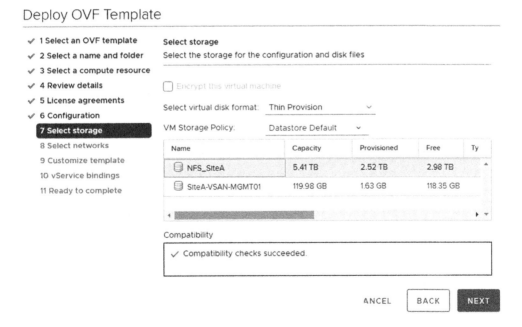

Figure 8.30 – Selecting a destination datastore and disk format

10. Select a network port group from the list of destination networks, set **IP allocation** to **Static - Manual**, **IP protocol** to **IPv4**, and then click the **NEXT** button:

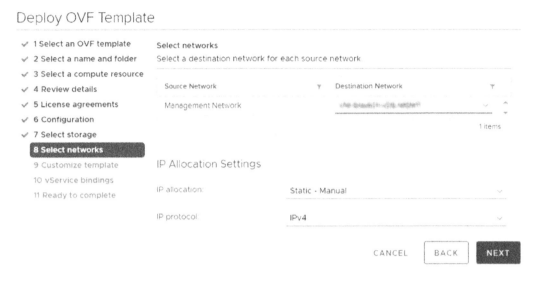

Figure 8.31 – Selecting a destination network for each source network

11. Specify the password for the root account, the NTP servers, and a hostname for the VR virtual appliance:

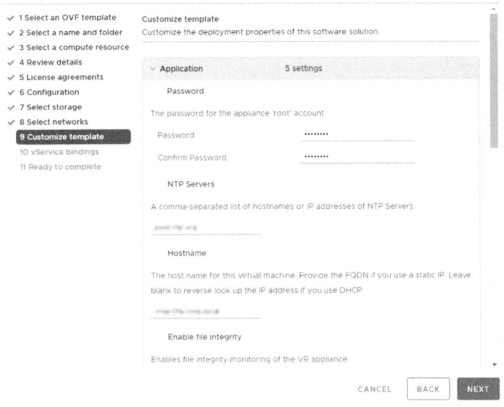

Figure 8.32 – Setting up the password for the root account on VR

12. Specify the domain name, domain search path, domain name servers, management IP address, and network netmask. Click the **NEXT** button:

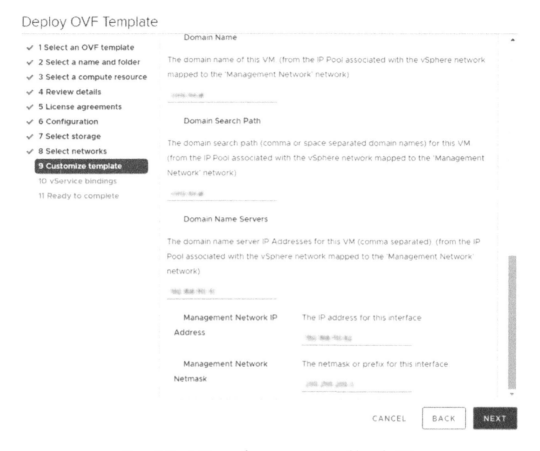

Figure 8.33 – Setting up the management IP address for VR

13. Select **vCenter Extension vService** from the **Provider** menu and then click the **NEXT** button:

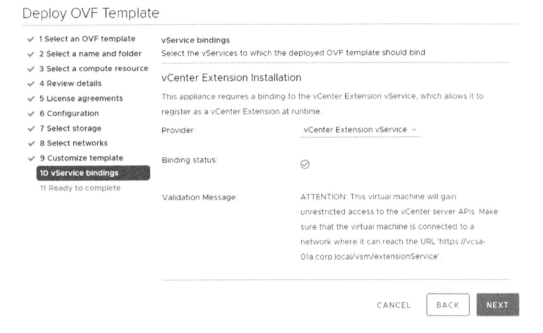

Figure 8.34 – Selecting the vService to which the deployed OVF template should bind

14. Review the settings and then click the **FINISH** button to confirm deployment:

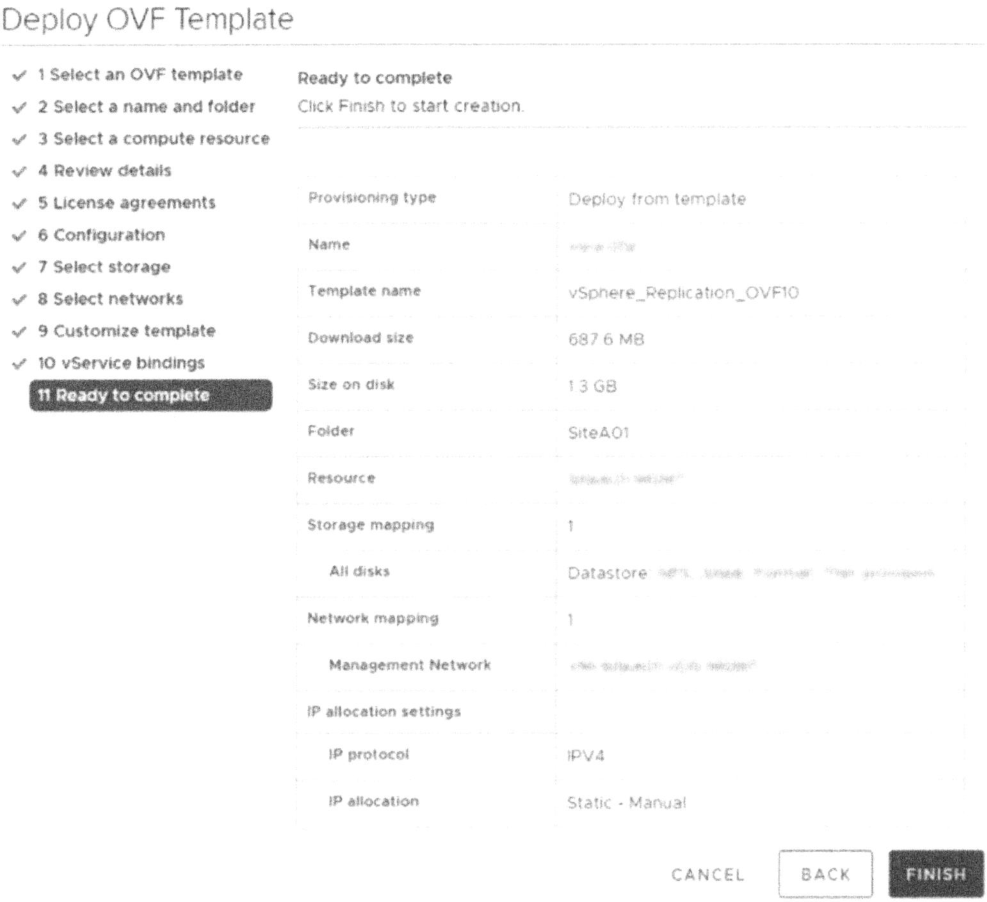

Deploy OVF Template

	Ready to complete
✓ 1 Select an OVF template	Click Finish to start creation.
✓ 2 Select a name and folder	
✓ 3 Select a compute resource	
✓ 4 Review details	
✓ 5 License agreements	Provisioning type
✓ 6 Configuration	
✓ 7 Select storage	
✓ 8 Select networks	
✓ 9 Customize template	
✓ 10 vService bindings	
11 Ready to complete	

Provisioning type	Deploy from template
Name	
Template name	vSphere_Replication_OVF10
Download size	687.6 MB
Size on disk	1.3 GB
Folder	SiteA01
Resource	
Storage mapping	1
All disks	Datastore
Network mapping	1
Management Network	
IP allocation settings	
IP protocol	IPV4
IP allocation	Static - Manual

CANCEL   BACK   FINISH

Figure 8.35 – Reviewing the settings of VR

15. Go to the web browser and input the management IP address of the VR **Virtual Appliance Management Interface** (**VAMI**); we set it up in *step 12*. Select the **VR** tab and then click **Configuration**:

Figure 8.36 – The VAMI of VR

16. Verify the domain name or IP address of the lookup service, which is also the VMware PSC (VxRail system virtual machine), and the SSO administrator and password for PSC.

Specify the vCenter Server IP address (VxRail system virtual machine) and admin email. Then, click the **Save and Restart Service** button:

| Getting Started | Configuration | Security | Support |

Startup Configuration

Configuration Mode:
- ◉ Configure using the embedded database
- ○ Manual configuration
- ○ Configure from an existing VRM database

Actions

| Save and Restart Service |
| Unregister VRMS |
| Reset Embedded Database |

LookupService Address:	
SSO Administrator:	Administrator@vsphere.local
Password:	••••••••
VRM Host:		Browse...
VRM Site Name:	Last login: Tue Jun 19 07:27:19 UTC 2018 on tty1
vCenter Server Address:	
vCenter Server Port:	80
vCenter Server Admin Mail:	

IP Address for Incoming Storage Traffic: [   ]

| Apply Network Setting |

SSL Certificate Policy

☐ Accept only SSL certificates signed by a trusted Certificate Authority
(You must click the 'Save and Restart Service' button after changing this setting)

Install a new SSL Certificate

Generate a self-signed certificate | Generate and Install |

Upload PKCS#12 (*.pfx) file | Choose File | No file chosen

| Upload and Install |

Service Status

| Start | VRM service is   **stopped**
| Restart | Tomcat service is **running**

Powered by VMware Studio

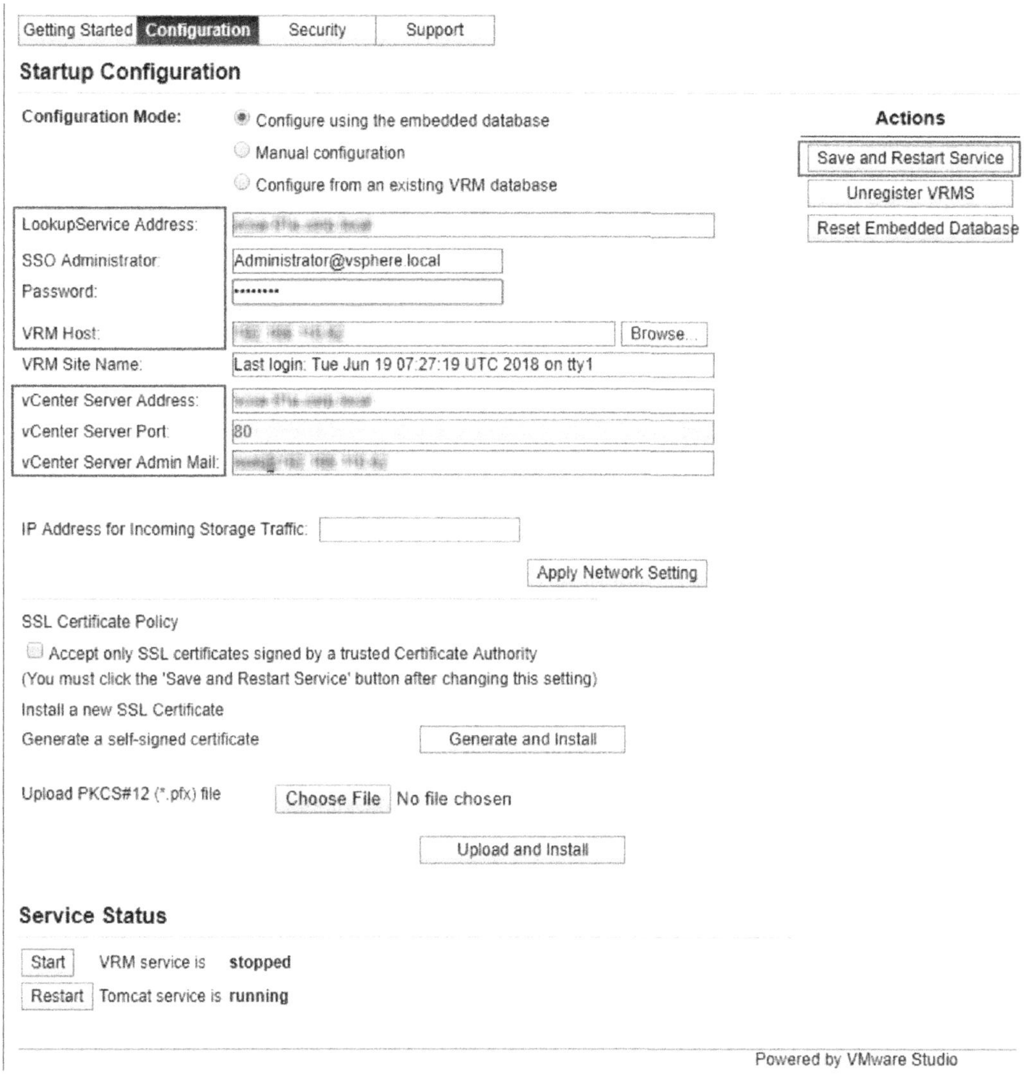

Figure 8.37 – VR configuration

17. Click the **Accept** button to confirm the vCenter certificate:

Figure 8.38 – Accepting the vCenter certificate on VR

After a few minutes, we can see that the **vSphere Replication Management (VRM)** and Tomcat services are running:

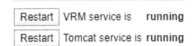

Figure 8.39 – The service status of VR

18. Log in to vCenter Server (site A) with the administrator account and choose **Site Recovery**:

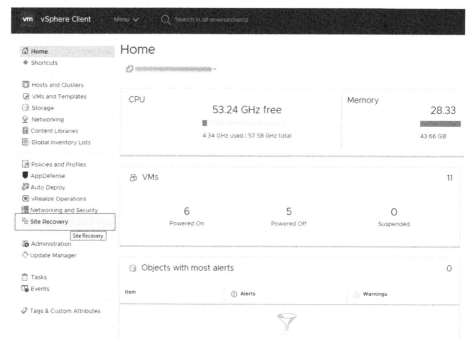

Figure 8.40 – The SRM plugin on the vCenter home page

19. We can see that the statuses of VR and SRM are **OK**. Now we can deploy VR at site B (repeat *steps 2* to *18*):

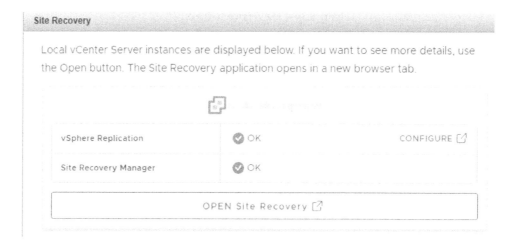

Figure 8.41 – The management dashboard for SRM

Once we finish the deployment of SRM and VR at both sites (sites A and B), then we can move on to the next section for configuring SRM inventory mappings across two sites.

Configuring SRM inventory mappings

In this section, we will discuss how to create the SRM mapping; this includes the network settings, folder mapping, resources mapping, storage policy, and placeholder datastore. The SRM inventory mappings provide the default objects in the inventory on the recovery site (site B) for the recovered virtual machines to use when we execute the SRM recovery plan.

The following is the procedure for creating the SRM inventory mappings:

1. Log in to vCenter Server (site A) and click **Site Recovery | OPEN Site Recovery**:

Figure 8.42 – The SRM dashboard

2. We select a site pair (sites A and B), and then click the **VIEW DETAILS** button:

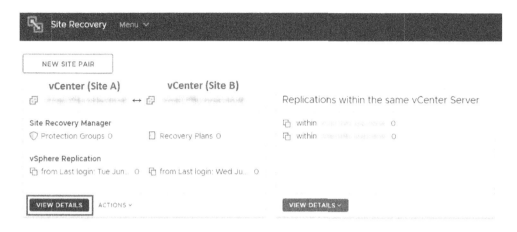

Figure 8.43 – The SRM site pairing dashboard

3. Select **Network Mappings** and click the **NEW** button to create a new mapping:

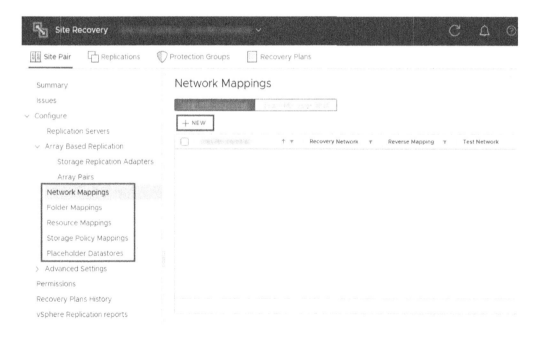

Figure 8.44 – SRM Network Mappings

4. Select **Prepare mappings manually** and then click the **NEXT** button:

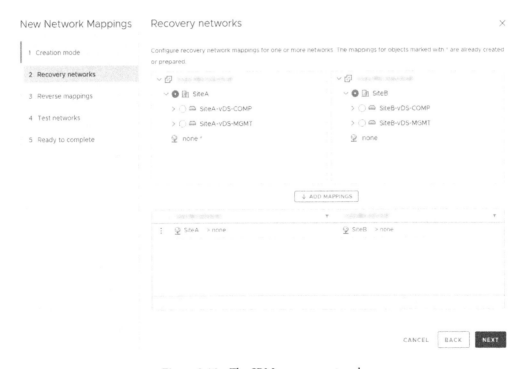

Figure 8.45 – The creation mode of SRM network mappings

5. In recovery networks, we select the network port group on the protected site (site A) to map to the network group on the recovery site (site B). Click the **ADD MAPPINGS** button to add the network mappings and then click the **NEXT** button:

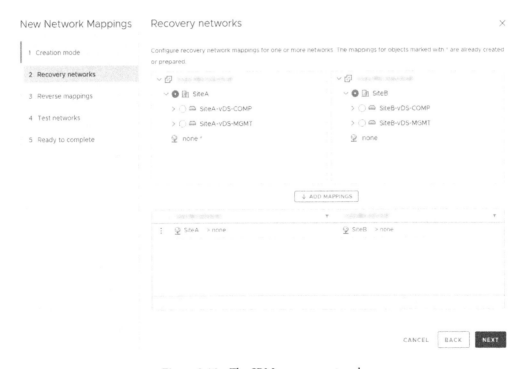

Figure 8.46 – The SRM recovery networks

6. Leave the default settings as they are and click the **NEXT** button:

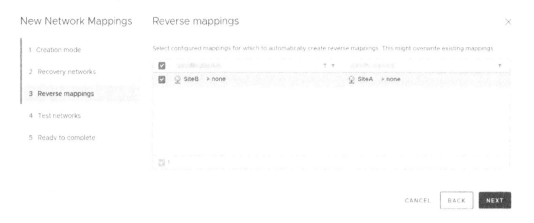

Figure 8.47 – Network reverse mappings

7. Keep the default setting (**Isolated network (auto created)**) and then click the **NEXT** button:

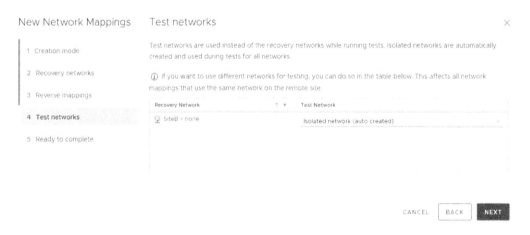

Figure 8.48 – SRM test network mappings

8. Click the **FINISH** button to create the mappings:

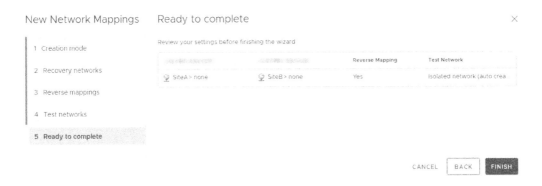

Figure 8.49 – Reviewing the network mappings

9. Back to the **Site Pair** dashboard, we continue creating the folder mappings. Choose **Folder Mappings** and then click the **NEW** button:

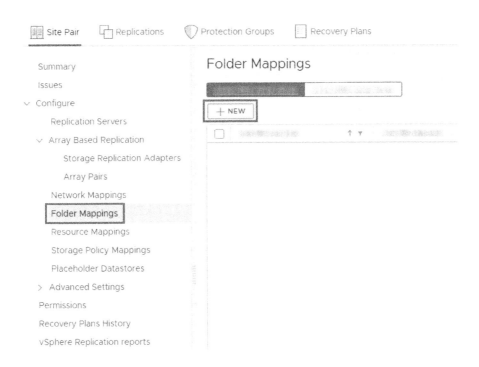

Figure 8.50 – Creating new folder mappings

10. The procedure for creating the folder mappings (selecting the virtual machine folder on the protected site to map to the virtual machine folder on the recovery site) is similar to the procedure for creating the network mappings. Once we have finished creating these mappings, we can move on to creating the resource mappings.

11. Back to the **Site Pair** dashboard, we continue creating the resource mappings. Choose **Resource Mappings** and then click the **NEW** button:

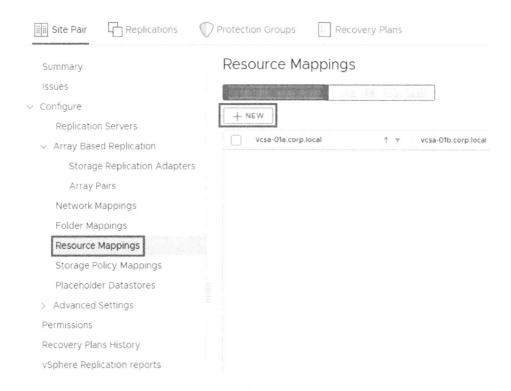

Figure 8.51 – Creating the new resource mappings

12. The procedure for creating the resource mappings (selecting the resource pool on the protected site to map to the resource pool on the recovery site) is similar to the procedure for creating the network mappings. Once we have finished creating these mappings, we can move on to creating the storage policy mappings.

13. Back to the **Site Pair** dashboard, we continue creating the storage policy mappings. Choose **Storage Policy Mappings** and then click the **NEW** button:

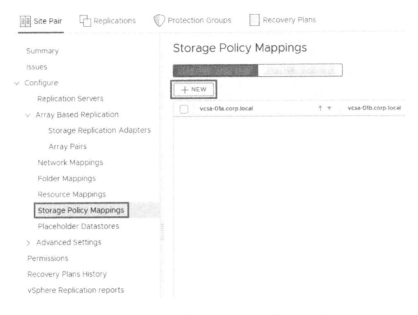

Figure 8.52 – Creating the new storage policy mappings

14. Select **Automatically prepare mappings for storage policies with matching names** to automatically map the resource folders and then click the **NEXT** button:

Figure 8.53 – Creation mode of storage policy mappings

15. We can see all the virtual machine storage policies on each vCenter Server (sites A and B). Select them all and click the **NEXT** button:

Figure 8.54 – Recovery storage policies

16. Keep the default settings of the reverse mappings and then click the **NEXT** button.

17. Review the storage policy mappings and then click the **FINISH** button to create the mappings:

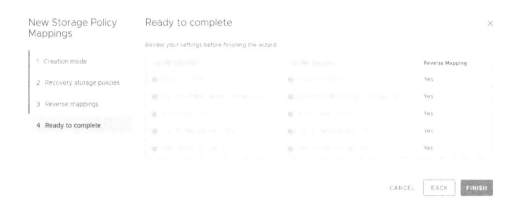

Figure 8.55 – Reviewing the storage policy mappings

18. Now we can create the last SRM mappings. Back to the **Site Pair** dashboard, we continue creating the placeholder datastores' mappings. Choose **Placeholder Datastores** and then click the **NEW** button:

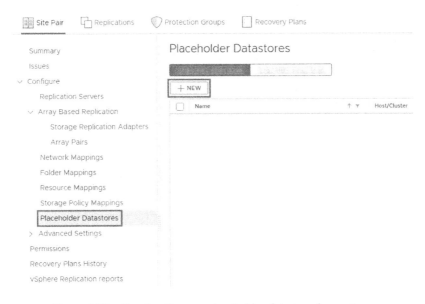

Figure 8.56 – Creating the new placeholder datastores' mappings

19. Select a non-replicated datastore (non-vSAN datastore on the VxRail cluster) on the recovery site (site B) to store the placeholder virtual machines, and then click the **ADD** button:

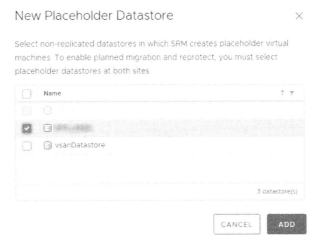

Figure 8.57 – New placeholder datastore

Once we have finished with all the above SRM inventory mappings, we can move on to the next section regarding the protection of virtual machines.

Protecting virtual machines

In this section, we will discuss how to protect virtual machines in the VxRail cluster with VR at site A, and then replicate the protected virtual machines to the VxRail cluster at site B:

1. Go to the **Site Recovery** dashboard. Choose the **Replications** tab, select **Forward replications**, and then click the **NEW** button:

Figure 8.58 – New forward replications

2. In the **Configure Replication** wizard, we can see that all the virtual machines are running on the VxRail cluster at site A. Select the virtual machines we want to replicate and click the **NEXT** button:

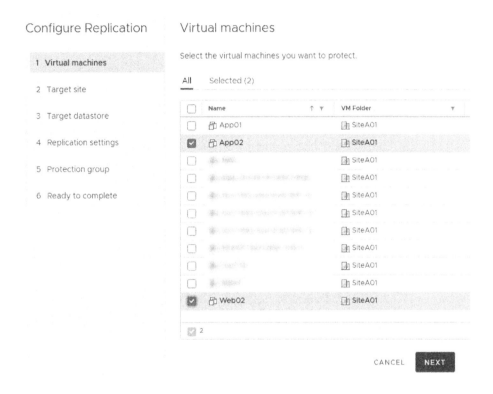

Figure 8.59 – Selecting the virtual machines for replication

3.   It will auto-select the vCenter Server at site B. We select **Auto-assign vSphere Replication Server** on the target site and click the **NEXT** button:

Figure 8.60 – Selecting the VR server

4.   Select the vSAN datastore on which to replicate the virtual machines. Then, click the **NEXT** button:

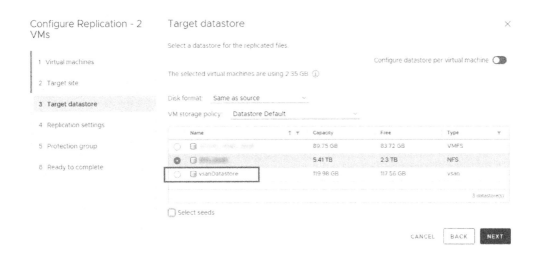

Figure 8.61 – Selecting the target datastore

5.   We can adjust the **Recovery point objective (RPO)** slider to set the acceptable period within which data can be lost if a site failure occurs. Keep the other configurations as the default settings. Click the **NEXT** button:

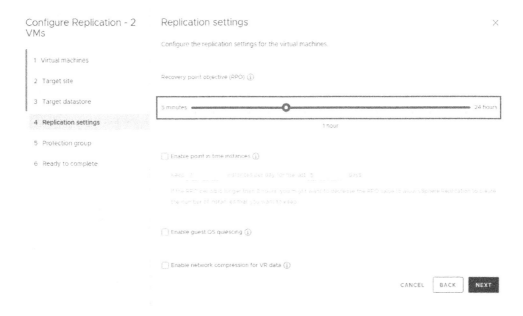

Figure 8.62 – The RPO settings of VR

6. On the **Protection group** step, we create a new protection group for the SRM recovery plan, specify the protection group name, and then click the **NEXT** button:

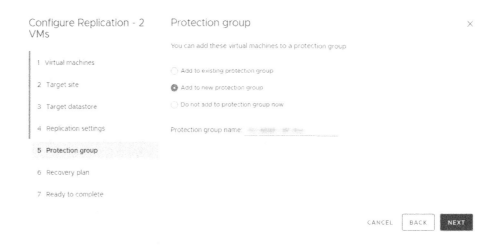

Figure 8.63 – Creating the protection group

7. Review the replication settings and then click the **FINISH** button:

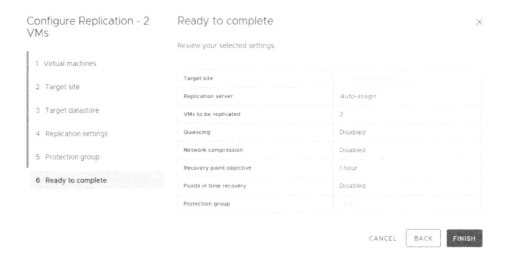

Figure 8.64 – Reviewing the replication of virtual machines

Once we have finished creating the virtual machine replication and protection group, we can proceed to the next section concerned with creating an SRM recovery plan.

Creating SRM recovery plans

In this section, we will discuss how to create an SRM recovery plan:

1. Go to the **Site Recovery** dashboard. Choose the **Recovery Plans** tab and then click the **NEW** button:

Figure 8.65 – Creating a new SRM recovery plan

2. Specify the name of the recovery plan and select the direction (site A to site B). Then, click the **NEXT** button:

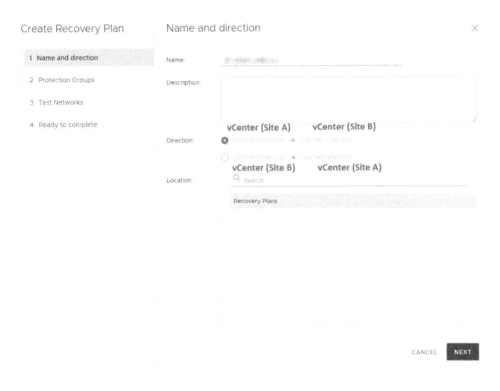

Figure 8.66 – Specifying the recovery plan name

3. Select all the SRM test networks in the VxRail cluster at site B (setup covered in *step 7* of the *Configuring SRM inventory mappings* section), and then click the **NEXT** button:

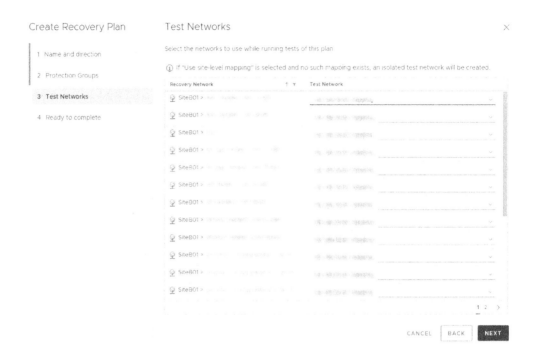

Figure 8.67 – Setting up the SRM test network in recovery plans

4. Review the recovery plan settings and then click the **FINISH** button:

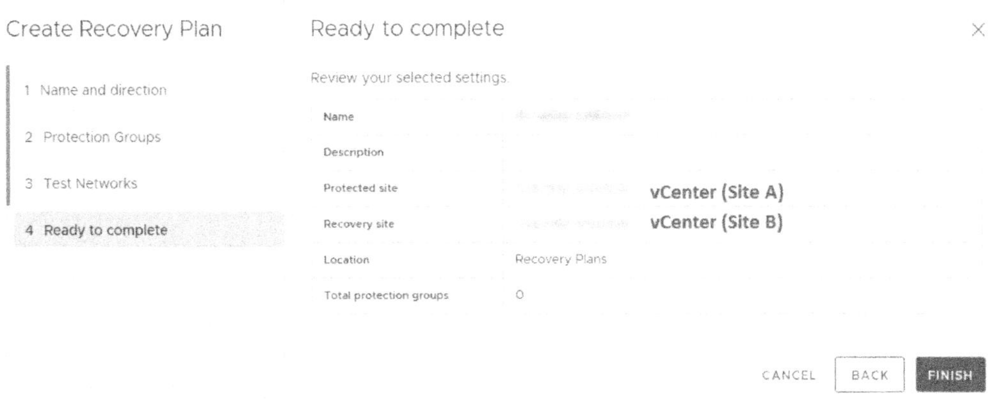

Figure 8.68 – Reviewing the recovery plan settings

Once we have finished with the SRM recovery plan, the configuration of the active-passive solution for VxRail is complete.

Having completed this chapter, we now understand what the disaster recovery solution for VxRail is and how to deploy an active-passive solution for VxRail across two sites.

Summary

In this chapter, we learned about the advantages of the active-passive solution for VxRail. We learned how to use both VMware SRM and VR to extend the disaster recovery feature on VxRail appliances across two locations. We also learned what core components are included in an SRM recovery plan, such as protection groups and RPO settings.

In the next chapter, we will learn about an advanced solution in the VxRail system. We will learn what the active-active solutions for VxRail are. This includes the active-active-passive solution with VMware SRM. We will learn how to plan and design this solution in the next chapter.

Questions

Test the knowledge you've gained from this chapter by answering the following questions:

1. Which data protection software is bundled on a VxRail appliance?

    a. VMware Site Recovery Manager

    b. vSphere Replication

    c. VMware vCenter Server

    d. VMware vSphere

    e. All the above

2. What is the minimum RPO setting on VMware vSphere Replication?

    a. 10 minutes

    b. 1 minute

    c. 15 minutes

    d. 1 hour

    e. 2 hours

    f. None of the above

3. Where can we download the vSphere Replication appliance?

    a. Dell EMC website

    b. VMware website

    c. Dell Support portal

    d. Dell Technologies website

    e. None of the above

4. Where can we monitor the services of vSphere Replication?

    a. vCenter Server monitoring

    b. vSphere hosts

    c. vSphere Replication Management

    d. Virtual Appliance Management Interface

    e. All the above

5. Which two services run on the vSphere Replication appliance?

   a. vCenter services

   b. VRM services

   c. MSSQL services

   d. Tomcat services

   e. None of the above

6. How many vCenter Server instances are required in an active-passive solution for VxRail?

   a. One

   b. Two

   c. Three

   d. Four

   e. Five

7. What is the file format of the vSphere Replication appliance?

   a. OVF

   b. OVA

   c. VMDK

   d. VHD

   e. None of the above

8. Which data protection software can support RPO set to 0?

   a. vSphere Replication

   b. Dell EMC Avamar

   c. Dell EMC RecoverPoint for Virtual Machines

   d. Site Recovery Manager

   e. VMware vRealize Operations Manager

9. Which replication mode can support vSphere Replication?

a. Asynchronization

b. Synchronization

c. Asynchronization with RPO set to 0

d. Synchronization with RPO set to 0

e. All the above

10. How can you trigger virtual machine failover to the recovery site?

a. With vMotion

b. With Storage vMotion

c. Execute the SRM recovery plan

d. Shut down the virtual machines

e. All the above

11. Which software requires an optional license when we set up an active-passive solution for VxRail?

a. vCenter Server appliance

b. VxRail Manager

c. vSphere Replication

d. Site Recovery Manager

e. All the above

12. Which replication direction can support an active-passive solution for VxRail?

a. One-way replication only

b. Two-way replication only

c. Two-way replication and one-way replication

d. One-to-many replication

e. Many-to-many replications

f. All the above

9
Active-Active Solution for VxRail

In *Chapter 8, Active-Passive Solution for VxRail*, we understood the advantages of the active-passive solution for VxRail. We learned how to use both VMware Site Recovery Manager and vSphere Replication to extend the disaster recovery feature on VxRail appliances across two locations.

In this chapter, we will learn about the advanced solution in the VxRail system. We will learn what a vSAN stretched cluster on VxRail is. This includes the active-active-passive solution with VMware **Site Recovery Manager (SRM)**. We will learn how to plan and design this solution in this chapter, including the deployment of a VxRail vSAN stretched cluster, and how to extend the disaster recovery feature on a VxRail vSAN stretched cluster.

In this chapter, we're going to cover the following main topics:

- Overview of the active-active solution for VxRail
- Deploying the active-active solution for VxRail
- Overview of the active-active-passive solution for VxRail

Technical requirements

In this chapter, you'll need to make sure your workstation (laptop) is running on the Windows platform, and that a web browser is installed on your laptop. The latest versions of Firefox, Google Chrome, and Microsoft Internet Explorer 10 or above are all supported. The VxRail software is running version 4.7.300 or above.

For the network requirements of the vSAN stretched cluster on VxRail, the latency or **Round-Trip Time (RTT)** between the primary and secondary sites hosting **virtual machine (VM)** objects should not be greater than 5 milliseconds, and the bandwidth between the primary and secondary sites should be a minimum of 10 Gbps or greater. In the vSAN stretched cluster configurations, the latency or RTT between the primary and secondary sites hosting VM objects and the witness node should not be greater than 200 milliseconds.

For the disaster recovery solution, there is a set of VxRail clusters (a minimum of four nodes each) running at both primary and secondary sites in a healthy state, and the VM replication network for vSphere Replication is deployed and ready across the primary and secondary sites. Additional licenses are required for VMware Site Recovery Manager when defining the SRM recovery plan.

The requirements of the SRM appliance configuration are that we must deploy an SRM appliance at each site. The version of the SRM appliance must be the same. The **Domain Name System (DNS)** name of the vCenter **Platform Service Controller (PSC)**, vCenter Server, and the SRM appliance must be configured with an appropriate DNS and IP address.

As regards the requirements of the vSphere Replication configuration, we must deploy a vSphere replication appliance at each site. vSphere Replication is configured with a dual-core or quad-core CPU, a 13 GB and a 9 GB hard disk, and 8 GB of memory. The DNS name of the vCenter PSC, vCenter Server, and vSphere Replication appliance has been configured to incorporate the DNS with the relevant IP address.

Overview of the active-active solution for VxRail

The vSAN stretched cluster on VxRail can deliver an active-active cluster between two geographically separate locations and synchronously replicate data between sites. This feature allows an entire site failure to be tolerated. It extends the concept of fault domains to data center awareness domains. The vSAN stretched cluster must build on between two separate sites (the preferred and secondary site). Each stretched cluster includes two data sites and one witness site. The witness host contains the witness components of the VM objects. The witness host is used as a decision maker that monitors the availability of datastore components when the network connection between the preferred and secondary sites is lost. The witness host can either be a VM or a physical machine.

Now we will have an overview of the logical diagram of the active-active solution for VxRail. In *Figure 9.1*, we can see that there are three separate sites: they are **Preferred Site**, **Secondary Site**, and **Witness Site**. The VxRail cluster must be deployed across the primary and secondary sites in an active-active configuration (vSAN stretched cluster), with four VxRail nodes deployed at each site. There are two 10 GB top-of-switches for VxRail network connections at the primary and secondary sites. At the witness site, there is a vSAN witness appliance deployed. The VxRail cluster with eight E560 nodes is managed by the vCenter Server Appliance. The VxRail system's VMs are running on this VxRail cluster, that is, the vCenter Server Appliance, vCenter PSC, VxRail Manager, and vRealize Log Insight:

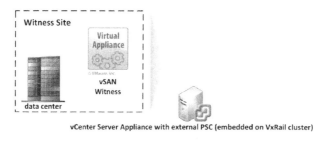

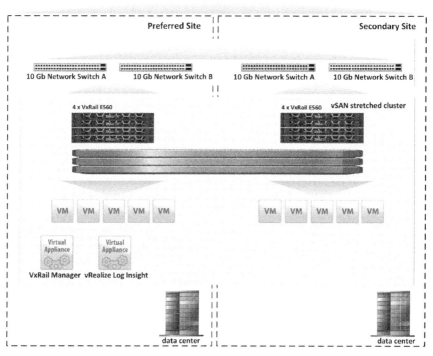

Figure 9.1 – A logical diagram of the active-active solution for VxRail

In the next section, we will discuss the requirements for this solution.

VxRail cluster configuration

The VxRail cluster must be deployed across two separate sites in an active-active configuration. The following table shows the configuration of each VxRail appliance in the vSAN stretched cluster. The witness host must be installed on a witness site that has independent data paths to each data site. The maximum supported configuration of the vSAN stretched cluster is 15+15+1 (30 nodes + 1 witness). The witness host must be running the same version as the VxRail cluster; for example, if the VxRail cluster is running in vSphere 6.7, the witness host must be version 6.7. The stretched cluster supports the **Failure Tolerance Method (FTM)** of RAID-5/6 and RAID-1. RAID-5/6 must be in the configuration of vSAN All-Flash:

Sites	Server	Fault Domain
Preferred	VxRail E560 Node	Fault Domain 1
Secondary	VxRail E560 Node	Fault Domain 2
Witness	vSAN Witness Appliance	Fault Domain 3

A vSAN stretched cluster uses **fault domain (FD)** technology to provide redundancy and failure protection across sites. Fault domains provide the core functionality of the vSAN stretched cluster. The supported number of fault domains in a vSAN stretched cluster is three. A stretched cluster requires **three fault domains**; these are the **Preferred Site**, the **Secondary Site**, and a **Witness Host**. The preferred and secondary sites are the data sites that are configured in a vSAN fault domain. The vSAN witness host can be either a physical host or a virtual appliance. The witness components are stored on the witness host and provide a quorum to prevent a split-brain scenario if the network is lost between the two data sites. This is the third fault domain. The following table shows the minimum number of VxRail nodes that depend on the VxRail software version and vSAN stretched cluster configuration.

> **Important note**
> VxRail appliances support vSAN stretched clusters with vSphere Standard edition. A vSAN Enterprise license is required for DRS.

In the following table, **PFTT** stands for the **Primary Level of Failures to Tolerate**, and **SFTT** stands for the **Secondary Level of Failures to Tolerate**:

VxRail Version		Minimum Nodes: Preferred Site + Secondary Site + Witness Host
VxRail 4.5.070 and above	PFTT = 1; SFTT = 1; Failure Tolerance Method = RAID-1 (Mirroring)	3 + 3 + 1
	PFTT = 1; SFTT = 2; Failure Tolerance Method = RAID-1 (Mirroring)	5 + 5 + 1
	PFTT = 1; SFTT = 3; Failure Tolerance Method = RAID-1 (Mirroring)	7 + 7 + 1
	PFTT = 1; SFTT = 1; Failure Tolerance Method = RAID-5/6 (Erasure Coding)	4 + 4 + 1
	PFTT = 1; SFTT = 2; Failure Tolerance Method = RAID-5/6 (Erasure Coding)	4 + 4 + 1

> **Important note**
> Erasure coding can only be enabled on an All-Flash vSAN cluster.

In the next section, we will discuss the vCenter Server requirements for a vSAN stretched cluster for VxRail.

vCenter Server requirements

Starting with VxRail 4.5.200 and above, either the embedded vCenter Server Appliance or an external vCenter Server can be supported for vSAN stretched clusters. If we choose an external vCenter Server for vSAN stretched clusters on VxRail, the following are the external vCenter Server requirements:

- The external vCenter Server version **must** be identical to the VxRail vCenter Server Appliance version.

- The **Fully Qualified Domain Name (FQDN)** of an external vCenter Server is required.

- If the vCenter **Platform Services Controller** (**PSC**) is non-embedded, the FQDN of an external PSC is required. Please include vCenter license requirements as well.

- The **Domain Name System** (**DNS**) server must resolve all VxRail ESXi hostnames prior to initialization.

- Create a data center on the external vCenter Server before joining the VxRail cluster.

- Create a *VxRail management* user in **Single Sign-On** (**SSO**) that has no role and permission assigned. VxRail will make a new role and assign it to this user account.

In the next section, we will discuss the network requirements for a vSAN stretched cluster on VxRail.

Network requirements

A vSAN stretched cluster in VxRail requires Layer 2 connectivity for the management network between the preferred and secondary sites. Starting with VxRail 4.7.300, Layer 3 is also supported between the two data sites (preferred and secondary). As regards vSAN network connectivity, we can use either Layer 2 or Layer 3. It recommends a minimum of 10 Gbps or greater bandwidth between the preferred and secondary sites. The network connectivity between two data sites and the witness site must be in Layer 3. *Figure 9.2* shows a supported network topology in the vSAN stretched cluster. The RTT, roundtrip latency, should not be more than 5 msec (one-way less than 2.5 msec). The data site to the witness RTT should not be more than 200 msec (one-way, less than 100 msec is acceptable). For 10+10+1 configurations, however, less than RTT-100 msec is preferred. For deployments bigger than 10+10+1, an RTT of less than 100 msec is required.

A vSAN stretched cluster includes the management network, vSAN network, vMotion network, and VM network. The management and vSAN networks must be connected to all three sites (the data sites and witness). In *Figure 9.2*, we can see that the connectivity for management and the vSAN network is in Layer 2 (the same VLAN ID) between the preferred and secondary sites. The network connectivity between the two data sites and the witness site is in Layer 3 (network routing):

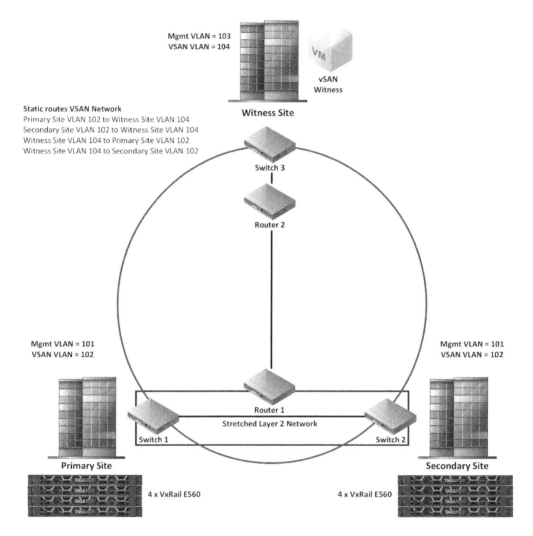

Figure 9.2 – The supported network topology in the vSAN stretched cluster

In the next section, we will discuss how to deploy the active-active solution for VxRail.

Deploying the active-active solution for VxRail

In this section, we will discuss the deployment of an active-active solution for VxRail. This includes the deployment of a vSAN stretched cluster witness and the configuration of a VxRail vSAN stretched cluster. Let's assume that we are deploying a VxRail cluster (with eight E560 nodes) across the preferred site and the secondary site, and that a vSphere cluster is running at the witness site.

Deploying a vSAN stretched cluster witness

We will deploy a vSAN witness appliance in a vSphere cluster at the witness site. The following is the procedure for deploying the vSAN witness appliance:

1. Go to the VMware website (`https://my.vmware.com/web/vmware/downloads/info/slug/datacenter_cloud_infrastructure/vmware_vsphere/6_7#drivers_tools`) and select the corresponding version on the **Select Version** menu. For VxRail version **4.7.x**, select **6.7**. We can download the latest version of the **VMware Virtual SAN Witness Appliance 6.7U3j** OVA file on the **VMware vSAN Tools, Plug-ins and Appliances** menu:

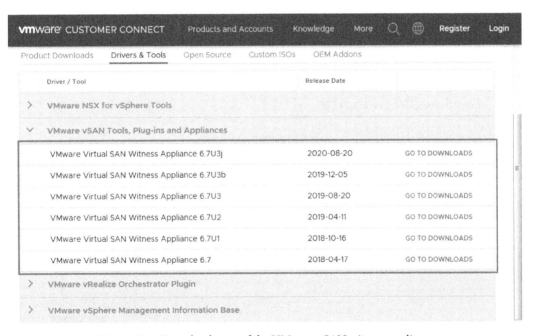

Figure 9.3 – Download page of the VMware vSAN witness appliance

2. Assume there is a vSphere cluster running at the witness site. We upload the vSAN witness OVA file and deploy it into this vSphere cluster. Then, click the **NEXT** button:

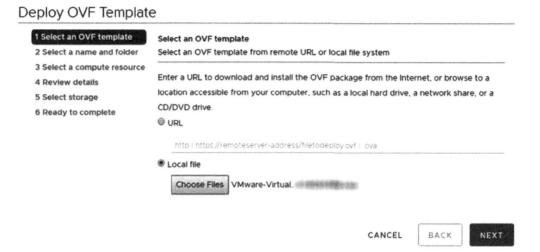

Figure 9.4 – Deploy OVF Template

3. Specify the witness hostname, select the target location, and then click the **NEXT** button:

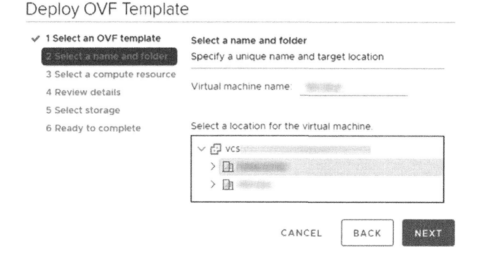

Figure 9.5 – Selecting a target folder

4. Select the target data center. Then, click the **NEXT** button:

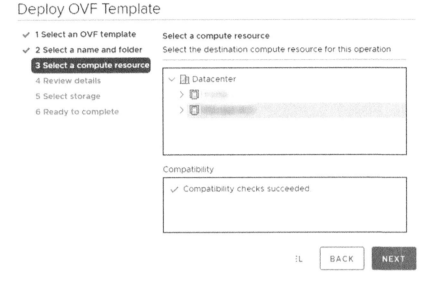

Figure 9.6 – Selecting a target data center

5. Review the template details. Then, click the **NEXT** button:

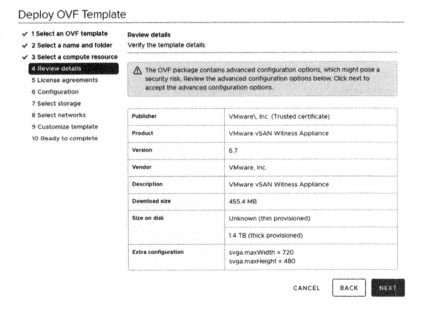

Figure 9.7 – Reviewing the template details

6.   Accept all license agreements. Then, click the **NEXT** button:

Figure 9.8 – Accepting all license agreements

7.   Select the **Medium** configuration for deployment. Then, click the **NEXT** button:

Figure 9.9 – Selecting the deployment configuration of the witness host

8. Select the target datastore. Then, click the **NEXT** button:

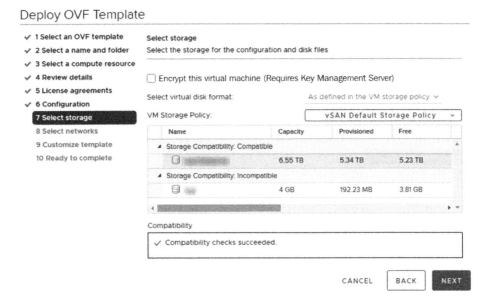

Figure 9.10 – Selecting the target datastore

9. Select the network port group for **Management Network** and **Witness Network** on the **Destination Network** menu. Then, click the **NEXT** button:

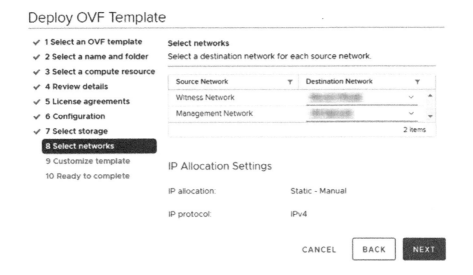

Figure 9.11 – Selecting the target network

10. Specify the root account password and click the **NEXT** button:

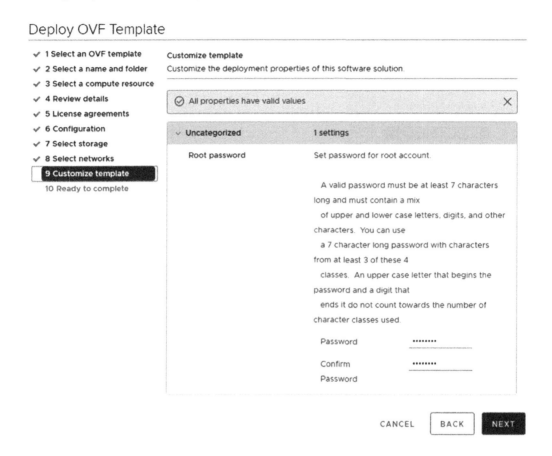

Figure 9.12 – Specifying the root account password

11. Review the configuration and click the **FINISH** button to deploy the vSAN witness host:

Figure 9.13 – Reviewing the configuration

12. Once the vSAN witness appliance is deployed, we need to power on this virtual appliance. We log in to the appliance as a root account. The vSAN witness appliance has two virtual network adapters (vmnic0 and vmnic1). vmnic0 is used for the vSphere management network, while vmnic1 is used for the vSAN network. Go to **Configure Management Network** and select vmnic0:

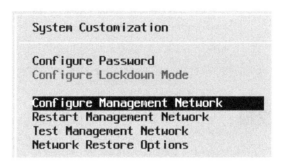

Figure 9.14 – Configure Management Network on a vSAN witness appliance

13. Choose **Set static IPv4 address and network configuration** and specify the IP address, subnet mask, and default gateway. Then, press **Enter**:

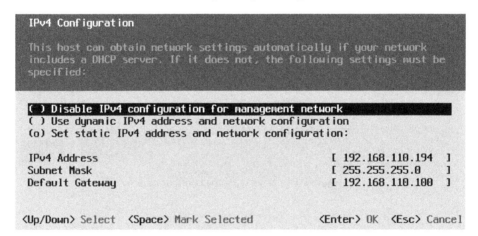

Figure 9.15 – Set static IPv4 address and network configuration

> **Important note**
>
> The management network on the witness host must be able to reach the vCenter Server Appliance on VxRail.

14. Configure the DNS servers and hostname and then press **Enter**:

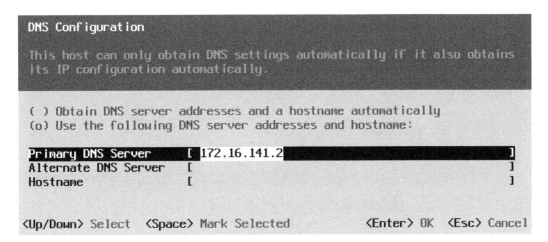

Figure 9.16 – DNS Configuration

15. Go to **Testing Management Network** to verify that all the tests have passed:

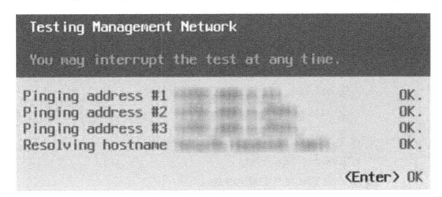

Figure 9.17 – ESXi management network testing

16. Go to the vCenter server that manages the VxRail cluster across the preferred and secondary sites and then create a new data center, **VxRail-Witness-Datacenter**, for the witness host. Use the **Add Host** wizard to add the vSAN witness host to this new data center:

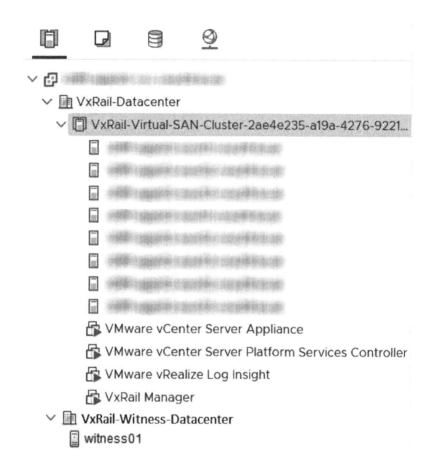

Figure 9.18 – Adding the witness host to a data center

17. Select the witness host and go to the **Configure** tab, choose **vmk1** on the **witnessPg** port group, and then click the **Edit…** button:

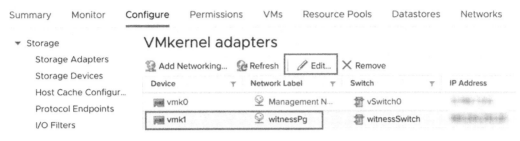

Figure 9.19 – vSAN witness port group

18. Select the vSAN service and set the **MTU** as 1500:

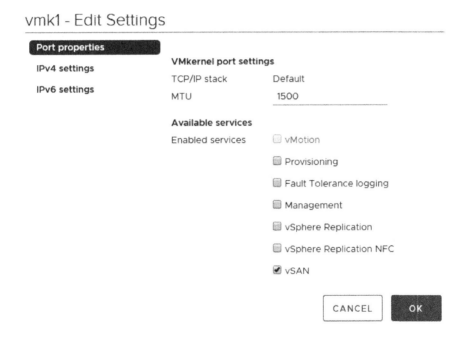

Figure 9.20 – Port properties on vmk1

19. Go to the IPv4 settings and select **Use static IPv4 settings**. Specify the IP address and the subnet mask for the vSAN network, and then click the **OK** button:

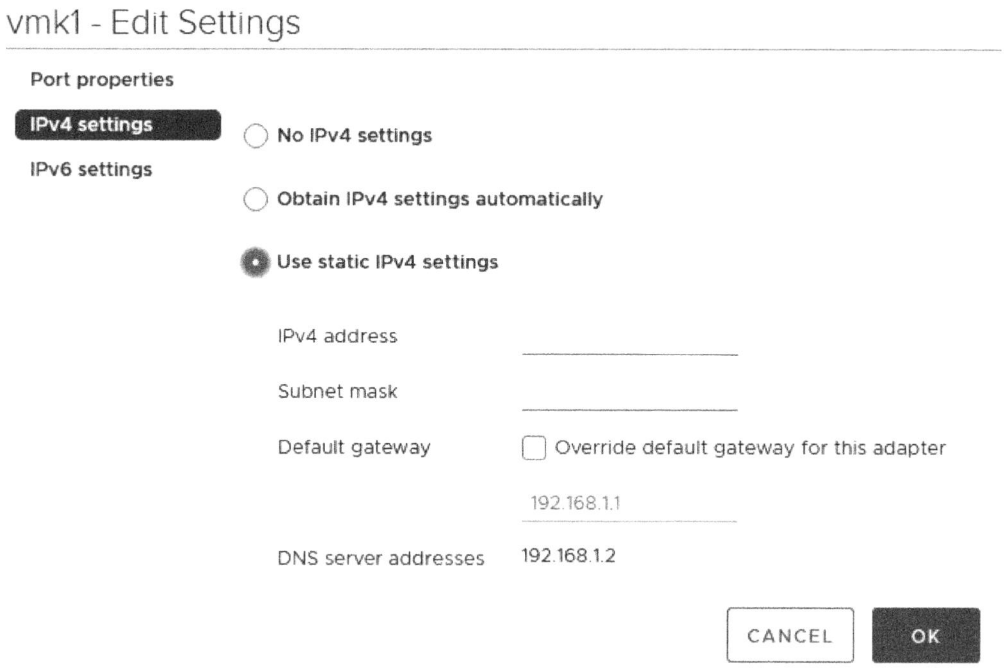

vmk1 - Edit Settings

Port properties

IPv4 settings   ○ No IPv4 settings

IPv6 settings

                            ○ Obtain IPv4 settings automatically

                            ● Use static IPv4 settings

        IPv4 address   _____

        Subnet mask   _____

        Default gateway   ☐ Override default gateway for this adapter

                            192.168.1.1

        DNS server addresses 192.168.1.2

                                            CANCEL   OK

Figure 9.21 – IPv4 settings on vmk1

Now that we've concluded management of the network and the vSAN network for the vSAN witness host, we will discuss the configuration of the VxRail vSAN stretched cluster in the next section.

Configuring the VxRail vSAN stretched cluster

In this section, we will discuss the configuration of the VxRail vSAN stretched cluster. The following is the procedure for deploying the VxRail vSAN stretched cluster:

1. Go to the vCenter server on the VxRail cluster, choose the **Configure** tab, and select **Fault Domains** under **vSAN**. Then, click the **CONFIGURE STRETCHED CLUSTER** button:

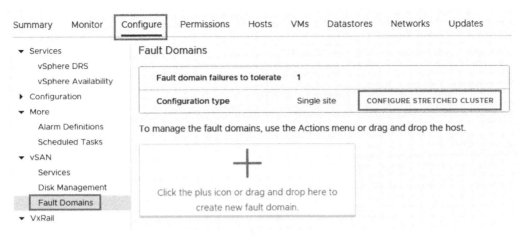

Figure 9.22 – Creating the stretched cluster

2. We must create two fault domains, **Preferred** and **Secondary**. Move the corresponding VxRail nodes into each fault domain and click the **NEXT** button:

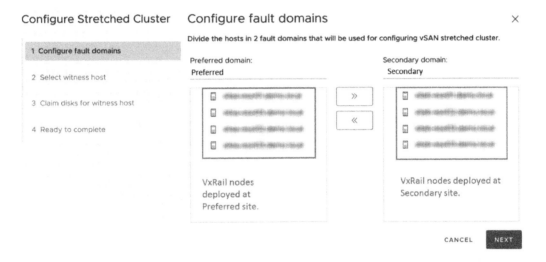

Figure 9.23 – Configuring the fault domains

3.   Select the witness host, and then click the **NEXT** button:

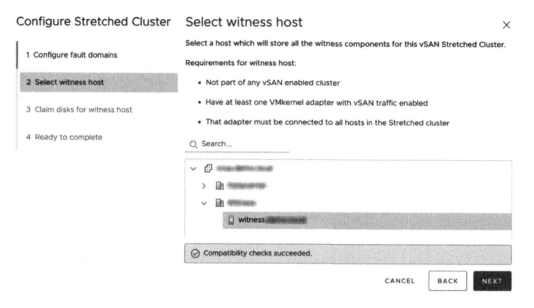

Figure 9.24 – Selecting the witness host

4.   Claim disks for the witness host. Select a cache tier and a capacity tier. Then, click the **NEXT** button:

Figure 9.25 – Claim disks for witness host

5. Review the configuration and then click the **FINISH** button:

Figure 9.26 – Confirming the configuration of the stretched cluster

6. Once the configuration of the stretched cluster is completed successfully, we go to the **Monitor** tab and select **vSAN health**. Make sure that all the tests have passed:

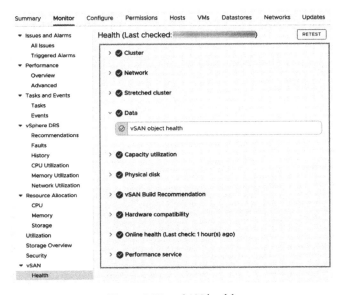

Figure 9.27 – vSAN health

7. Once the vSAN stretched cluster has been created successfully, we will create two stretched cluster host groups: one is used for the preferred site, and the other is used for the secondary site. Go to the **Configure** tab and select **VM/Host Groups**, click the **Add** button to add to the hosts from the preferred site to the host group's **Preferred Site**, and click the **OK** button. Then, select the hosts from the secondary site to add to the other host group's **Secondary Site**:

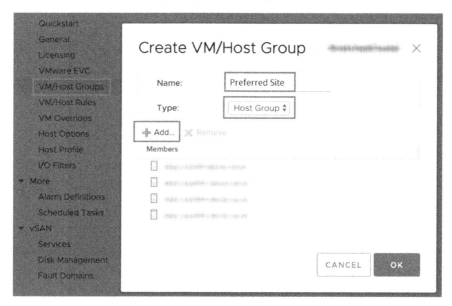

Figure 9.28 – Create VM/Host Group

8. Once the host group has been created, we can see two host groups:

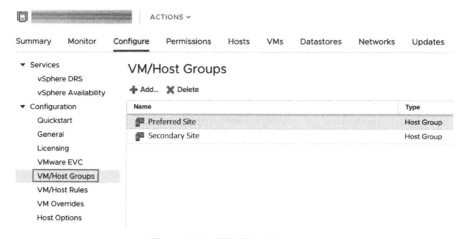

Figure 9.29 – VM/Host Groups

9. We will create two stretched cluster VM groups: one is used for the preferred site, and the other is used for the secondary site. Click the **Add** button to select the VMs from the preferred site to add to the VM group's **PreferredSite_VM** and click the **OK** button. Then, select the VMs from the secondary site to add to the other host group's **SecondarySite_VM**:

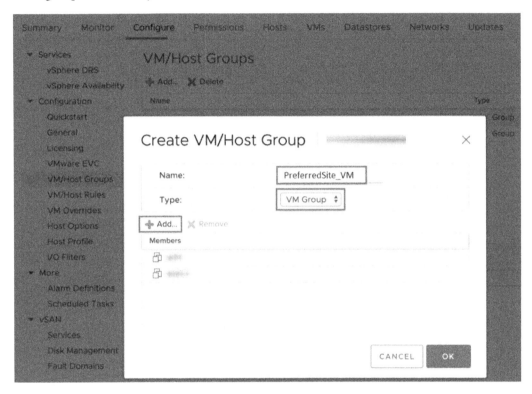

Figure 9.30 – Create VM/Host Group

10. Once the VM groups have been created, we can see two VM groups:

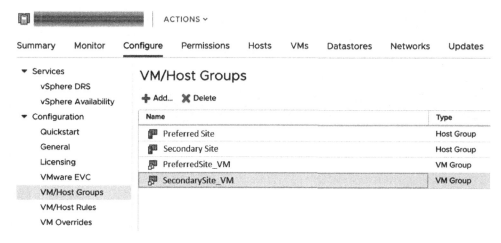

Figure 9.31 – Creating host groups and VM groups

11. Once we have created two host groups and two VM groups, we need to create two VM/host rules to associate VM groups with host groups and ensure that selected VMs run on a particular site (preferred or secondary). Go to the **Configure** tab and select **VM/Host Rules**, click the **Add** button to create the should rule for the preferred and secondary sites, specify the rule name **ShouldRunPreferred**, and choose the host and VM groups that were created in *Steps 7 and 9*:

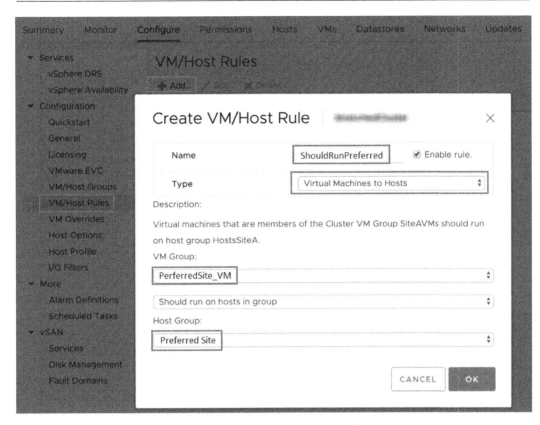

Figure 9.32 – Create VM/Host Rule

12. Once two VM/host rules have been created, we can see two **Should** rules:

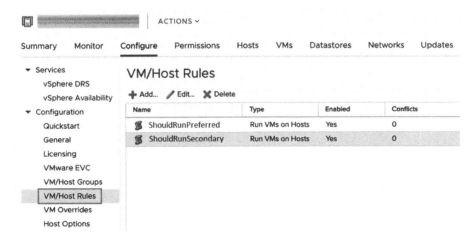

Figure 9.33 – Creating the two "should" rules

13. Now we will set up **Admission Control**, ensuring that HA has sufficient resources available to restart VMs when a site failure occurs (preferred or secondary). Select **Override calculated failover capacity.**. Specify 50% of **CPU** and **Memory**. Then, click the **OK** button:

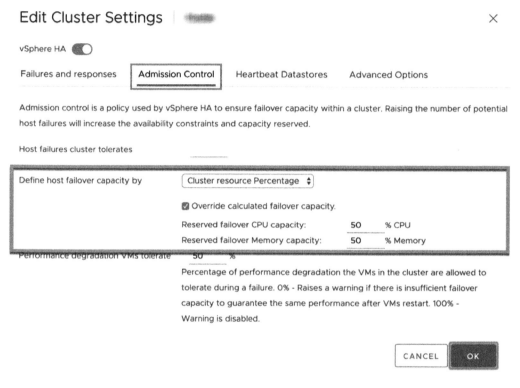

Figure 9.34 – Admission Control settings

14. When using **vSphere HA** on a vSAN stretched cluster, we need to ensure that the isolation address for both preferred and secondary sites is configured. If we have only one default vSAN gateway, set only **das.isolationaddress0**; if we have two default vSAN gateways, set both **das.isolationaddress0** and **das.isolationaddress1**. Click the **Add** button and enter each **Option** and **Value**:

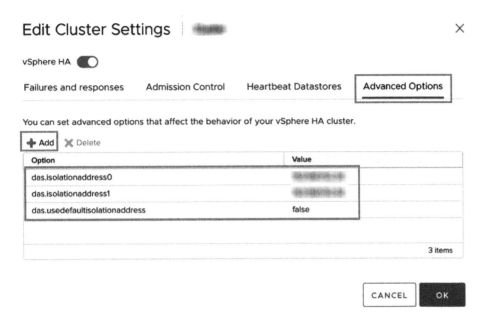

Figure 9.35 – Advanced Options on vSphere HA

15. If we are using Layer 3 switchings for the **witnessPg** port group in the vSAN stretched cluster witness (*Step 18* in the *Deploying a vSAN stretched cluster witness* section), we must add the static routes of the witness and the VxRail nodes for communication.

Enable SSH on each VxRail node. The SSH service is disabled by default on VxRail. SSH into each VxRail as root (the preferred and secondary sites). Execute the following command:

```
esxcli network ip route ipv4 add -n <Witness VSAN subnet/24> -g
<Local VSAN gateway>
```

Enable SSH on the witness host. The SSH service is disabled by default on the witness host. SSH into the witness host as root. Execute the following command:

```
esxcli network ip route ipv4 add -n <VxRail node VSAN
subnet/24> -g <Local VSAN gateway>
```

16. When we've finished the configuration of the static route on the vSAN stretched cluster, we will set up the VM storage policy for the vSAN stretched cluster. Make sure **Site disaster tolerance** is set to **Dual site mirroring (stretched cluster)** and **Failures to tolerate** is set to **1 failure - RAID-1 (Mirroring)**:

Figure 9.36 – Creating a VM storage policy

17. Once the VM storage has been created, we can assign this policy to the VMs.

In the next section, we will discuss an overview of the active-active-passive solution for VxRail.

Overview of the active-active-passive solution for VxRail

If we deployed the vSAN stretched cluster on VxRail between the primary and secondary sites, how could the disaster recovery solution for the vSAN stretched cluster be extended? VMware **Site Recovery Manager** (**SRM**) also supports extending the site-level protection to other sites. In *Figure 9.37*, we can see that there are four separate sites: they are **Preferred Site**, **Secondary Site**, **Witness Site**, and **Remote Site**. The vSAN stretched cluster builds on VxRail across the preferred and secondary sites, and the vSAN witness host is running at the witness site. The VxRail cluster is running at the remote site. The SRM is enabled with vSphere Replication between the vSAN stretched cluster and the VxRail cluster. If the vSAN stretched cluster has a fault, we could execute the SRM recovery plan to recover all the protected VMs on the vSAN stretched cluster in the VxRail cluster at the remote site:

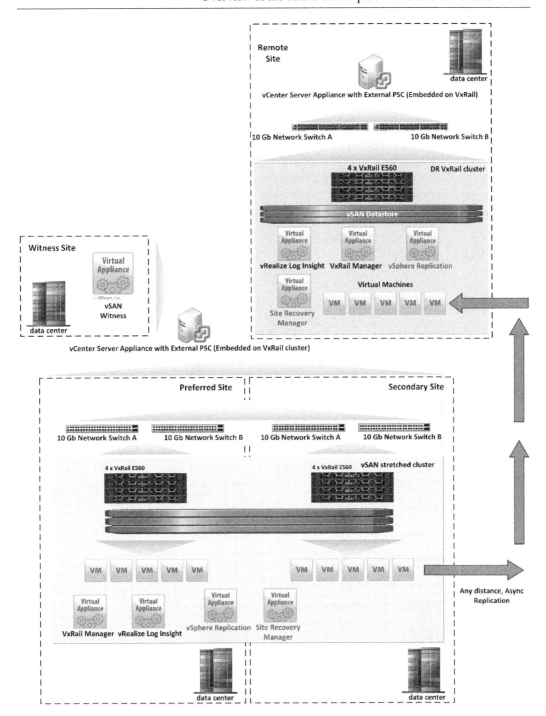

Figure 9.37 – The logical diagram of the active-active-passive solution for VxRail

If you want the details of deploying the SRM solution with vSphere Replication on VxRail, you can go to *Chapter 8, Active-Passive Solution for VxRail*.

Summary

In this chapter, we learned the advantages of the active-active solution for VxRail. We learned how to deploy and configure a vSAN stretched cluster on VxRail, using VMware Site Recovery Manager and vSphere Replication to extend the disaster recovery feature on VxRail appliances across three locations. We acquired the skills to deploy a VxRail vSAN stretched cluster and facilitate the disaster recovery solution across three separate locations in this chapter.

In the next chapter, we will learn about the migration methodology for migrating VMs into the VxRail system.

Questions

1. Which feature provides the active-active solution on VxRail?

    a. VMware Site Recovery Manager

    b. vSphere Replication

    c. A vSAN stretched cluster

    d. Dell EMC RecoverPoint for Virtual Machines

    e. All the above

2. What is the minimum number of sites required for a vSAN stretched cluster?

    a. Two data sites

    b. Three data sites

    c. One data site and one witness site

    d. Two data sites and one witness site

    e. Three data sites and two witness sites

    f. None of the above

3. What is the network requirement for a vSAN stretched cluster between the preferred and secondary sites?

    a. The network latency between two data sites should be more than 5 milliseconds.

    b. The network latency between two data sites should not be more than 5 milliseconds.

    c. The network latency between two data sites should not be more than 10 milliseconds.

    d. The network latency between two data sites should be more than 10 milliseconds.

    e. None of the above.

4. What is the bandwidth requirement for a vSAN stretched cluster between two data sites?

    a. 1 GB

    b. 10 GB or above

    c. 10 GB or above, and network latency should not be more than 5 milliseconds

    d. 1 GB and network latency should not be more than 10 milliseconds

    e. All the above

5. Which deployment configuration does it support for the vSAN witness host?

    a. Only a virtual server

    b. Only a physical server

    c. Either the virtual server or the physical server

    d. OVF format

    e. All the above

6. Where can we download the installation file for the vSAN witness host?

    a. The Dell EMC website

    b. Make a request to the Dell EMC support team

    c. Make a request to the VMware support team

    d. The VMware software website

    e. None of the above

7. How many virtual network adapters do we need to set up following vSAN witness appliance deployment?

    a. One virtual network adapter is used for the management network.

    b. Two virtual network adapters: one is used for the management network, and the other is used for the VM network.

    c. Two virtual network adapters: one is used for the management network, and the other is used for the vSAN network.

    d. One virtual network adapter is used for the vSAN network.

    e. None of the above

8. Which data protection software can support RPO set to zero?

    a. vSphere Replication

    b. Dell EMC Avamar

    c. Dell EMC RecoverPoint for Virtual Machines

    d. Site Recovery Manager

    e. VMware vRealize Operations Manager

9. Which replication mode can support vSphere Replication?

    a. Asynchronization

    b. Synchronization

    c. Asynchronization with RPO set to 0

    d. Synchronization with RPO set to 0

    e. All the above

10. How many vCenter servers and SRM servers does the SRM solution on VxRail require?

    a. One vCenter server and one SRM server

    b. Two vCenter servers and one SRM server

    c. Two vCenter servers, two SRM servers, and one vSphere Replication appliance

    d. Two vCenter servers, two SRM servers, and two vSphere Replication appliances

    e. None of the above

11. Which software requires an optional license when we set up the active-active-passive solution for VxRail?

    a. vCenter Server Appliance

    b. VxRail Manager

    c. vSphere Replication

    d. Site Recovery Manager

    e. All the above

12. How do we configure a VM storage policy for a vSAN stretched cluster on VxRail if PFTT is set to 1, SFTT is set to 1, and TDM is set to mirroring?

    a. We select **Dual site mirroring (stretched cluster)** on the **Site Disaster Tolerance** menu and select **1 failure - RAID-1 (Mirroring)** on the **Failure to tolerate** menu.

    b. We select **Dual site mirroring (stretched cluster)** on the **Site Disaster Tolerance** menu.

    c. We select **1 failure - RAID-1 (Mirroring)** on the **Failure to tolerate** menu.

    d. We select **None - keep data on Preferred (stretched cluster)** on the **Site Disaster Tolerance** menu and select **1 failure - RAID-1 (Mirroring)** on the **Failure to tolerate** menu.

    e. We select **None - keep data on Non-preferred (stretched cluster)** on the **Site Disaster Tolerance** menu and select **1 failure - RAID-1 (Mirroring)** on the **Failure to tolerate** menu.

10
Migrating Virtual Machines into VxRail

In *Chapter 9, Active-Active Solution for VxRail*, we had an overview of VxRail vSAN stretched clusters and their advantages. We learned how to deploy a vSAN stretched cluster on VxRail and how to use both VMware Site Recovery Manager and vSphere Replication to extend the disaster recovery feature on VxRail appliances across three locations.

In this final chapter, we will learn how to migrate virtual machines into VxRail appliances from the vSphere environment, including different migration methodologies based on various scenarios.

In this chapter, we're going to cover the following main topics:

- Understanding migration methodologies for VxRail
- Migrating a virtual machine into VxRail with vSphere Replication
- Migrating a virtual machine into VxRail with Storage vMotion

Technical requirements

For this chapter, you need to make sure your workstation (laptop) is running a Windows platform and a web browser is installed onto your laptop. The latest versions of Firefox, Google Chrome, and Microsoft Internet Explorer 10 or above are all supported. The VxRail software should be run in version 4.7.300 or above.

For the requirements of the vSphere Replication configuration, we must deploy a vSphere Replication appliance into a vSphere cluster and VxRail cluster. vSphere Replication is configured with a dual-core or quad-core vCPU, two virtual disks with 13 GB and 9 GB usable capacity, and 8 GB of memory. The **Domain Name System** (**DNS**) name of the vCenter **Platform Service Controller** (**PSC**), vCenter Server, and the vSphere Replication appliance have been configured to incorporate the DNS with the relevant IP address.

For the requirements of storage migration, the vMotion network can be enabled and accessed across both the vSphere cluster and the VxRail cluster. The speed of the vMotion network must be 1 GB or above.

Understanding migration methodologies for VxRail

Data migration involves the transfer of data and host connectivity from one platform to another. When considering which migration methodology to use, there are many requirements and dependencies to be considered. Actually, there are a lot of migration methodologies for VxRail appliances, such as using vSphere Replication, VMware Storage vMotion, or Dell EMC RecoverPoint for Virtual Machines, or backing up and restoring the data. In this chapter, we will consider how to migrate a virtual machine from a vSphere cluster into a VxRail cluster and will discuss the migration methodologies for VxRail appliances in two different scenarios. In the first scenario, we will migrate a virtual machine from a vSphere cluster into a VxRail cluster, and both clusters will be managed by different vCenter Server instances. We will use vSphere Replication to migrate the virtual machine into the VxRail cluster. In the second scenario, we will migrate a virtual machine from a vSphere cluster into a VxRail cluster, and both will be managed by the same vCenter Server instance. We will use VMware Storage vMotion to migrate the virtual machine into the VxRail cluster. Finally, we will discuss the advantages and disadvantages of these two migration methodologies.

> **Important note**
> VxRail-embedded vCenter Server appliances only support the management of VxRail clusters; non-VxRail clusters are not supported.

In the next sections, we will discuss these two migration methodologies – data migration with vSphere Replication and VMware Storage vMotion.

Migrating a virtual machine into VxRail with vSphere Replication

In this section, we will discuss the migration method of migrating a virtual machine by using vSphere Replication. In *Figure 10.1*, we can see that there are two vSphere clusters. One is a standard vSphere cluster that is connected to a storage array through two SAN switches. The other is a VxRail cluster with four E560 nodes. Each cluster is managed by a vCenter Server appliance:

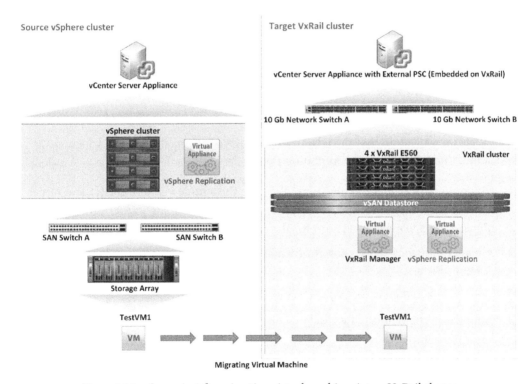

Figure 10.1 – Scenario 1 for migrating virtual machines into a VxRail cluster

Environment

Now we will discuss the hardware and software configuration for the scenario. The following table shows the hardware and software configuration in this environment. In this scenario, we will migrate a virtual machine into a VxRail cluster by using a vSphere Replication appliance:

	vCenter Server Appliance	vSphere	SAN Topology	vSphere Replication Appliance	Virtual Machine
Source vSphere cluster	vCenter Server appliance 6.7	Four vSphere 6.7 instances	Two 16 GB SAN switches	vSphere Replication 8.2	TestVM1
Target VxRail cluster	Embedded vCenter Server appliance 6.7	Four E560 VxRail nodes	Two 10 GB network switches	vSphere Replication 8.2	VxRail Manager 4.7

In the next section, we will discuss this migration process.

Migration flow

In this section, we will discuss the flow of migrating virtual machines with vSphere Replication. The following is the migration flow:

1. To deploy the vSphere Replication OVF into the source vSphere cluster and target VxRail cluster, refer to *Chapter 8, Active-Passive Solution for VxRail* (the *vSphere Replication deployment* section) for the deployment procedure.

2. Create the replication session for the virtual machine required to migrate into the VxRail cluster.

3. Start the virtual machine replication session.

4. Shut down the replicated virtual machine and execute the failover operation of a virtual machine.

5. Do a health check on the status of the virtual machine on the VxRail cluster following the failover operation.

Creating a virtual machine replication session

In this section, we will discuss how to create a virtual machine replication session across a vSphere cluster and VxRail cluster. The following is the procedure for creating virtual machine replication:

1. Log in to the source vCenter Server with an administrator account and go to **Site Recovery** on the home menu. Then, click the **VIEW DETAILS** button:

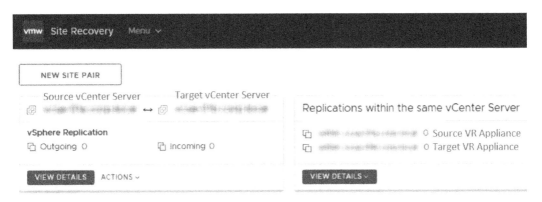

Figure 10.2 – Site Recovery dashboard

2. Go to the **Replications** tab, and then click the **NEW** button to create a new virtual machine replication session:

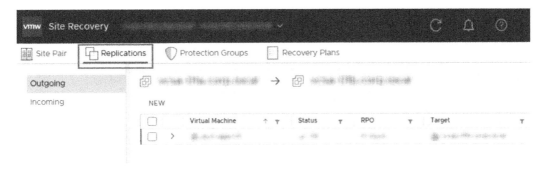

Figure 10.3 – Creating a virtual machine replication session

3. Select **Auto-assign vSphere Replication Server** for the target site, and then click the **NEXT** button:

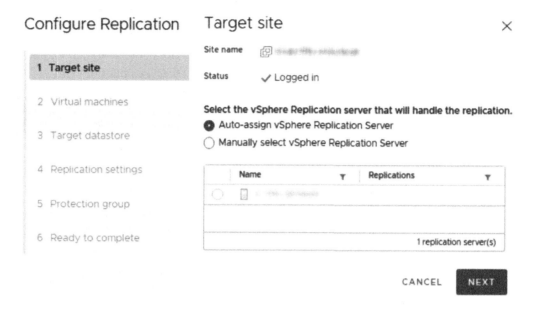

Figure 10.4 – Selecting vSphere Replication Server as the target site

4. Select the virtual machine required to replicate into the VxRail cluster, **TestVM1**, and then click the **NEXT** button:

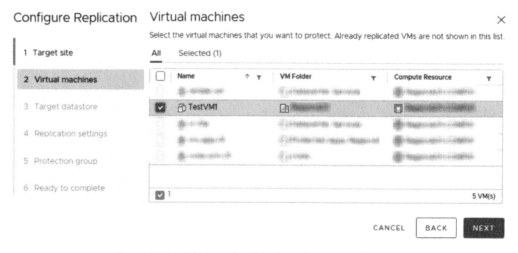

Figure 10.5 – Selecting the virtual machine for replication

5. Select the target datastore on the VxRail cluster and then click the **NEXT** button:

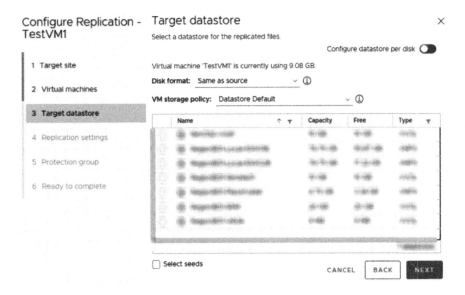

Figure 10.6 – Selecting the target datastore for virtual machine replication

6. Set the recovery point objective (the minimum is 5 minutes), and then click the **NEXT** button:

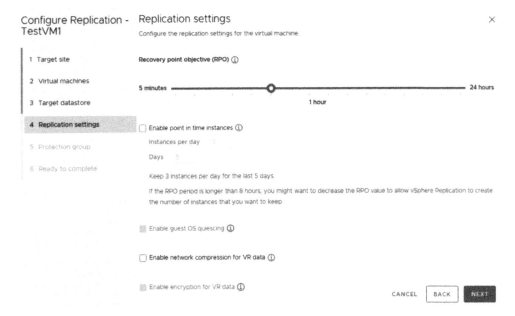

Figure 10.7 – Setting the recovery point objective for virtual machine replication

7.   Select **Do not add to protection group now**, and then click the **NEXT** button:

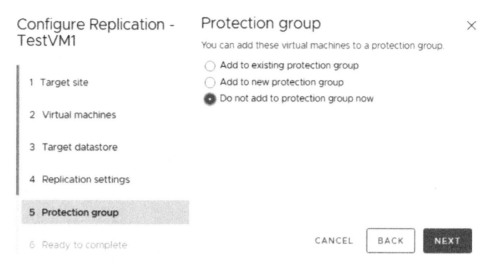

Figure 10.8 – Setting the protection group setting for virtual machine replication

8.   Review the settings to create the virtual machine replication session, and then click the **FINISH** button:

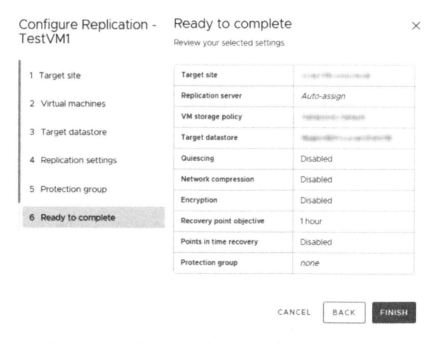

Figure 10.9 – Reviewing the settings for virtual machine replication

9. Once the virtual machine replication is created, it will initialize the virtual machine replication session across the source and target clusters:

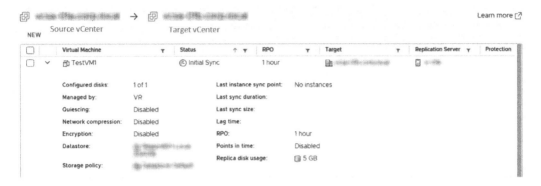

Figure 10.10 – Initializing the virtual machine replication session

10. Once the virtual machine replication has completed successfully, we can see that the status shows **OK**:

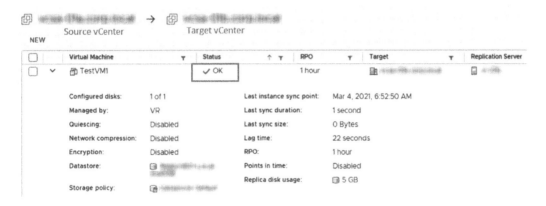

Figure 10.11 – The status of the virtual machine replication session

Once the **TestVM1** virtual machine has replicated into the VxRail cluster, we will trigger the virtual machine failover, and this virtual machine will activate into the VxRail cluster.

In the next section, we will discuss how to fail over a replicated virtual machine into a VxRail cluster.

Failing over a virtual machine

In this section, we will discuss how to failover a replicated virtual machine into a VxRail cluster. We must verify that the virtual machine at the source cluster is powered off before recovering the virtual machine at the target VxRail system. The following is the failover procedure of virtual machine replication:

1. Log in to VxRail's vCenter (the target vCenter server) and shut down the replicated virtual machine. Then, go to **Site Recovery** and choose **Incoming**, so that we can check that the replication status of the **TestVM1** virtual machine is **OK**. Then, click the **RECOVER** button:

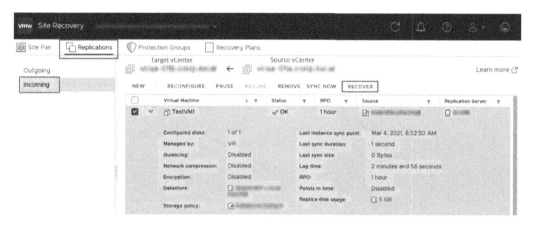

Figure 10.12 – Recovering the virtual machine for virtual machine replication

2. Select **Synchronize recent changes**, and then click the **NEXT** button:

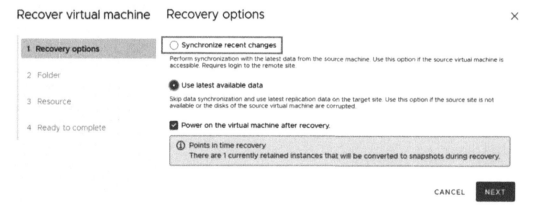

Figure 10.13 – Choosing the recovery options for virtual machine replication

3. Select the target folder on the VxRail cluster and then click the **NEXT** button:

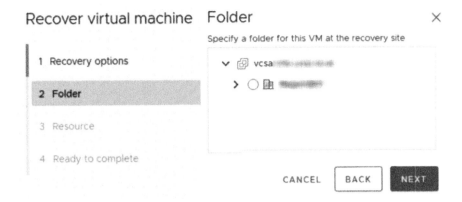

Figure 10.14 – Selecting the recovery folder for virtual machine replication

4. Select the target VxRail node on the VxRail cluster and then click the **NEXT** button:

Figure 10.15 – Selecting the recovery VxRail node for virtual machine replication

5. Review the virtual machine recovery summary and then click the **Finish** button to confirm the recovery operation:

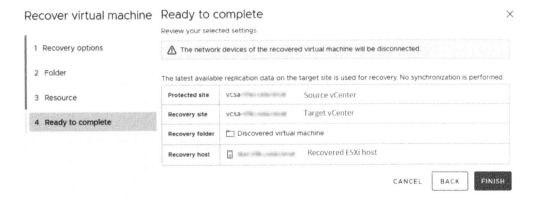

Figure 10.16 – Reviewing the virtual machine recovery summary

6. Once the recovery operation for the **TestVM1** virtual machine is completed, we can see that the status displays as **Recovered**:

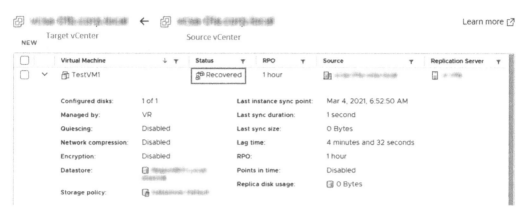

Figure 10.17 - The virtual machine is recovered into the VxRail cluster

Now, let's look at another migration mechanism of virtual machines into a VxRail appliance.

Migrating a virtual machine into VxRail with Storage vMotion

In this section, we will discuss the migration method of migrating a virtual machine by using VMware Storage vMotion. In *Figure 10.18*, we can see that there are two vSphere clusters. One is a standard vSphere cluster that is connected to a storage array through two SAN switches. The other is a VxRail cluster with four E560 nodes. Both clusters are managed by the same vCenter Server appliance:

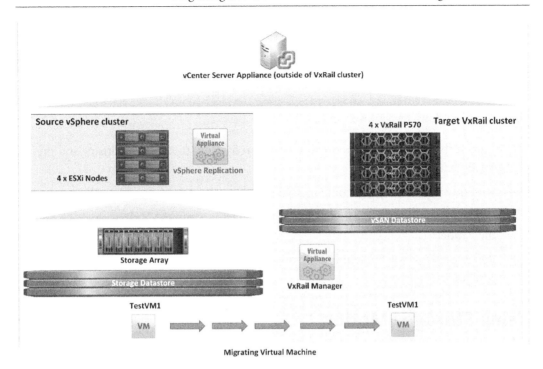

Figure 10.18 – Scenario 2 for migrating virtual machines into a VxRail cluster

Environment

Now we will discuss the hardware and software configuration for the scenario. The following table shows the hardware and software configuration in this environment. In this scenario, we will migrate a virtual machine into a VxRail cluster by using VMware Storage vMotion:

	vCenter Server Appliance	vSphere	SAN Topology	Datastore	Virtual Machine
Source vSphere cluster	VMware vCenter appliance	Four vSphere 6.7 instances	16 GB SAN fabric	VMFS datastore	TestVM1
Target VxRail cluster		Four E560 VxRail nodes	10 GB vSAN network	vSAN datastore	VxRail Manager 4.7

In the next section, we will discuss this migration process.

Migration flow

In this section, we will discuss the flow of migrating virtual machines with Storage vMotion. In this migration method, there is no shared storage for virtual machine migration.

The migration flow is as follows:

1. Ensure that the vMotion network is connected across the vSphere cluster and the VxRail cluster.

2. Shut down the virtual machine that you plan to migrate into the VxRail cluster.

3. Use Storage vMotion to migrate the virtual machine into the VxRail cluster from the vSphere cluster.

4. Power on the virtual machine after migrating the virtual machine into the VxRail appliance.

Using Storage vMotion

In this section, we will discuss how to migrate a virtual machine with Storage vMotion between the vSphere cluster and the VxRail appliance. The following is the procedure for using Storage vMotion:

1. Log in to vCenter Server, right-click the source virtual machine, and select the **Power** menu. Then, choose **Shut Down Guest OS** to shut down the source virtual machine:

Figure 10.19 – Shut Down Guest OS

2. Once the source virtual machine shuts down successfully, right-click the virtual machine and select **Migrate…**:

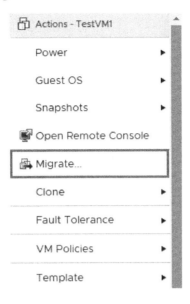

Figure 10.20 – Triggering the virtual machine migration

3. Select **Change both compute resource and storage** for the migration type, and then click the **NEXT** button:

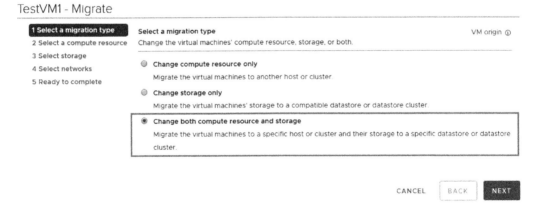

Figure 10.21 – Selecting the migration type

4. Choose the target cluster (the VxRail cluster) and then click the **NEXT** button:

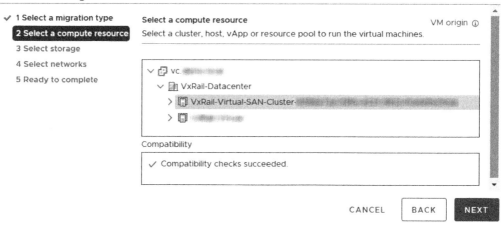

Figure 10.22 – Selecting the target location for migration

5. Choose the target datastore (**VxRail-Virtual-SAN-Datastore**) on the VxRail cluster and then click the **NEXT** button:

Figure 10.23 – Selecting the target datastore for migration

6. Select the destination network port group on the VxRail cluster and then click the **NEXT** button:

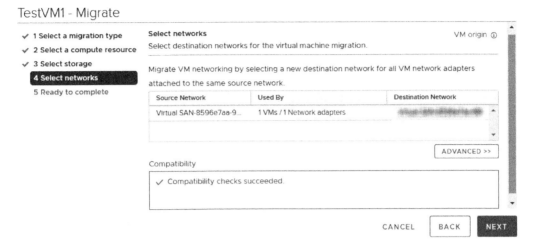

Figure 10.24 – Selecting the destination network for migration

7. Review the migration summary of the virtual machine and then click **FINISH** to confirm the virtual machine migration:

Figure 10.25 – Reviewing the migration summary

8. Once the virtual machine migration is completed successfully, we can power on this virtual machine on the VxRail cluster. Right-click the virtual machine and choose **Power On** to power on this virtual machine:

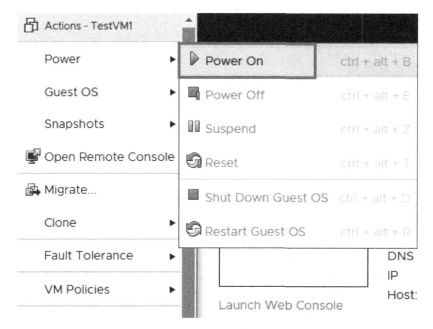

Figure 10.26 – Powering on the virtual machine

After completing this chapter, we have learned how to carry out virtual machine migration with Storage vMotion across a vSphere cluster and VxRail cluster. We did not install any software or tools on the source vSphere cluster; it is easy to migrate a virtual machine into the VxRail appliance with the embedded feature (Storage vMotion).

Summary

In this chapter, we learned about the virtual machine migration methodologies for VxRail in different scenarios, such as using vSphere Replication or VMware Storage vMotion. When we plan to migrate virtual machines into the VxRail system, we need to consider which method is best for our environment.

Over the past 10 chapters, we have covered an overview of the VxRail appliance and how to prepare the deployment of the VxRail appliance. We learned how to manage the virtual machine storage policy in a VxRail cluster, system scale-out, software upgrades, and so on. Finally, we acquired the skills for deploying both an active-passive solution and an active-active solution for VxRail.

Questions

1. Which feature provides virtual machine migration in VxRail?

   a. VMware Site Recovery Manager

   b. vSphere Replication appliance

   c. VMware vMotion

   d. VMware Storage vMotion

   e. All the above

2. What is the minimum number of vCenter Server instances for enabling a vSphere Replication session on VxRail?

   a. One

   b. Two

   c. Three

   d. Four

   e. Five

   f. None of the above

3. What is the status of the replicated virtual machine when the replication session is started?

   a. The replicated virtual machine requires a power down.

   b. The replicated virtual machine requires a shutdown.

   c. The replicated virtual machine requires power on.

   d. The replicated virtual machine requires being stopped.

   e. None of the above.

4. What action is required before the failover of the replicated virtual machine into the target cluster?

   a. No action.

   b. Reboot the replicated virtual machine.

   c. Shut down the replicated virtual machine.

   d. Stop the virtual machine replication session.

   e. All the above.

5. What is the status of the virtual machine replication session when the replication is completed?

   a. Started

   b. Stopped

   c. Recovered

   d. OK

   e. None of the above

6. What is the status of the virtual machine replication session after executing the recovery operation?

   a. Started

   b. Stopped

   c. Recovered

   d. Initial Sync

   e. None of the above

7. What is the migration type used for Storage vMotion across two vSphere clusters?

   a. Change compute resource only.

   b. Change storage only.

   c. Change both compute resource and storage.

   d. Change either compute resource or storage.

   e. None of the above.

8. Which data protection software can support the recovery point objective set to 0?

   a. vSphere Replication

   b. Dell EMC Avamar

   c. Dell EMC RecoverPoint for Virtual Machines

   d. Site Recovery Manager

   e. VMware vRealize Operations Manager

9. Which replication mode can support vSphere Replication?

   a. Asynchronization

   b. Synchronization

c. Asynchronization with the recovery point objective set to 0

d. Synchronization with the recovery point objective set to 0

e. All the above

10. Which editions of vSphere 6.7 are supported on VMware Storage vMotion? (Choose two)

a. vSphere Standard Edition

b. vSphere Enterprise Edition

c. vSphere Enterprise Plus Edition

d. vSphere Advanced Edition

e. All the above

11. Which configuration is not supported on VxRail's embedded vCenter Server appliance?

a. VxRail scale-out

b. VxRail software upgrade

c. Managing a VxRail cluster

d. Managing a non-VxRail cluster

e. All the above

12. Which VMware product supports integration with the vSphere Replication appliance, besides vCenter Server appliances and vSphere?

a. VMware vRealize Operations Manager

b. VMware Site Recovery Manager

c. VMware vSAN

d. VMware vRealize Log Insight

e. All the above

Assessments

In the following pages, we will review all practice questions from each of the chapters in this book and provide the correct answers.

Chapter 1 – Overview of VxRail HCI

1. a
2. a, b, c, e
3. e
4. d
5. a
6. b
7. a, d, e
8. a, c
9. e, d
10. c
11. c
12. d

Chapter 2 – VxRail Installation

1. a
2. a, b
3. a, b
4. b
5. d
6. b, c

7. d

8. b

9. c

10. c

11. c

12. b

Chapter 3 – VxRail Administration Overview

1. c

2. d

3. e

4. a

5. a

6. c

7. b

8. a, b, c

9. b

10. e

11. c

12. f

Chapter 4 – VxRail Management Overview

1. d

2. e

3. d

4. c

5. c

6. a, c

7. a, c, e

8. e
9. b
10. a
11. e
12. b

Chapter 5 – Managing VMware vSAN

1. e
2. f
3. b
4. b
5. d
6. e
7. a, c
8. e
9. b
10. e
11. b
12. c

Chapter 6 – VxRail Upgrade

1. c
2. d
3. b
4. d
5. c
6. c
7. b
8. e

9. b, c

10. a, b, c

11. a, b, d

12. a, b, d

Chapter 7 – VxRail Scale-Out Operations

1. c

2. b

3. b

4. c

5. c

6. b

7. c

8. b

9. c

10. b

11. b

12. b

Chapter 8 – Active-Passive Solution for VxRail

1. b

2. f

3. b

4. d

5. b, d

6. b

7. a

8. c

9. a

10. c

11. d

12. c

Chapter 9 – Active-Active Solution for VxRail

1. c

2. d

3. b

4. c

5. c

6. d

7. c

8. c

9. a

10. d

11. d

12. a

Chapter 10 – Migrating Virtual Machines into VxRail

1. e

2. a

3. c

4. c

5. d

6. c

7. c

8. c

9. a

10. a, c

11. d

12. b

`Packt.com`

Subscribe to our online digital library for full access to over 7,000 books and videos, as well as industry leading tools to help you plan your personal development and advance your career. For more information, please visit our website.

Why subscribe?

- Spend less time learning and more time coding with practical eBooks and Videos from over 4,000 industry professionals

- Improve your learning with Skill Plans built especially for you

- Get a free eBook or video every month

- Fully searchable for easy access to vital information

- Copy and paste, print, and bookmark content

Did you know that Packt offers eBook versions of every book published, with PDF and ePub files available? You can upgrade to the eBook version at `packt.com` and as a print book customer, you are entitled to a discount on the eBook copy. Get in touch with us at `customercare@packtpub.com` for more details.

At `www.packt.com`, you can also read a collection of free technical articles, sign up for a range of free newsletters, and receive exclusive discounts and offers on Packt books and eBooks.

Other Books You May Enjoy

If you enjoyed this book, you may be interested in these other books by Packt:

Mastering Veeam Backup & Replication 10

Chris Childerhose

ISBN: 978-1-83898-044-3

- Discover the advanced concepts of Veeam Backup & Replication 10

- Master application optimizations based on Veeam best practices

- Understand how to configure NAS backups and work with repositories and proxies

- Explore different ways to protect your backups, including object immutability and cloud backup and recovery

- Discover how DataLabs works

- Understand how Instant VM Recovery allows you to restore virtual machines

- Become well versed in Veeam ONE for monitoring and reporting on your environment

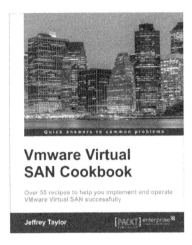

VMware Virtual SAN Cookbook

Jeffrey Taylor

ISBN: 978-1-78217-454-7

- Prepare your infrastructure for VMware Virtual SAN

- Plan and build infrastructure solutions to suit your needs

- Implement VMware Virtual SAN

- Exploit the power of policy-based management

- Increase or decrease the scale of your Virtual SAN as needs change

- Monitor your Virtual SAN infrastructure effectively

- Respond to and troubleshoot problems

Packt is searching for authors like you

If you're interested in becoming an author for Packt, please visit `authors.packtpub.com` and apply today. We have worked with thousands of developers and tech professionals, just like you, to help them share their insight with the global tech community. You can make a general application, apply for a specific hot topic that we are recruiting an author for, or submit your own idea.

Leave a review - let other readers know what you think

Please share your thoughts on this book with others by leaving a review on the site that you bought it from. If you purchased the book from Amazon, please leave us an honest review on this book's Amazon page. This is vital so that other potential readers can see and use your unbiased opinion to make purchasing decisions, we can understand what our customers think about our products, and our authors can see your feedback on the title that they have worked with Packt to create. It will only take a few minutes of your time, but is valuable to other potential customers, our authors, and Packt. Thank you!

Index

A

active-active-passive solution, for VxRail
  overview 304-306
active-active solution, for VxRail
  overview 277, 278
active-active solution, for
    VxRail deployment
  about 283
  vSAN stretched cluster witness,
    deploying 283-294
  VxRail vSAN stretched cluster,
    configuring 294-304
active-passive solution
  deploying, for VxRail 222
All-Flash configuration 75
Analytical Consulting Engine (ACE) 10
Application Programming
    Interfaces (APIs) 130

B

Bring-Your-Own (BYO) 12

C

Continuous Data Protection (CDP) 10

D

data migration 312
Dell EMC 4
Dell EMC PowerEdge servers 5
Dell Technologies Knowledge Base articles
  reference link 204
disaster recovery solution 222
disk group 75
Domain Name Server (DNS) 37
Domain Name System (DNS) 35, 281

E

End User License Agreement (EULA) 229
Enterprise License Agreement (ELA) 12

F

Failure Tolerance Method (FTM) 79, 279
Failure To Tolerate (FTT) 78
fault domain (FD) 279
Fully Qualified Domain Name
    (FQDN) 280

G

Graphics Processing Unit (GPU) 5

H

Hard Disk Drive (HDD) 109
HCIA Management role
  user account, creating with 114-116
High Availability (HA) 9, 44
hybrid configuration 75

I

Input/Output Operations Per
  Second (IOPS) 76, 126
Integrated Dell Remote Access
  Controller (iDRAC) 15, 70

J

Joint Photographic Experts
  Group (JPEG) 123

K

Key Management Server (KMS) 89, 125

L

LCM 20
light emitting diode (LED) 48
Live Optics 5

N

Network Daughter Card (NDC) 14
Network Time Protocol (NTP) 37

Network Validation Tool (NVT) 36

O

One-Unit (1U) 6
Out-of-Band (OOB) 41

P

Platform Service Controller
    (PSC) 15, 38, 281
port groups 86
Pre-Engagement Questionnaire (PEQ)
  URL 36
Primary Level of Failures to
    Tolerate (PFTT) 280

R

RecoverPoint for Virtual
    Machines (RP4VM) 222
Recovery Point Objective (RPO) 267
Recovery Time Objective (RTO) 223
Remote Office Branch Office (ROBO) 12
replicated virtual machine
  failing over, into VxRail cluster 320-322

S

Secondary Level of Failures to
    Tolerate (SFTT) 280
Secure Remote Services (SRS) 10, 72
Single Sign-On (SSO) 281
Site Recovery Manager (SRM) 11, 304
Software Defined Data Center (SDDC) 5
Software-Defined Storage (SDS) 4
Solid-State Drive (SSD) 109
SolVe Desktop

reference link 26

SolVe Online
  reference link 25

SPBM 21

SRM inventory mappings
  configuring 255-263

SRM recovery plans
  creating 269-271

Storage Policy-Based Management
    (SPBM) 9, 75

stretched cluster, fault domains
  Preferred Site 279
  Secondary Site 279
  Witness Host 279

T

Top of Rack (ToR) 16, 44

Two-Unit (2U) 6

V

vCenter
  VxRail Manager plugin 107-110

vCenter Server
  requirements 280

vCenter Server Appliance (VCSA) 4

Virtual Appliance Management
    Interface (VAMI) 251

Virtual Desktop Infrastructure (VDI) 6

virtual machine
  building 158-163
  building, with deployment
      methods 158, 159
  migrating, into VxRail with VMware
      Storage vMotion 322
  migrating, into VxRail with
      vSphere Replication 313

migrating, with VMware Storage
    vMotion 324-328

migration flow, with VMware
    Storage vMotion 324

migration flow, with vSphere
    Replication 314

protecting 264-268

Virtual Machine Disks (VMDKs) 77

virtual machine replication session
  creating 315-319

Virtual SAN (vSAN) 5, 74

VM network 282

vMotion network 282

VM storage policies
  applying 139, 140
  creating 133-139
  overview 130-132

VMware 4

VMware Cloud Foundation (VCF) 5

VMware SRM 223

VMware SRM appliance
  deploying 225-240
  reference link 225

VMware SRM solution
  for VxRail 223, 224

VMware SRM solution, VxRail
  deployment procedures 224, 225

VMware Storage vMotion
  used, for migrating virtual
      machine 324-328
  used, for migrating virtual
      machine into VxRail 322

VMware vCenter Server 4, 72

VMware VR 222

VMware VR appliance
  deploying 240-254
  reference link 240

VMware vRealize Log Insight 74

VMware VR solution
  for VxRail 223, 224
VMware VR solution, VxRail
  deployment procedures 224, 225
VMware vSAN
  about 74
  overview 75-77
  vSAN object 77, 78
  vSAN storage policy 78-84
VMware vSAN service
  advanced parameters 128, 129
  configuration 122
  vSAN Deduplication and
      Compression 123, 124
  vSAN Encryption 124-126
  vSAN iSCSI target service 127, 128
  vSAN Performance Service 126, 127
VMware vSphere 9, 10
VMware vSphere Client 71
VMware vSphere Web Client (Flex) 200
vSAN cluster
  availability 147
  capacity 144
  cluster level 144, 145
  health checks 140, 141
  host level 145, 146
  monitoring 140
  objects, resyncing 143
  virtual objects 142
  VM level 146, 147
vSAN Deduplication and
    Compression 123, 124
vSAN Encryption 124-126
vSAN fault domains
  creating 150-152
  overview 147-149
vSAN iSCSI target service 127, 128
vSAN maintenance mode

  about 152-156
  advantages 157, 158
  disadvantages 157, 158
vSAN network 282
vSAN object 77, 78
vSAN Performance Service 126, 127
vSAN services 89
vSAN storage policies
  defining 130
vSAN storage policy 78-84
vSAN stretched cluster
  about 277
  network, requirements 281
vSAN stretched cluster witness
  deploying 283-294
vSphere APIs for Storage
    Awareness (VASA) 130
vSphere Distributed Switch (vDS) 86
vSphere Replication
  used, for migrating virtual
      machine into VxRail 313
vSphere Replication Management
    (VRM) 253
vSphere Storage vMotion 9
vSphere Web Client 71
VxRail
  active-passive solution,
      deploying for 222
  migration methodologies 312
  VMware SRM solution 223, 224
  VMware VR solution 223, 224
VxRail Appliance
  about 4-8
  cabling 44, 45
  cluster status, at hardware level
      monitoring 110, 111
  Continuous Data Protection
      (CDP) 10, 11

DNS requirement 42
hardware and software status,
    monitoring 106
hardware installation 43
initialization 46
licensing 11-13
mounting 44
option 9
power and rack space, requisite 43
resources 24-27
roles and permission
    management 112-114
site preparations 35, 36
system architecture 14-18
system features 18-22
system management 23, 24
Top-of-Rack switch, requisite 36-41
VMware SDDC 9, 10
VxRail HCI System Software 10
VxRail cluster
  building 48-61
  environment 314, 323
  replicated virtual machine,
      failing over into 320-322
  validating 61-63
VxRail cluster configuration
  about 85, 279, 280
  port groups 86
  vDS 86
  vSAN services 89
  VxRail disk groups 87-89
  VxRail storage policy 90
  VxRail system virtual machines 85, 86
VxRail cluster expansion
  about 199
  preparing 200-203
  scale-out operation 203-214
VxRail disk group

configuration 168
  drive expansion procedures 169-171
  drive, upgrading in 171-175
VxRail disk groups 87-89
VxRail HCI System Software 10
VxRail management
  user account, creating with HCIA
      Management role 114-116
VxRail management interface
  about 70, 71
  VMware vCenter Server 72
  VMware vRealize Log Insight 74
  VMware vSphere Client 71
  vSphere Web Client 71
  VxRail Manager 72, 73
  VxRail Manager plugin for vCenter 71
VxRail Manager
  about 72, 73
  overview 96
VxRail Manager connectivity
  laptop, configuring from 47, 48
VxRail Manager plugin
  about 4
  at cluster level 97-104
  at host level 104-106
  for vCenter 107-110
VxRail Manager plugin for vCenter 71
VxRail scale-out rules
  about 198
  environment 198, 199
VxRail software
  components 175, 176
  downloading 180-182
  upgrading 175, 176
  upgrading, from version 4.7
      to version 7.0 183-192
VxRail storage policy 90
VxRail system virtual machines 85, 86

VxRail upgrade procedure
  accessing 176-180
VxRail vSAN stretched cluster
  configuring 294-304

Made in the USA
Las Vegas, NV
29 June 2021